Praise for
THE 27TH MILE

"*The 27th Mile* captures the deeply personal moment when the thing that once defined you is suddenly out of reach. Dimity writes with honesty, humor, and so much heart. This book is a companion for anyone navigating the loss of a long-held identity—and a hopeful guide to discover who you are beyond what you do. It is tender, wise, and profoundly relatable."

—**Siri Lindley,** world champion triathlete, coach, and author

"Dimity McDowell puts words to the grief that runners feel when they're forced to give up an activity that's so much more than mere exercise—it's also a source of community, identity, and release. *The 27th Mile* offers comfort, commiseration, and useful coping advice to waylaid runners. Whether their break from running is temporary or permanent, runners involuntarily separated from their beloved sport will find support and a sense of hope in McDowell's book."

—**Christie Aschwanden,** author of *Good to Go: What the Athlete in All of Us Can Learn from the Strange Science of Recovery*

"So many titles exist about the joy of running or how to become a runner, but rarely has there existed a book honoring the choice and necessity to take leave of the sport. Not only does she pay homage to all that the sport has done for her and her community, but Dimity also takes time and space to honor her own body and spirit, inviting other longtime runners to offer their stories as well. When you are ready to make that decision, make sure to read this book first."

—**Mirna Valerio,** runner, adventurer, and author of *A Beautiful Work in Progress*

"Runners tie their identities to their hobby like few others. It serves us well—until it doesn't. Then what? The grief and loss are real when running is no longer an option. *The 27th Mile* is the gentle, kind, and sound advice we didn't know we needed to move on to the next phase of life."

—**Erin Strout,** journalist and author

"This scenario is every runner's nightmare: The day when it ends, when the body says the glory days are gone, or—even worse—when it says 'no more.' It's like losing your best friend. Preparation is everything, so read this now!"

—**Kathrine Switzer,** pioneering marathon runner and author

THE
27TH
MILE

ALSO BY DIMITY MCDOWELL

Run Like a Mother: How to Get Moving—
and Not Lose Your Family, Job, or Sanity with Sarah Bowen Shea

Train Like a Mother: How to Get Across Any Finish Line—
and Not Lose Your Family, Job, or Sanity with Sarah Bowen Shea

Tales from Another Mother Runner: Triumphs, Trials,
Tips, and Tricks from the Road with Sarah Bowen Shea

THE 27TH MILE

How to Smooth the Rough Transition Out of Your Running Years

DIMITY McDOWELL

balance

NEW YORK BOSTON

Copyright © 2026 by Dimity McDowell
Cover design by Kayla Areglado
Cover image by Nadezda AUDIGIE/Shutterstock
Cover copyright © 2026 by Hachette Book Group, Inc.

Balance
Hachette Book Group
1290 Avenue of the Americas
New York, NY 10104
GCP-Balance.com
@GCPBalance

First Edition: February 2026

Balance is an imprint of Grand Central Publishing. The Balance name and logo are registered trademarks of Hachette Book Group, Inc.

The publisher is not responsible for websites (or their content) that are not owned by the publisher.

The Hachette Speakers Bureau provides a wide range of authors for speaking events. To find out more, visit hachettespeakersbureau.com or email HachetteSpeakers@hbgusa.com.

Balance books may be purchased in bulk for business, educational, or promotional use. For information, please contact your local bookseller or email the Hachette Book Group Special Markets Department at Special.Markets@hbgusa.com.

Print book interior design by Sheryl Kober

Library of Congress Cataloging-in-Publication Data has been applied for.

ISBNs: 9780306837357 (trade paperback); 9780306837364 (ebook)

Printed in the United States of America

LSC-C

Printing 1, 2025

FOR GRANT.

CONTENTS

INTRODUCTION

We're in This Together

As the author, I shouldn't say this, but I'm sorry you picked up this book.

Maybe it's in your hands because you're wondering how many miles are left in your body, which isn't cooperating like it used to. Perhaps this injury—your latest setback—feels more permanent, more stubborn than ones before. Or maybe you heard the words *knee replacement* bandied around at a recent orthopedist appointment and you're petrified.

Maybe it's in your hands because you've physically stopped running, but mentally, you're far from over it. You glare at runners through your car window, wondering whether they appreciate how good they've got it. You tell yourself you've moved on, that you're okay with the fact that you'll never cross another finish line, but you still bristle when a well-meaning friend asks when your next race is.

Maybe it's in your hands because you now hike, cycle, or strength train with the vigor you previously reserved for running, yet a cavity still aches in your soul as you finish a workout. *Why doesn't this feel as good as running did? What am I missing?*

Or maybe it's in your hands because you are still running strong, but something inside you is asking: *What happens when I can't do this anymore?*

Quitting running is like contemplating a divorce or the death of a loved one: something we think about a lot but don't want to verbalize, lest doing so actually gives the thought momentum. Still, running has shaped your days, your friendships, your sense of self, and you need to know what's on the other side. What does life look like without race bibs and tempo efforts, wasted legs and routes so soothing you run them in your dreams?

Whatever reason landed this book in your hands, I'm glad you're here. Nobody should have to figure out their final miles by themselves. Letting go of running is more grueling than the last 10K of a marathon—and there's none of the glory waiting for you at the finish line. There is, however, a virtual hug and lots of love from me, your unofficial therapist and official guide to the other side of running. Which, I realize, compared to a marathon medal, feels like being served fruit for dessert: fine, but disappointing.

I was a runner for almost three decades. I quit our beloved sport in January 2020, about three years—thirty-eight months or 1,186 days, not that I was counting—after my trusted orthopedist, upon examining my complicated hamstring situation that had confounded my physical therapist for ten months, gently suggested that I "consider not running anymore."

My body, although athletic, is not ideal for running. I've got a lot of mass to move. I'm extremely tall—almost six foot four—and although you, like everybody who sees me for the first time, might think I was a basketball prodigy, you would be wrong. Coordination is not my forte, and being the tallest person in almost every class from kindergarten to twelfth grade—and, yes, I'm including the teacher here—made me extremely self-conscious. I would rather have read the entries from my Judy Blume diary to a packed school assembly than dribble a basketball up the court in front of the seven spectators at the JV games.

My height, however, came in handy when I got to college and was recruited to the rowing club. Height is an asset in rowing; the taller you are, the more leverage you get on the oar and the faster and farther the boat goes. Better yet, your feet are tied in to the boat and eight rowers repeat the same motion again and again. No coordination necessary, and no individual sticks out. For the first time in my life, I felt like an athlete. Instead of being picked last for dodgeball in gym class—my sheer surface area made me a liability—I was now five seat, the center of the boat's powerful engine room. Walking around at regattas among other tall, strong rowers, I carried myself like a star.

Still, I didn't have a great proprioceptive sense. "Dimity, your head is as heavy as a bowling ball," one coach continually yelled at me, trying to correct my leftward lean. "Can't you just keep it straight?" No, actually, I couldn't. After college, I dialed up my training to pursue Olympic dreams. But nearly every practice laid bare my technical flaws. No matter how fiercely I focused, I couldn't find the finesse to move in perfect sync with my elite teammates. And despite strength sessions that ended with multiple rounds of jump squats and sit-ups, my core never felt solid enough to anchor my long torso at the end of hours on the water.

When I traded my oar for running shoes, I thought I'd found athletic freedom; after all, running is an individual sport that requires little to no coordination. And for a few glorious years in my early twenties, I had exactly that: smooth, joyful miles that made me feel unstoppable. But my physical foundation remained fragile, and some of my key anatomical parts were faulty. Direct quote from my podiatrist, an ultrarunner, after fitting me for my *fourth? fifth?* set of orthotics: "Your feet are not genetically blessed." Yes, I needed a full medical team—orthopedist, physical therapist, podiatrist—to help me stay on the road.

To be clear: I wasn't chasing prize money or trophies or sponsorships. I never won a dollar, never even cracked an age-group podium in any race distance, not even a neighborhood 5K. When I finished in the top third of my age group, I floated for days after the race. Mostly, I loved how running made me feel, both inside and out, and that was enough for me to keep going.

During my twenties, my only issue was a blitzing Morton's neuroma in one foot, but my thirties and forties bloomed with all types of injuries.

After my first pregnancy, things kicked off with a stubborn bunion (and a failed bunionectomy) and multiplied from there. The most common were stress fractures in my unblessed feet. I lost count of exactly how many cloudy breaks doctors pointed out to me on X-rays over the years, but I am confident I spent the equivalent of at least twelve full months clomping around in one of those clunky black boots whose Velcro straps attract lint, pet hair, and other unsavory debris.

The rest of my lower body felt like a Jenga tower after too many turns; engage one ligament, muscle, or tendon the wrong way, and the whole thing would topple. Left-hip issues led to a tight lower back, which resulted in a strained right hamstring, which trotted down to my left knee, which ached like it had a railroad spike tunneling through it. Forget a race medal or a personal record: When I completed a training cycle for a half-marathon with sore muscles as my only issue, I considered that a win. Every long run felt like a gamble: Could I get through 12 miles? Usually I could, but that's because I became a champion at selectively blocking out pain. (Oh, that hot spot under the ball of my foot? Probably just a rock in my shoe.) And completing the long runs didn't put my nerves at ease. Would I pay the price for those dozen miles, hobbling to the soccer sidelines to watch my kid or stuffing an ice pack into my sweaty leggings to soothe my lower back? Yes, I usually would.

I was constantly on the hunt for something to tip me toward better, more efficient running. Thinking ChiRunning would lighten my elephantine landing, I clipped a beeping pedometer to the waistband of my running shorts to help me boost my sluggish cadence. Within a few months, I grew tired of both the relentless *beep-beep-beep* and imagining what passing runners thought of the noise—and me. I experimented with Newton shoes, which feature a built-up forefoot to naturally encourage correct running form; within a few runs, they earned me yet another stress fracture. I ran on a treadmill under the watchful eye of a physical therapist, who later pulled up a computer analysis to show how much my hips teeter-tottered. Not much, it turned out, but it was still too much to withstand my moderate weekly mileage. I tried Altras, shoes with a minimal, flat sole and a toe box wide enough to give my bunioned feet space. The natural fit felt so helpful I contemplated getting a pair of Barefoot Ted's running sandals, but that felt like a bridge too far. Instead, I ran barefoot, both forward and backward, in the grass at a local park, to get more in touch with my foot strike, more in touch with my whole body. Alas, nothing tipped the scale to becoming a resilient, hearty runner.

When benched, I continued my relentless, spirit-sucking search for that magic combination of healing advice and exercises that could end the injury cycle. Too many physical therapists to name and too many PT appointments to count; hundreds of hours of videos on YouTube, including fifty versions of *the ONE move you need to heal knee pain!*; Pilates and Feldenkrais; foam rolling and massages; clamshells for days; glute bridges for miles; dozens of broken resistance bands as I monster-walked back and forth in my basement; dry needling; cupping; chiropractic adjustments; and a pair of shoes with soles so thick they felt like the moon boots I wore in fourth grade.

The pain leaked into other aspects of my life, drying up my patience with my kids, my humor with my husband, my ease with the world. It also wasn't fabulous for our family's budget: We owned the kind of health insurance two self-employed, relatively young and healthy adults with two very young and healthy kids have. We were covered for emergencies, but a twinge in my left calf that doesn't really go away? Not so much.

Anybody who isn't a runner might ask, why? Why spend so much time, money, and effort loving a sport that clearly didn't love you back?

Anybody who is a runner already knows the answer: Because I'm a runner. Running structured my days and life, defined my quads, balanced my glass-half-empty perspective, and gave me an identity beyond the typical mother, sister, wife, daughter, worker. An identity that immediately marked me as strong and determined. An identity that made me believe in myself.

Running by parked minivans in suburban neighborhoods as the sun came up flooded my body with endorphins and my mind with hope. Doing so with other women created friendships so deep, no topic was off-limits. In my hardest seasons marked by depression, the rhythm of my feet and the simplicity of the forward motion gave me enough momentum to carry on. Standing in the corral of a half-marathon filled with like-minded people ready to challenge themselves and cheer for each other was the best party I could imagine. Coming home after an hour of pounding the pavement, I felt like Serena Williams at Wimbledon, like Bruce Springsteen at the Meadowlands: exactly where I was supposed to be.

Nothing—not yoga or meditation, not cycling or swimming, not a second glass of wine or an orgasm—brought me to the peaceful, settled, supportive land where running reliably transported me.

My connection to running wasn't just personal; it was also the center of my professional career. Back when people read magazines, not phones, I was a contributing editor at *Runner's World*. Personal narratives were my specialty. I wrote features about breaking two hours in a half-marathon and breaking my wrist on an icy trail run. Sarah Bowen Shea, a colleague of mine, and I ran the 2007 Nike Women's Marathon when our kids were ankle biters, and we chronicled our training and race in a story titled "The Marathon Moms." We expanded that feature into our first book: *Run Like a Mother: How to Get Moving—and Not Lose Your Family, Job, or Sanity*, published in 2010. We turned the success of that book into a small business: Another Mother Runner. Over the course of fifteen years, we wrote two more books, helped thousands of women train for everything from a 5K to a 50-miler, attended marathon expos where we gave prerace talks and sold shirts that proclaimed "It's all good. I ran today," recorded thousands of podcasts with everybody from brand-new triathletes to Antarctic marathon finishers, and otherwise thought, talked, and dreamed about running 24/7.

Sarah and I made it clear that we led from the middle of the pack, so I didn't feel pressure to rip it up with seven-minute splits. That said, as a cofounder of a running business with a very engaged community, I felt a quiet obligation to run often and document it. In my mind, I told myself I needed to cover enough weekly mileage to be able to jump into a half-marathon with little notice, to have my daily workouts show up on Strava, to post mid-run selfies with wide smiles and clever captions. Knowing how fragile my body was on a pure running diet, I spread my focus to triathlons within several years of *Run Like a Mother* being published. Mixing up my workouts with cycling and swimming prolonged my running career—and allowed me to finish an Ironman triathlon in 2014, the best race of my life—but deep down, I knew the end was always lurking. With our relationship rocky even in the best of times, it was just a matter of time before running and I parted ways.

Although my professional connection to running amplified the intensity of my transition, whether you're an ER doctor, a stay-at-home mom, or a desk jockey, ending your running years is tough, and not in that satisfying long-run way. Running is so sticky, so all-encompassing, that even when you're not actively logging miles, it permeates nearly every aspect of your life. Your T-shirt drawer is stuffed with race tees and your front hallway overflows with running shoes. You wear your GPS to a friend's wedding because you want to make sure you log all your steps on the dance floor. You're driving down a newly paved road, and you can't help but wonder what it would be like to run it. You make early dinner plans with friends—or duck out of them—because you've got a 5:15 alarm the next morning. Your weekend "vacations" involve running a half-marathon and, when you take a "real" vacation, you scout out several routes before you commit to an Airbnb.

And perhaps your bookcase is lined with books about running: training guides to your best marathon; strength programs to stay injury-free; personal narratives from pro runners. None, however, addresses how to stop running or helps you process the transition when your body can no longer handle this favorite activity, this near daily companion you're not sure you can live without.

That's where I—and plenty of other women who have been in your shoes—come in. While researching this book, I talked to over fifty accomplished women about their running years: the highs and the lows, the beginnings and the ends.* Some of us are making peace with significantly less mileage than we used to cover, some of us are freshly mourning running, and some of us, like me, haven't run in years. Some of us lost running suddenly because of a disease diagnosis, some of us willingly stepped away, and others of us have had running slowly fade away with joint issues. Our stories are woven throughout this book, both in the multifaceted chapters and in the Aid Stations, stand-alone essays between the chapters. No matter where you are on the losing-running spectrum, I am confident you will see yourself in and feel validated by the experiences and emotions of your fellow runners.

Before we dive in together, I want you to know two things.

First, this book does not take you on a linear, step-by-step process from just letting your Hokas gather dust in the garage to riding 20 miles on a new bike surrounded by sporty friends. Of course, we're going to dig into dejection and dusty shoes as well as new activities and communities. But I need to be clear: There's no crisp, simple, efficient formula, no *ONE thing*, that ushers in acceptance of losing a sport that gave you community and connection, inner power and mental peace. Likewise, finding your 27th mile, your next athletic chapter, is going to take some trial and error, some flexibility and grace.

Like any meaningful transition or closure, running can't be packed away neatly. "Runners pride themselves on the fact that not many people do it. And that it's the hardest, most pure sport: You're not hiding behind equipment or a team," says Kim Dawson, a sports psychologist who works with amateurs to Olympic-level runners. "If it's the purest thing in your life, it's also going to be the hardest thing to leave."

---

* For the purposes of this book, I basically froze time at the point I talked to them, which was in the second half of 2024. Writing, editing, and publishing a book is its own kind of marathon, so when you read this, they may be in a different spot with their running than when this was written. (If nothing else, they're definitely older.)

In case Dawson doesn't make it clear, here is the second thing you need to know: This is really freakin' hard. (Much harder than qualifying for the Boston Marathon if, you know, you don't have the ability to qualify for next year's Boston while running this year's Boston.)

I wish I could wave a magic wand, like the one I carried once at the Disney Princess Half, and create another physical outlet that could easily substitute for running. It would be low impact and guaranteed to never cause injures but still have the efficiency, endorphins, ease, friendships, and stylish, colorful gear that running does. We could all toss this book aside, smoothly insert ourselves there, and continue moving forward.

Instead, like a good country song so often reminds us, the only way out is through. Along the way, you're probably going to go through six-packs of Kleenex. (And, if you're like menopausal me, whose sleep can no longer withstand an evening drink, maybe a few six-packs of non-alcoholic beer.) You will likely lose some friends. You may become slightly depressed. You might think *walk* is the most vulgar four-letter word ever. You will likely want to throw your phone across the room multiple times when you see a social media post ("Just PR'ed!") from a running friend, perhaps one who ghosted you in real life. You will likely gain some weight. You might wonder, *Who is this person spitting venom out of her eyes at every runner she sees, and why is she driving my car?*

Over time, though, your running-related wounds won't feel so raw, and your body might even move with more ease and energy than before. More importantly, you will come to realize everything that made you a runner—inner drive, endurance, mental toughness, discipline, power, strength, a belief in yourself, just to name a few—is all still within you, just waiting to find its next purpose and goal.

Welcome to the 27th mile, friend. You've covered many, many miles to get here. Although the road ahead looks different from what's behind you, it's still wide open and full of potential, just like you.

CHAPTER 1

Running on Borrowed Time

The Meaning of Miles

On a July morning in 2024, Donna Nash sprays her muscular legs with bug repellent, pulls a visor over her blonde bun, double-knots her Sauconys, and heads out the door around 6:30 a.m. "About an hour later than I wanted to," the second-grade teacher who lives in Connecticut says with a laugh. "You know how that goes." It's summer vacation, and she doesn't have to fly out of bed as soon as the alarm screeches.

Donna, fifty-four years old, has 12 miles on her schedule today, a day when the humidity has her sweating before her GPS has locked onto a satellite signal. Her dark brown ranch house sits atop a steep hill on a gravel road: a boon at the start of the run, a beast at the end. Despite running for nearly thirty-five years, she is still lured in by the combination of gravity and fresh legs and goes out too fast.

Her feet find a rhythm on the downhill, and she's grateful for the ease. Despite the early hour, the sun already seems directly overhead and gnats swarm around her face. These are minor annoyances though. Her

1

real concern is her body and how it will hold up as she pounds her joints for over two hours. About two years ago, her right hip started to deeply ache and exhibited the same symptoms her mother, a longtime runner who eventually had a hip replacement, once had. "It's extremely uncomfortable right now," Donna says. "And it's not going away."

Turning left onto a paved road, she exhales when she feels flat, smooth pavement underfoot and cooling shade overhead. There's a scant six inches of shoulder on this typical New England road, but cars are few on a Saturday morning, and the maple trees throw shadows across most of it.

Today's run, despite the length, doesn't have any hallmarks of a typical long run: exploring new routes, watching splits to gauge fitness, or covering a loop instead of an out-and-back that forces her to trot by the same scenery twice. Donna has just one goal: to cover these dozen miles as smoothly as possible, and she's willing to trade novelty and performance for simply going the distance with minimal joint aggravation. On the pavement, Donna runs about two-tenths of a mile in one direction, does a U-turn, and runs back to the start. She repeats this pattern: back and forth, back and forth on a flat, shaded patch, until she covers about 5 miles.

Her hip is still quiet, but she's careful not to press her luck. For the next 6 miles, she gears down to run/walk intervals: two minutes of running, thirty seconds of walking. When absolute boredom with one location sets in, she trots to traverse a fresh stretch. Her route, when viewed from above, looks like a stick figure with one short arm and one long leg.

This monotony is far from her all-time favorite hilly run of 6 miles, one that she's covered hundreds of times preparing for eight marathons, over thirty half-marathons, and plenty of 5Ks, 10Ks, Spartans, Warrior Dashes, and Ragnar Relays. Then again, it's not as dull as her other option: a flat 0.4-mile loop around a local park that she laps again and again. There, the bugs aren't nearly as bad, and there's usually a breeze.

The modifications to today's run are part of the program she designed for herself to cross a finish line she can't refuse: the 2024 New York City Marathon in November. To be able to cover 26.2 miles in one stretch, Donna knows she needs to be judicious about how many miles she puts on that delicate right hip, a joint so tender she can't lie on it at night. Its fragility is always on her mind, whether she's lowering herself to the toilet or emptying the dishwasher. Don't even ask her to rate her pain when she has to maneuver in and out of a car, especially after a long road trip. "The absolute worst," she says.

A few years ago, as her two teenage daughters started their college searches, she found she suddenly felt old. A list maker, she decided to create a running bucket list since she soon would have more time on her hands as an empty nester. Although her right hip was quiet at the time, she felt a sense of urgency; she realized three decades of running combined with her active job that required her to stand on her feet all day created a cumulative physical effect she couldn't afford to ignore. "I was definitely wondering when the day would come when I couldn't run anymore," she says.

Items on Donna's bucket list: Beach to Beacon 10K in Maine; Chicago Marathon ("a little further down"); Disney's Dopey Challenge ("bit of a reach"); Vermont City Marathon in Burlington; a half-marathon in Nashville (completed a few months ago); and running the New York City Marathon for a charity, her current quest.

New York City became possible when Becky, her best running friend and a fellow second-grade teacher, was offered two charity bibs for Live On New York, which raises awareness for organ transplants and tissue donations.

Becky asked Donna whether she would run it with her.

"How do I say no to that?" Donna asks.

She didn't. Instead, she treats her running like fine china, pulling it out only when necessary. She runs three days per week, never on back-to-back days and often circling the breezy, bug-free park loop. Instead of employing a typical marathon training schedule, which includes incrementally longer runs every week, Donna is slicing that in half: She covers double digits twice per month. After today's 12-miler, her next long run won't be for another two weeks. And even though she thrives on racing, she won't pin on a bib until the marathon in November, not even for her favorite New Milford 8-Mile Road Race, a summer race with roller-coaster hills she's done almost every year. If she shows up at that race, she's scared she'll get swept up in the momentum and push herself—and her hip—too hard.

To mitigate the miles, she gets regular massages, regularly does pigeon pose and other hip-opening moves, and takes Advil "when it starts to get nasty." Her other workouts in the week are gentle on her joints: walks with a friend, yoga, and some strength training.

Making her situation feel more fragile is the knowledge that genetics are not on her side. Her father had a hip replacement at age eighty. Her mother, who started running in her fifties and ran into her seventies, got her replacement at age seventy-five.

Conveniently, her mom is also a former emergency room nurse. "Every time I share a symptom with my mom, she's like, 'Yep, I'm sure a replacement is going to be in your future,'" Donna says. Even though maternal advice can be hard to hear at age fifty-four, Donna is grateful for the sounding board. Her mom is the only medical professional she has consulted about her situation. "I admit I'm temporarily sweeping it under the rug," she says. "I'm scared of what my doctor will say. I don't want to be told no."

I'm guessing you wouldn't want to be told no either.

I certainly wasn't going to say no when I had the chance to run the New York City Marathon in 2010. At that time, I had two marathons under my belt. The first was the 1997 New York City Marathon, which I finished injury-free thanks to my twenty-five-year-old body. Ten years and two kids later, I eked my way through the 2007 Nike Women's Marathon. The training cycle was brutal, featuring a stress fracture in my heel and a sprained ankle when I temporarily came out of the boot. (Yes, I spent eight weeks of a sixteen-week training cycle not running.)

Despite having an expert coach writing my workouts and guiding my training for the 2007 marathon, I couldn't stay healthy. Knowing how much the marathon meant to me, my coach revised my program so that I spent most of my time preparing for a high-impact marathon via low-impact cycling. Looking back, if I'd been a little more self-aware—or more open to the idea that running served as my antidepressant and way to feel okay in my own skin—that mid-program switch could have been a clear warning sign: Maybe long-distance running wasn't the best choice for me.

Finishing the Nike marathon wasn't just about getting a sparkly Tiffany's finisher's necklace from a hunky firefighter though. Sarah Bowen Shea, a fellow freelance writer who would become my business partner, and I were documenting our training and race day for *Runner's World* magazine. People were commenting on our blogs, watching our training, cheering us on. We represented a group of women who were, at the time, kind of tossed aside in the running world: middle- and back-of-the-pack women who weren't necessarily natural runners, who came to the sport as adults, and who thrived on the structure, community, and identity the sport gave them. The idea of *not* finishing and either losing the assignment or—worse yet—documenting my failure in what was then the bible for running just wasn't an option.

Holding my sister's hand, I crossed the line, and the banana-wide smile on my face said it all: I had done it. Elation. My clothes were streaked with white lines of dried sweat, my short hair was soaked, and I felt like a complete and total badass. Our feature story, called "Marathon Moms," resonated with runners who were just like us: women who set high goals and, despite crazy schedules and unrelenting demands, got it done. Three years later, our book *Run Like a Mother* was published. Within a few more years, we had a company focused on running: Another Mother Runner. It became my exclusive source of income and a huge source of my personal and professional fulfillment.

The book was released a few months before Asics, then a partner with the New York City Marathon, offered me a spot in the 2010 race. My coach for this training cycle was going to be Andrew Kastor, the husband of Olympian medalist and Asics-sponsored athlete Deena Kastor. Stress fractures and weak core be damned, I thought, of course I want to be trained by a celebrity coach and outfitted by Asics from head to toe. Would you say no? In the age before influencers (or even Instagram) were a thing, I, and our new book, had the chance to be put on a pedestal before one of the largest marathons in the world.*

Although my previous stress fracture was three years in my rearview mirror, I wasn't naive. I knew with certainty that my body would crack again if I took on another marathon training cycle. I also knew with certainty that I didn't have the guts to admit that to our quickly growing community. What kind of leader would I be if I couldn't run a marathon?

So, in June, six months before race day, I skirted around it. In a blog post centered on my excitement for the marathon, I also publicly gave myself guidelines:

- *I am going to listen to my body.* If a training session hurts too much, I'm done. If I wake up hobbled in pain, no workout except stretching and maybe light yoga.†
- *My biggest concern when I run is going to be my form, not my time.* For at least a few months, my Garmin is staying in the random electronics basket, where I'm pretty sure my Walkman, a gift from 1999, is fermenting.
- *I want to cross the finish line in NYC as a stronger, healthier, more efficient, smarter runner who's got a rock-solid body to prove it.* If I do that, I won't care what the clock reads.
- *My training is going to be unconventional.* I learned, through the Nike marathon adventure, that you can prepare numerous ways for a marathon. So, I'm planning on running trails for time, not miles, for most of my long runs;‡ I'm going to

---

* To be clear, this pedestal was not an official race podium. Asics put no time qualifications or expectations on my entry or those that it offered to other journalists.
† This intense description makes me think I *might* have known the hobbled feeling all too well.
‡ I searched and searched for my preliminary emails with Coach Andrew and couldn't find them. But I definitely recall an exchange in which I passed this trail idea by him, and he wasn't keen on it. His message: You've got to train on pavement if you're going to run for four plus hours on pavement. Smart coach.

swim and bike pretty heavily; I'm in for Pilates at least two times a week; I'm going to strength train starting tomorrow.*

- *Did I mention I am going to listen to my body?* I really am. When I told Sarah of my decision to run the marathon, with all these conditions, she said, "Can you put that in writing? Because I know you have the ability to just tough it out." None of that. There will be no toughing it out, except maybe on race day.

One month later, in July, after celebrating a pain-free 5 miles, I laid on another layer of strict conditions: a public proclamation doubling as private protection. "I've told myself that if I can run 10 miles by early August with a pain level of 3 or below on a scale of 1 to 10, then I'll take on the marathon training for NYC full throttle," I wrote. "Like I've said before: no marathon grind this time. My body and mind can't hack it."

Coach Andrew at the helm, I embarked on my official marathon training. I made it to day 14—two whole weeks—before having to trade in my running shoes for bike pedals with, yes, another stress fracture.

I'm confident my fate so many years ago will not be Donna's fate this year.† She'll get her ninth marathon medal, and I bet she'll even complete the finish-line cartwheel she promises if she finishes in under six hours.

That said, her quest for a finish line in New York City is about trying to push back another finish line, a much bigger one that, when crossed, rips up a daily routine, slashes an identity, and upends decades of exercise and endorphins. "Running is pretty much everything to me," she says. "It makes me feel fantastic and accomplished. It's therapy, mental clarity, a stress reliever, time for reflection, a mood booster all wrapped in one."

---

* Tomorrow? LOL.
† She's solid. She's rarely had any running injuries over the course of thirty-five years and has finished eight marathons already. And although height has no scientific correlation to marathon success, she's five two, over a foot shorter than I am.

Without knowing much about Donna, given only these three details you can picture the daily routine she's had for decades: She's a runner, she's a mother, she's a second-grade teacher.

You see her workout clothes laid out on the bathroom floor so she doesn't wake her husband ("absolutely not a runner") and kids as she rallies before dawn for her miles. You watch her slip out the door into the crisp fall air, switching on a headlamp as she heads down the hill as familiar to her as the smell of each daughter's hair. The quiet darkness feels pristine, not scary, and when the sun rises directly ahead of her, you know exactly what she's thinking: *How lucky am I to be the only one alive witnessing this?* She thinks through her day, through her problems, through nothing. Five miles down, her sports bra is soaked. As the run wraps up, goosebumps prick her skin in the chill, and you can almost feel them too. She steps into the kitchen just as the rest of the house begins to stir.

She's not ready to shower yet though. Feel-good endorphins coursing through her body, she buzzes around the kitchen, making sure her two girls are ready for a day of school and sports practices. She's not fazed by one of them worrying about a biology test and the other griping about peanut butter and honey sandwiches *again*. "Really, Mom?"

She's fresh off a run, after all. You know the feeling: You float above most of the complaints and worries that trip you up when you're merely a human on earth. After a quick shower, during which she flexes her calves just to check out her ripped muscles, she heads to school brimming with energy, more than enough to face a day of reminding her students where a period goes in a sentence and hunting down errant lunch boxes. Her legs feel satisfyingly tired as she squats at a desk or climbs a flight of stairs. They're strong; she's strong. The run's high has worn off by the time she heads home, but something deeper remains: the quiet steadiness of someone who claimed a victory close to twelve hours ago, before most people woke up. She's got enough natural endurance to make it through to bedtime, before which she'll lay out her clothes in the bathroom so she can do it all over again tomorrow.

Although the simultaneously exhilarating and exhausting pace of the day might be overwhelming for most, it is perfect and fulfilling for Donna, a runner who is also, in her own words, "not a good sit stiller."

Back on the road, Donna's run/walk intervals get her to mile 11, a mile short of her 12-mile target. For the final mile, she runs the few down-hills and walks the rest. The humidity is a bear, and she is toast. As she climbs the hill to her house, she gives herself a little pep talk: "I'm doing it. I'm doing the work. I'm going to be able to put a sticker on my training chart."*

She walks inside, pulls off her visor and shoes, and sends a download text to Becky, her running buddy and biggest cheerleader. "You're doing great," Becky, a decade younger than Donna, writes back. "Get yourself a popsicle and put your feet up."

Donna, as we've already established, is not one who puts her feet up. But maybe this afternoon she'll investigate adult swimming lessons, an activity she's contemplated starting after the marathon. "It's imperative I find an activity that will replace running," she says. "I'm having a hard time imagining my life without being able to move my body in a way that helps keep my mental health in check." She's not interested in bike riding—the terrain around her house is too hilly—and she knows that, when her running days come to a hard stop, strength training, yoga, and walking will not fill the void that running leaves.

She can't imagine herself doing laps in a pool just yet. She's not a nat-ural swimmer and is nervous about the skill involved. "I think I'd need to start with inflatable swimmies on my arms," she says with a laugh. Still, the idea of pivoting to the pool feels slightly agreeable, as does setting up a doctor's appointment post-marathon to get a true diagnosis and timeline on her right hip.

---

* Once, as a joke, Donna's husband hid her sticker chart. "I almost lost my mind."

Before all that happens, of course, she's got 26.2 miles in New York City to cover, which might be the easiest of the tasks set before her. She doesn't seem visibly worried about any of them. "If running has taught me anything," she says, "it's taught me that I can do hard things."

Putting Running in Context: What's the Big Deal?

As a working mom, my stream of daily thoughts can be classified, at best, as mundane. *What time, again, is that meeting today? Is Dave's Killer Bread cheaper at Costco or on sale at the grocery store? Is the dog's prescription for arthritis meds about to run out? Did anybody replace the toilet paper in the kitchen bathroom?*

When I am in motion, though, my thoughts elevate. Yes, I've made plenty of mental grocery lists during my miles, but I also listened to Eckhart Tolle read *The Power of Now* during one of my run/walk phases. I spent a full hour turning over his koan: *You are not the voice in your head; you are the one who hears it.* Other times, I rooted myself in the world around me. *I share DNA with that woolly caterpillar inching across the path. I am breathing oxygen produced by the trees shading me. The sun I see rising now in Colorado will soon be setting over Japan.*

One major question that consistently pinged around my brain: *Why does running matter so much?* I mean, I knew why it mattered on a practical level: It got me up early, gave structure to my day, kept my quads strong and my mind clear. But there are plenty of other reasons to set an early alarm, other ways to anchor a daily routine, to stay healthy. Why did running feel so essential to my being?

My grandiose thoughts are much sparser now that I'm no longer running, but I wanted to remind myself how I thought of the sport when I was in motion. Sitting still, I racked my brain for philosophical nuggets from my college years. I don't recall how many circles of hell Dante created, but I do remember snippets from three renowned psychological theories from Psych 101: Maslow's hierarchy of needs, Yalom's existential theory, and Csikszentmihalyi's flow. Revisiting those ideas helped me understand why running means so much—and why losing it can feel like a personal unraveling. Running fulfills some of our deepest human needs. It gives us space to wrestle with life's biggest questions. And it regularly delivers the kind of flow-state experience that makes us feel fully alive.

If you're struggling to pinpoint why your missed miles have completely rocked your world or to explain the depth of your loss to somebody who categorizes your runs the same way she thinks about her knitting, here's the rundown.

Maslow's Hierarchy of Needs

What It Is

A five-level pyramid created by psychologist Abraham Maslow, the hierarchy stacks up the bulk of human needs: the first level is basic needs, the second is safety, the third is love and belonging, the fourth is esteem, and the fifth is self-actualization.*

How Running Relates

Running is loosely connected to the pyramid's first level of physiological needs. Although running isn't shelter or air or any other basic need, being a committed runner means you take the essentials of food, sleep, and water seriously.

Move up one level to safety needs, and running is fully relevant. It boosts all aspects of your physical health, helps regulate anxiety, and makes you feel like you've got some control over your body, your stress, and, on the best days, even your life.

Running shines in the third level: love and belonging. *Community* could be running's middle name. The sport serves up connection in myriad ways: friendships with a trusted training partner; weekly workouts

---

* Fun fact: Maslow was a runner. Not-so-fun fact: He died from a heart attack at age sixty-two while out for a jog.

with a running club; the prerace buzz at an expo; even a smile shared with a fellow runner also wearing a Big Sur Marathon sweatshirt at the airport.

Climb up one more rung to esteem: feeling valued by yourself and others. Running comes in here hot, meeting needs like achievement, confidence, mastery, recognition, and, although they came after Maslow's time, kudos on Strava.

Finally, Maslow defined the fifth level—self-actualization—as realizing one's full potential and being the most that one can be. That's our sport in a nutshell: soaking up the mile you're in while believing the next one can be better.

Yalom's Existential Theory

What It Is

Psychiatrist Irvin Yalom theorized that to live a fulfilling life, we must confront four ultimate concerns: death, freedom, isolation, and meaninglessness.*

How Running Relates

Starting with a big one: death. That mid-run feeling, with your pores pouring and your legs flying, is pure vibrancy and presence; it makes you feel alive with a capital A. On the flip side, aching knees, favorite routes that become too challenging, and splits that get slower gently remind us that our running days—and indeed all our days—are limited.

Next up is freedom, or the idea that you carry the burden of responsibility for your choices. Nobody forces you to run. Every time you set out, you are deliberately making a choice about your health, time, and priorities. You are writing the direction of your day and your life, building inner power with every mile.

We often run solo, which gives us space to experience and contemplate isolation, the third biggie on Yalom's list. You run alone, and, yes, you

---

* Yalom was also a runner.

will die alone. Morbid but true. Still, running offers valuable moments of camaraderie with training partners, group runs, and races. A sweaty hug at the end of a 10K makes those miles incredibly meaningful, ones you may use to power through a solo run.

Finally, running takes on meaninglessness—*What am I even here for?*—through the act of running itself. You choose to run. You choose to do a hard thing, even when nobody is watching, when nobody really cares. With every mile, you ground your presence in this world, solidify your identity, and define what matters to you.

Csikszentmihalyi's Flow

What It Is

Psychologist Mihaly Csikszentmihalyi coined the term *flow* to define a state of deep immersion while doing any activity. Essential elements of flow include an optimal challenge, full focus, clear goals with immediate feedback, and intrinsic rewards.

How Running Relates

Whether you're relatively new or a master athlete, running continually offers up the first flow essential: optimal challenge, the place where you feel skilled enough to stretch yourself, but not excessively. As you focus on a pace, a personal record (PR), or a race distance, you're in that sweet spot where your confidence builds as your feet run beneath you. It feels like growth, not a grind.

Full focus, the second flow essential, naturally blooms with the cadence of your strides and your steady inhales and exhales. Thoughts aren't pinging around anymore, and your mind isn't running away from you. It's exactly where your feet are.

Running's linear structure provides a chance to perceive clear goals and get immediate feedback, another flow essential. You plan to run 4 miles, and thanks to your GPS, you know exactly how long it took you.

Zooming out, you can have multiple goals going at once: monthly mileage goals, completing a 10K in three months, a lifetime goal of finishing a half-marathon in every state. All easy—and satisfying—to measure.

Finally, the fourth element of flow is intrinsic reward, or running for how it makes you feel. You may have started running to lose weight or on the invitation of a friend, but you stayed for yourself. You run in pursuit of a clearer head, a sense of power, an inner calm, that smile that naturally appears around mile 2. It never gets old.

AID STATION

Jen Says No to One More Marathon

Jen Rucker knew she was in trouble when, about halfway through the Brooklyn Half-Marathon, her left knee blew up. "The pain was excruciating," she says. "I could hardly put any pressure on my leg." She staggered to the finish line, dragging her left leg as best she could.* "I knew I pushed it too far," says the former collegiate soccer player.

About five months earlier, a lightning rod of pain went through her hamstring as she was sitting at the dinner table. She visited her doctor, who suggested the pain might be stemming from her back, not her hamstring, but Jen wasn't convinced. A steroid pack calmed things down enough for her to continue to run—and not check in with him again. She trained with no memorable pain for the Brooklyn Half, a bucket-list run; her dad was born and raised in Brooklyn, and Jen is a native New Yorker herself.†

At that point, Jen, an elementary school reading specialist, had finished twelve marathons—and plenty of half-marathons during the marathon training cycles—in seven intense years, when she barely took a break from training. Five of those marathons were the Marine Corps, a favorite near her hometown in Maryland.

Some might consider that schedule a little aggressive, but Jen found her people, purpose, and connection in the Montgomery County Road Runners, particularly its First Time Marathon (FTM) program. She was a runner with FTM for five years, then became a pace coach. Along the way, she bonded with three guys—fellow coaches Jeff and John and runner Jason—and the four of them branded themselves the J's. In their prime, the J's road-tripped to Corning, New York, for the Wine Glass

---

* Yes, she finished a half-marathon without being able to lift her heel. Not recommended, of course, but racing can sometimes elicit in-the-moment behaviors that, in hindsight, you realize weren't super healthy.

† "Despite how horrible I felt, I still consider it one of my favorite races. The course and crowds were fantastic."

Marathon. "I had a monster marathon PR of seventeen minutes," she remembers. Their post-race celebration dinner also included Jen blowing out birthday candles. "All the gifts were running related, of course."

Back home in Maryland after the Brooklyn race, the doctor she'd ghosted a few months earlier got her in to see a back specialist, stat. Turns out, a disc was pressing on a motor nerve, and she had to have surgery to repair the issue.

She tried to return to running after surgery, but it didn't feel great. Although she was mentally ready for a gentle ease back into the sport, her nerve-damaged heel was still healing. Her fellow J's were in similar situations; all their bodies needed a break. "We all just did too much," she says. "We got burnt out."

Six months after surgery, an advertisement for a Pure Barre class caught her eye. She reluctantly went. "I never thought I'd enjoy studio classes." The sixty-minute session was surprisingly challenging for a marathon runner, and she loved the variations of classes. Over time, she found a new community. "It took a little longer because you're not really talking like you can on a run," she says. Now forty-five years old, she's hitting the barre at least three times weekly.

Back in the spring of 2024, the J's got a group text from Jeff: *Should we get the band back together? Marine Corps one more time?** The query arrived the same day Jen's soon-to-be ex-husband was moving out of their house. "Our divorce is amicable," she says. "Still, it felt serendipitous."

She took a day to think it over, then texted back: *I'm* in. In fact, they were all in, and the J's were so excited about it, they all paid the Marine Corps registration fee before one of them even ran a single training mile.

Jen signed up for a half-marathon, ready to repeat a half-then-full marathon training pattern that had worked for her in the past. Except that she didn't really embrace the preparation like she used to. "My

---

* If you run the Marine Corps Marathon five times, you get an annual guaranteed entry.

training was not consistent or fun," she says. "I felt like my body was rejecting running." For seven years, Barre had made her feel strong, fluid, and whole, and just a few months of running nearly broke her. Her knees and feet were in constant pain.

Standing at the half-marathon starting line, she felt pangs of joy; she had missed the energy and anticipation of the starting line. By the finish line, though, her mood had definitely downshifted. She realized she was done with her second chapter of running. Her sixth Marine Corps Marathon would not happen.

She texted the J's and told them so. Two followed her path: One never got started, and the other was injured early in his training. Only Jeff took a 26.2-mile victory lap around Washington, DC. The other three J's volunteered at a water stop during a July training run. Jen loved handing out Gatorades and chatting with Jeff and other FTM friends, but she didn't leave with a feeling of regret for the path she had traveled.

"Some of the biggest benefits were the friends and memories running brought me," she says, "and I still have those."

CHAPTER 2

Making the Decision

Should I Stay or Should I Go?

When it comes to races, Ruthie McCartney is a rule follower. Which is how she found herself standing on a windy pier on a Wilmington, Delaware, beach at 5 a.m. on a February morning. "The race director was very clear," she says. "Get on an early shuttle."

So, Ruthie, fifty-five years old, set her alarm for four o'clock. She rose, pulled on her favorite black Under Armour tank top, and double-knotted her Karhu Synchrons, a style she'd been loyal to for three years. Before she closed the door to the hotel room, she zipped a Honey Stinger vanilla waffle, her favorite prerace snack, into her jacket pocket and made her way down to the lobby. For fifteen years, she had run two half-marathons annually, so she knew exactly what prerace routine worked for her. This morning, she was doing her best to shift to race-day autopilot so she could tune out the diagnosis she just received: arthritis in her right knee.

Despite getting a cortisone shot from her doctor recently and a professional taping at the expo yesterday, her knee would not be ignored. "The pain was undeniable," says Ruthie, who had started running to celebrate her fortieth birthday. ("I'd already been skydiving, so I thought, 'I need to find something else.'") Sitting alone on the mostly empty shuttle, she looked out the window as the bus passed mile markers 6 and 7. She winced, forecasting how painful her knee would feel mid-race.

She got off the bus and, to kill time, wandered out to the pier, which was too windy for her minimal layers. Ruthie had two choices to get warm: a porta-potty or the tiny gift shop, opened early to let the rule-following runners get warm. A "nervous tinkler," she'd typically head to the loo. "If there's a chance to use a bathroom, I take it." Instead, she slowly walked back toward the parking lot, where more-populated shuttles were dropping full buses of excited, chatty runners. "I just knew. I knew," she recalls. She couldn't eke out 13.1 miles. She lied, telling a volunteer she wasn't feeling well, and asked whether she could get back on the bus. She could. Sliding into a seat, the voices in her head wouldn't stop. *Who goes to a starting line but doesn't start?*

To quiet her mind on the ride back to the Hampton Inn, Ruthie called her friend Sarah, who traveled with her from Virginia, to explain she didn't have her own key to the room. It wasn't even six o'clock yet, but she had faith in Sarah, whom she'd met a decade ago on a group run. "Sarah's my run, ride, or die: the kind of friend who helped me and my children move out of my ex-husband's house when I left him," she says, adding that she realized at mile 8 of her first half-marathon that her marriage was over.

When Sarah opened the door, she pulled Ruthie into a bear hug. Ruthie immediately broke down, her body shaking as she sobbed. Sarah held her close, reassuring her that she'd made the right decision. Although Sarah was hoping to crawl back into bed, grab breakfast, and ease into the day, Ruthie was already moving. "I knew hanging around Wilmington was a bad decision for my mental health. I did not want to be reminded of my not running." They were on the road home by 7 a.m. Speeding home as they talked more about Ruthie's predicament, Sarah said she would tell people whatever Ruthie wanted her to about the race.

"Better yet, she told me she would kick anybody's ass who judged me," Ruthie says. "Every woman needs a Sarah in her life."

Although Ruthie's story feels like a polished Hollywood version of the end of a running career, it's not that tidy for most of us. It certainly wasn't for me.

When I got the *you-should-consider-not-running-anymore* diagnosis from my orthopedist, I had done exactly five short-for-me runs in ten months and had already skipped out on both a half-Ironman and a half-marathon I was registered for. "It feels like somebody poured hot coffee into the motherboard of my back," I told my doctor. I was convinced most of my lower body muscles, ligaments, and tendons didn't know how to function properly anymore.

Compounding the physical issues were three other factors: I was a full-time working mom of two; my husband was also self-employed, so our health benefits were skimpy; and, after nearly fifteen years of riding the injury cycle, I wasn't keen on embracing months of tedious steps to totally rewire my running form that might or might not work. In other words, my time, resources, and patience were extremely limited.

But our business was riding high. Sarah Bowen Shea and I had published three running-centric books, appeared regularly at race expos, and had a podcast so popular I was recognized by my voice at 2 a.m. while pacing a friend at the Rocky Raccoon 100-miler in Huntsville, Texas. Even though I spoke and wrote frequently about my injuries and being sidelined from running, I hadn't yet publicly talked about being permanently done with the sport. I was terrified of how it would land. If cheering for runners at mile 24 six hours into the marathon has taught me anything, it's this: Runners don't quit.

The orthopedist tempered his diagnosis by letting me know I could "continue to run 5Ks now and then." When I first heard that, I was enraged—I was *so* much more than a Turkey Trotter—but after a few minutes of sitting with the idea, a sense of relief flooded my nervous system. Here was an expert I respected, a thoughtful man who knew that both my professional life and emotional well-being centered around running. He was bold enough to suggest that this thing I loved to do was causing more harm than good, and if I continued to chase after it, my body would suffer bigger repercussions down the line. I gave him a hug, my tears soaking his light blue oxford.

In the same way I told my kids to "blame it on me" when they didn't feel confident enough to back out of an exorbitant pre-prom dinner, I could blame my exit on the doctor. Which I did almost immediately in a post on the Another Mother Runner website and in a podcast with Sarah. That said, I tiptoed around it. I couldn't stomach saying or writing the word *quit*, and I also wasn't ready to permanently lock the door on running. "I am consciously redirecting my energy away from my running" was the phrase I returned to repeatedly to explain my situation.

Feeling lighter than I had in a year, I continued to swim, strength train, hike, and cycle. Eventually, the fried motherboard calmed down enough so I could even run a little bit: twenty to thirty-five minutes on the Highline Canal, a flat, gravel path near my house. I rationalized it by telling myself I was running less than a 5K no more than once per week. Knowing my back couldn't hack the 2-mile round trip to the path, I drove the five minutes down to the trail, my bruised ego sitting in the passenger seat next to me.

Bolstered by these short runs, I wanted one more swing at a race, one more chance to remind myself that I could go big. I was intrigued by a competition called SwimRun, a hybrid race in which teams of two cover a racecourse by alternating between swimming and running segments. My friend Katie, whose swimming and running skills surpass mine—she was the one I was pacing in the Rocky Raccoon 100—was kind enough to be my teammate. We'd swim between islands in Casco Bay, Maine, then run through them.

I prepared minimally for the runs, which totaled about 13 miles on race day. On the ferry over to the island start, I traced diamonds around my knees with KT Tape—my body felt like a sandcastle at high tide at that point—and during the race, I gritted, hobbled, and badly bruised some ribs when I slipped on an especially rocky island. Carnage notwithstanding, I had a blast. I took in all the details: swimming through patches of seaweed as large as a semi; running down island roads dotted with cabins with quaint screened porches; urging myself to take ten more strokes, then ten more when the chilly waters started to freeze my motivation. Afterward, though, everything ached, and my hamstring swelled bigger than it ever had. Got it, Universe: Thirteen miles in one day—and even in one week—was too ambitious.

Once my body calmed down *again*, I mentally drafted a run-forever plan. I didn't really talk publicly about my running anymore, but I still craved the rhythm of my feet underneath me, which quieted my mind like a lullaby. Two easy runs per week on the Highline would fill my cup, I thought, without allowing me to cross back into dangerous physical territory. I wouldn't ever race again, but I'd keep enough skin in the game to have another cardio option when a bike ride or swim felt too onerous and to not feel like a poser when I dispensed running advice.

On a thirty-minute run, my hamstring typically started groaning around twenty minutes, so I often ran/walked the last ten minutes. *Good enough*, I told myself, repeating a mantra I'd often use around Another Mother Runner when we talked about adjusting perfectionist tendencies when life got too chaotic. If the workout has eight intervals, six is good enough. If I really should consider not running anymore, sixty minutes total a week is good enough.

For a full year—spring, summer, fall, winter—I ran once or twice per week. The runs were fine: They fired up my endorphins and boosted my mood, but they also made me feel like I was wandering around at the end of a party, clutching an empty beer bottle. The fun was over. A little over three years after that fateful appointment, good-enough running just didn't hold my interest anymore.

As I drove down to the Highline on a January afternoon, I didn't mentally proclaim it as my last run. I didn't try to mentally timestamp each mile for posterity. I didn't cry on the way home either.

Like Ruthie, I just knew. I didn't have some great epiphany that I was finally calm, content, and confident enough to be done. By the end of it,

I simply sensed I no longer needed to run. I also realized this: I couldn't have arrived at that spot without running thousands of miles first.

In between Ruthie's cinematic moment and my slow fade lie thousands of factors that influence the decision to step back. These four women followed winding roads that all ended at considerably less mileage and a new perspective on moving forward.

Pam: "Running Made Me Feel Really Awful About Myself"

When Pam Harris was in her late twenties, her best friend—"a very forceful personality"—decided they both needed to start running to lose weight. "The first time I ran a mile without stopping was a high like no other. I quite literally wanted to keep going farther and farther," says Pam, now forty-three. Crossing her first marathon finish line in Melbourne, Florida, her childhood hometown, she gave a virtual finger to her middle school PE teacher who mocked her in gym class. Crossing her second marathon finish line confirmed what she suspected: Training for 26.2 miles played to her strengths of patience, persistence, and consistency.

Six months after her third marathon—a virtual Boston Marathon, thanks to COVID—Pam was diagnosed with thyroid cancer. At the time, she was already signed up for Wine Glass, a flat and fast marathon in Corning, New York, then five months away. After getting the go-ahead from her doctors to continue training, she kept the race on the calendar; worst-case scenario, she figured she'd drop to the half-marathon. But the surgery to remove half her thyroid sapped all her endurance. She couldn't go 4 miles without multiple walk breaks. She scrapped her Wine Glass plans and took some time to regroup.

About eight months later, Pam, a research manager, signed up for her current hometown's signature race: Atlanta's Peachtree, a 10K. A distance, she notes, she could have once run in her sleep. She slogged through the training cycle, hoping for a moment when an easy 3-miler didn't feel like a heavy lift. It never came. The drain wasn't just physical. "Instead of running feeding my soul and making me feel good like it used to, it just made me really feel awful about myself," she admits.

Still, on July 4, she rode the light rail to downtown Atlanta with running friends, hoping for some race-day magic and momentum. "Collective effervescence: when you have the same surge of emotion as your fellow participants, like at a concert or a race," she says. "The feeling that we're all in this together. I've always loved that about races." Unfortunately, she felt little connection to her fellow runners or her former running self. She found herself feeling flat, just going through the motions. "It was nothing like my former races," she says.

Pam had come to a metaphorical fork in the road. She could keep running, hoping that with more patience, persistence, and consistency, she could get back to her sweet spot where she could run for hours. Or she could step back.

"Nothing about running felt good," she says, "I couldn't tell whether it was physical or mental, but I decided I didn't care. I didn't want to keep making myself feel bad." She opted to trade her running shoes for boxing gloves and a fresh start in a brand-new activity where no comparisons with her former self—or sport—lingered.

When the voice of regret came calling, telling her she should reconsider running, she reminded herself that she was still working out five days per week and taking care of her body and mind. "I pivoted when it was the healthy thing to do for all of me," she says, "and I'm so proud of myself for that."

Paige: "I Was Running Myself into the Ground"

Perhaps one of the only twelve-year-olds who loved the President's mile in middle school, Paige Kaptuch started running as a tween and didn't look back. She ran through grad school at the University of Arizona as she got her MFA in fiction; she ran as she taught English at a boarding school in Connecticut to support her husband, then in medical school; and as a "medium-fast master's runner," she ran while working as a sales rep for Goodr sunglasses, Picky Bars, Oiselle, and other boutique brands in the running industry, with a goal to qualify for Boston. She got her second Boston Qualifier (BQ) on the day she turned forty, flying down Utah's Wasatch Mountains at the 2018 Ogden Marathon in a time of 3:33.*

When she arrived in Boston the following spring, Boylston Street didn't quite have the allure she anticipated. "It's embarrassing," she admits. "I worked so hard to qualify, but the race was so unfulfilling to me." The streets seemed jammed, the urban scenery didn't compare to the natural beauty of Utah, and the crowded finish line felt too empty to her; her family wasn't there to cheer her on. The race left a physical aftertaste too: She gained weight, felt bloated, and couldn't think clearly for weeks and weeks afterward.

A few months later, Paige felt like she had a broken toe. Physical therapists gave her foot exercises, but they provided no relief. As the summer wore on, her hip started talking to her, then sciatica set in. The nerve pain running down the back of her leg became brutal when Paige was alone with her kids, then ages two and four, on a road trip to Flagstaff, Arizona. "I felt like I was nearly paralyzed," she says. She gutted out a ten-hour drive home and "ugly cried" when she turned into her driveway.

An MRI revealed a herniated disc and pinched nerve. Although she was wary of back surgery, she opted for it instead of unknown months of drawn-out recovery. Her son was about to start kindergarten, and she was in so much pain, she could barely get off the floor to help him pack a backpack.

Thankfully, the surgery was a success, and she was able to resume her regular running within a few months. Her miles exploded when the pandemic hit; she and her friends found connection and refuge running among the sandstone canyons and bighorn sheep of the Colorado National Monument in Grand Junction, Colorado.†

---

* She also ran a 3:33 in 1997—twenty-one years prior—but was injured before she could cross the starting line in Boston.
† "You're not allowed to mountain bike or even walk your dog there. It was just quiet trails. A total luxury."

As her time on the trail added up, Paige started craving another shot at a marathon. This time, though, she wanted the anti-Boston: the Desert RATS Trail Running Marathon in Fruita, Colorado, which is part of a small trail running festival. She would be surrounded by familiar faces and be racing on trails that overlook the Colorado River, routes she knew intimately.

Despite her extensive preparation and the beloved setting, it was her worst marathon yet.* The same exhaustion that plagued her after Boston came roaring back: weight gain, brain fog, overall fatigue. This time, she connected some dots between long, hard efforts and her postrace mega-slump. She had recently read about pro runner Ryan Hall's early retirement because of low testosterone levels, and she wondered if she could be in the same place.† After all, she had been running for thirty-three years. A hormone panel showed she, at age forty-two, had no testosterone—a significant absence, given that the hormone contributes to bone density, muscle mass, cognitive function, daily energy, and overall mood. "I was running myself into the ground," she says. (The impending hormone disruption of perimenopause was also on the horizon, she notes, so her body was serving up a volatile cocktail.)

The lab results forced a reckoning for Paige. She wasn't just worried about when the next back flare-up might leave her flattened again. She was also confronting a deeper shift: the steep hormonal decline that was draining her energy, blunting her mood, and reshaping her sense of self. "I remember thinking, 'I don't like how I look. I don't like how I feel,'" she says. "I just decided, I don't want to do this to myself anymore."

A thirty-three-year-old habit dies hard though. These days, Paige will join a friend for a short trail run now and then, but it takes a team—chiropractor, massage therapist, dry needler—to make those miles possible. More often, she finds strength through lifting weights and barre classes,

---

* "It was on the trail, so you can't compare finishing times to the road, but I felt reaaaalllly bad the whole time."
† Relatively same place, of course. "Not that I was performing at his level, but the idea of hormone imbalance from overtraining was a new idea to me."

and challenge in a different kind of marathon: writing the novel that took root during all those years on the run.

Ingrid: "I Broke Up with Running on Valentine's Day"

While in law school in Chicago, Ingrid L. both started and solidified her running habit on the Lakefront Trail, as she soaked up views of the silver skyline against the blue waters of Lake Michigan. "Running gave me an escape portal from my own mind," she says. "There's nothing I love more than lacing up my shoes and letting my worries drop from me one by one."

As a mom working full-time while raising two kids back-to-back, her miles became even more integral to her mental health. Although her doctor didn't officially diagnose her with postpartum depression after the birth of her first son—"it wasn't so well known then"—he told her he wouldn't prescribe anything until she exercised outside three times per week. So Ingrid kept running. The rhythm of her feet felt as soothing to her spirit as diaper cream was to her baby's bottom.

Three decades later, Ingrid, now an attorney, continued to find salvation on her familiar Chicago streets during the pandemic. "We were in new territory; there were no laws in place for situations like COVID," the fifty-six-year-old says. "It was super stressful." At the time, Ingrid was working demanding hours from home, alongside her husband, whose office was also closed. Her two college kids, whom she'd driven across the country to pick up in Colorado and California, were now Zooming into their classrooms from the living room. Even though her knees often ached during and after runs, the mental release was worth a few postrun minutes with frozen peas on her joints. "I told myself, 'I've got to keep running.' I couldn't handle it otherwise."

She designed a training pyramid: 4 miles four times per week in April (the fourth month of the year), 5 miles five times per week in May, and so on. "I made myself a cardboard medal with my kids' old markers at the end of every month," she says. "Anything to make sure I kept going." She also joined Run Oak Park, a club that gave her much-needed community.

Her club friends encouraged her to sign up for her first—and second—half-marathon. With just one weekend in between, the two races were nearly back-to-back. By the time Ingrid crossed the second 13.1-mile finish line, she couldn't straighten her knee.

The diagnosis: not just one but both knees featured bone-on-bone severe arthritis. Thus began a three-year search for something to keep her joints out of pain and in good enough shape to continue running.

She tried, in no particular order:

Physical therapy
Previnex
Joint capsules
Cherry juice
Magnesium
Turmeric
No sugar, to lower inflammation
Appointments with three different orthopedists*
Platelet-rich plasma (PRP) injections
Steroids
Yoga and Pilates classes
Braces
NSAIDs
KT Tape
Following the Knees-Over-Toes Guy on YouTube
A closet full of shoes†
Heavy-duty orthotics‡

---

* The consensus: She needs at least one knee replacement, but at age fifty-six, she's too young and active to get one yet.
† "I had every single brand of running shoes, thinking that one pair was going to be my magic bullet. That clearly wasn't the issue."
‡ Made by a medical pedorthist, a professional who matches her gait and her foot to create orthotics for optimal support. She brought in two garbage bags full of all her shoes (running and otherwise) and they went through every pair to see whether they would ease her pain or at least not create more pain. "Most pairs were a no."

Nothing provided the relief she craved.

Hoping to hold onto some regular miles, Ingrid spread her athletic wings. She completed a sprint triathlon, continued Pilates, and walked with friends and her dog. Twice, she trained to hike down into the floor of the Grand Canyon. The first time, her doctor told her she'd make it to the bottom of the canyon but her friends would have to carry her out. She canceled that trip and started a series of injections of PRP and steroids to fortify her joints. A new—and now current—doctor gave her the go-ahead to complete the whole hike. "You can't do any more damage," he told her. She descended the 5,000 feet to the canyon floor, camped for two nights, and climbed back to the rim, where her knee once again ballooned like it did after her second half-marathon.

Still, she couldn't accept the idea of never running again. She adored her running friends, who offered a safe space to vent and connect; she valued running's heart-healthy benefits, especially with her family history of cardiac issues; and she couldn't imagine life without the efficient, clarifying mental release running had given her for over thirty years. So she toughed out a few short run/walks weekly, paying for her limited mileage by icing her knees for hours on the living room couch. Her husband, seeing her struggle, gave her a reality check. "This is ridiculous," he told her. "You have to stop."

Her doctor gave her another reality check when he suggested that she needed to think about her athletic life in buckets. Her running bucket was really, really, *really* small. "You can't expect it to fulfill what you need any longer," he said.

The vision of a thimble-sized bucket, combined with the fact that she didn't want to suffer through training for an upcoming hiking trip to Alaska, made Ingrid realize she finally needed to be done. "I knew it was coming," she says. "It was just a really slow grind to get there." She makes it sound simple, but no breakup is simple, especially one that happens in a complicated, decades-long relationship. "I broke up with running on Valentine's Day," she says. "I loved myself enough to know I needed to do it."

Jeanne: "I Should Have Done It Ages Ago"

When Jeanne Hanisko was a chubby fourteen-year-old, she'd slip out her front door at night and run laps around her block in Saginaw, Michigan. "I didn't want anybody to see me," she says. "It felt like such a weird thing to be doing." At the time, her parents were going through a long, acrimonious divorce, and the fresh air and steady rhythm of her feet gave Jeanne a much-needed feeling of control over her life and body.

In college, away from the tension in the house, she kept running; it was the easiest way to control her weight.* She was taller and heavier than her petite older sister, a comparison that took up too much space in her brain. Not naturally athletic or competitive, she wasn't drawn to races. The few 10Ks she did in her twenties made her feel uncomfortable, like she wasn't good enough to be there.

Things changed when she and her husband entered a duathlon with their young daughter in tow, which led to doing their first marathon together: the 1991 Detroit International Marathon. On a rainy, freezing day, she wore a long-sleeve cotton shirt, didn't eat any prerace breakfast, and spent the last 6 miles dry heaving before collapsing into bed for hours afterward.† When she finally made it to the shower, she couldn't lift her arms to wash her hair.

Still, Jeanne, now sixty-four years old, was hooked. She loved the difficulty of the training, pitting herself against her body and winning, and the high after the race. Improving her training tactics, gear choices, and nutrition, she went on to complete fifteen total marathons over fifty years, qualifying for the Boston Marathon five times—something she never would've believed was possible, given her inauspicious start.

Her last race, a half-marathon with her daughter, was over eight years ago. But stepping away from racing didn't mean stepping away from running. For Jeanne, running remained a constant: a steady rhythm in her day, an anchor

---

* "If I behaved now the way I behaved then, I'd be diagnosed as an anorexic," she admits. "But it wasn't a big thing in the early seventies."
† Her mom, who was a nurse and was waiting for her at the finish line, said, "You hear about people who are sick looking green. I never saw that until I saw your face today."

that helped her feel grounded and "right within my own body." For decades, she ran nearly every day, usually logging about 6 miles. "It's just the kind of person I am," she says. "If I say, today I don't feel like it, then the next time I say I don't feel like it, it's easier. Before you know it, I'm never doing it."

Perhaps not surprisingly, Jeanne isn't a big fan of rest days, so when she caught COVID early during the pandemic, she continued her daily miles. She didn't feel the virus's effects while she was running, but after she recovered from being sick, her legs took on a heaviness she hadn't experienced before. "It felt like they weren't getting the oxygen they need," she says, adding that her feet no longer push off the way they're supposed to.

She shuffled around as best she could for about another year. Reading one of my Another Mother Runner blog posts about how I was redirecting my energy from running, she started crying and finally conceded that she had to face the facts. Her morning runs with her dog are now mostly morning brisk walks. "I keep thinking the walking is temporary, like I just need to fix something: pick up my knees more, not let my hips drop," she says. "But I'm not sure that's realistic."

Letting go wasn't a single decision. It was a slow, reluctant unraveling. "I should have done it ages ago, but the drive to run every day is so strong after fifty years of doing it, I just couldn't make myself do it," she says. "I can't really explain it except that quitting felt like it was a betrayal of the person I created."

Making the Hard Decision (a Little) Easier

In a way, Mariah Gianakouros had it easy: Her doctor told her she could absolutely not run again. A runner for over a decade, she developed chronic sinus infections as she trained for all distances of races, working her way up to the 2011 New York City Marathon. "The more I ran, the sicker I seemed to get," she says. The sinus infections were treated with high doses of steroids, which helped her lungs, but not her joints. Long-term use of steroids decreases bone mineral density and interferes with calcium absorption, and Mariah's feet suffered multiple stress fractures. After a handful of hospitalizations and surgeries, her medical team found the miracle medicine that kept her lungs healthy, but the damage was done. She had to have major joint reconstructive surgery in her toe.

"My orthopedist told me I can row, I can ski, I can bike, I can swim, I can walk, I can do anything but run," says Mariah, now fifty years old. He repeated: "You cannot run. And you definitely cannot run outside."

Although this firm directive was brutal, it was also fortunate. After all, most of us don't get such clarity; instead, we're left to figure out for ourselves when it's time to step away or scale way back. And that decision is like trying to pick up a knife with no handle: No matter how you grab it, you're going to get cut.

Because we, as humans, resist change. Even if something is clearly not working like it used to, our natural inclination is to stay the course instead of letting go. When we switch things up, we dredge up a whole slew of unwanted feelings, including fear of the unknown, loss of control, and lack of confidence. The fact that running provides a familiar rhythm to the day, a sense of control in our body and mind, confidence that might not naturally be there makes this process infinitely more challenging. It's like that knife has inflicted a huge bloody wound on you, and you don't have any access to medical care—or even a Band-Aid.

Before we dive deeper into gore and wounds, let's zoom out a bit. Change can happen in two ways: proactively and reactively. The former is when you are in charge. You initiate a breakup, you leave one job for another, you decide to start running after being sedentary. "This kind of change can be empowering," says Shawn Snelgrove, a change agility consultant based in Denver, Colorado. "You retain autonomy and control."

Even though you consciously opted for this change and it sounds exciting, proactive change can still upend your sense of normal. "Letting go is at best an ambiguous experience," writes William Bridges in *Transitions: Making Sense of Life's Changes*. Even when you can't wait to move to a faraway city or start a fresh gig, your adventure begins with the loss of everything familiar. Things can feel a little shaky as you figure out your new normal, but the discomfort doesn't feel as disruptive as it could. After all, you've got new partners to meet, new skills to learn, new miles to run.

On the flip side, when change is reactive, or forced on you by circumstances out of your control—budget cuts at your company, a partner whose needs have shifted, a hip that can't take any more high-impact pounding—"that's grief, that's loss, that's being pissed at your body, at nature, at everything," says Snelgrove. You've been relegated to a space you didn't ask to be, and finding your way out requires recalibration, flexibility, patience, and potentially a new identity.

Research on elite athletes and retirement, says sports psychologist Erin Alaya, indicates that when an athlete feels like she has a choice about stepping back, the situation doesn't feel as negative as when she feels like she doesn't. This concept applies to athletes of all levels, says sports psychologist Kim Dawson. "The psychological experience of leaving sport is the same experience for an elite athlete as it is for a recreational athlete," Dawson clarifies, adding that very few of us, elite or amateur, exit a sport we love on our own terms.

Even though I've been a go-home-while-the-party-is-still-fun type for most things in my life (especially if I had a run scheduled for the next morning), it still took me nearly three years to leave the running fiesta. Firmly on the other side now, I find it easy to type this advice: If you're on the brink of breaking, you might want to consider making the intentional decision yourself instead of allowing the final day to be dictated by your body. You'll feel more in control of the situation and be able to say goodbye on your terms. I clearly didn't heed the directive, though, and respect and understand if you don't want to either.

If you're waffling, here are three ideas that might help you clarify your decision:

1. **Get an Outside Reality Check:** Asking somebody whether they think you should stay or go is going to make you feel super vulnerable. I get that. Make the conversation feel as safe as possible by picking somebody who understands your running is not just a hobby, not just exercise.

    Bolster your confidence for this query by telling yourself their response is not your final answer. In fact, instead of paying attention to their actual advice, focus on gauging your reaction to it. "If somebody tells you that it's probably best to stop running and you feel relief, that's good information," says Alaya, who is based in Minneapolis, Minnesota. "Your heart knows before your mind does."

You also might receive unsolicited advice; several women I spoke with mentioned that their partner helped them realize what they were doing was not serving them any longer.

Heather Escaravage, who spent more than eighteen months trying to rehab a knee, got a loving gut check from her husband. "I'd spend twenty minutes to get ready to run for thirty minutes, and then I'd come home and stretch. Some days, I'd be icing my knee for two hours postrun. The next day, it'd be sore going up and down the stairs," she says. "My husband was like, 'What are you getting out of this? You're not a sponsored athlete.'"

Heather, age forty-two, ultimately made the decision to quit herself, but if you're feeling mentally solid, soliciting direct, honest advice can be very helpful. Pick your source wisely; your best running friend who has a stake in you continuing to run might not be the best call. "They have to be someone who has our long-term best interests at heart and is willing to tell us what we need to hear, not what we want to hear," writes Annie Duke in *Quit: The Power of Knowing When to Walk Away.*

2. **Define Your Warning Track:** Softball players chasing a fly ball know they're about to hit a wall when the grass turns to gravel. Alaya recommends figuring out what your gravel looks like. "Is it a certain amount of money spent on medical bills? How you show up in your relationships? Your day-to-day mood?" Then tell a trusted friend, and, more importantly, give them permission to let you know if they see you hit it.

If you want something a little more defined, consider creating what Duke calls "kill criteria": a set of circumstances that define the point when it's healthier to abandon ship than to keep sailing. Kill criteria are detailed, including both states and dates. Examples could be: "If I'm not able to do a four-minute/one-minute run/walk ratio in three months, I will direct my energies elsewhere." And "If I can't run continuously in the 10K in eight months, I'm going to investigate other activities."

Be as generous with your kill criteria as you need to be. Having space to explore what it looks like to, say, stop training for long races and run for thirty minutes two times per week is a worthwhile endeavor.

3. **Consult the Matrix (and Your Values):** If the idea of thinking it through on paper is attractive to you, Alaya suggests making a four-square matrix, which is helpful when making big decisions. "It captures more nuances, which can be overlooked when making a simple pro-con list," she explains.

	Pros	Cons
Keep Running		
Stop Running		

Create a similar matrix for yourself. Give yourself at least ten quiet, distraction-free minutes, if not more, to list the physical, mental, social, and logistical reasons why you should and should not keep running.

I didn't fill in a matrix—or even a pros and cons list—during the three years I was transitioning out of running, and having just done so for the following example, I now wish I had. The experience of processing all aspects of the situation and writing them down is so much more enlightening than what I did. (Or, actually, didn't do, which was never taking time to give my endless thoughts any order or weight.) Everything is clearer in hindsight, of course, but seeing "I love how running makes me feel and look" across from "emotionally exhausted," I appreciate how explicit the matrix is. I was so weary, and I clearly needed an exit ramp, no matter how my body would react.

	Pros	Cons
Keep Running	• Easy access to work out anywhere • Feel legit at Another Mother Runner • I love how it makes me feel and look	• Emotionally exhausted • Very hard to stay injury-free and run regularly • Pain will continue • Expenses to fix pain will also continue
Stop Running	• Much less pain • No more mental spinning: Am I on the path back to healthy running? • No more physical therapy and related expenses • More time for swimming and biking, which both have room for improvement • Less overall anger and frustration	• Can't do triathlons anymore • Potential to feel like an imposter at Another Mother Runner—like I can't hack it • Will need to find new workout friends • Need more time for bike rides, commuting to pool

After you fill your own matrix, you can find edification in a few ways. Volume is one way to look at it: My "stop running" pros and "keep running" cons total nine; my "keep running" pros and "stop running" cons total seven. The depth of the reasons is also helpful. My "stop running" cons (no more triathlons, finding new workout friends) are arguably easier hurdles to overcome than my "keep running" cons (emotional exhaustion, difficulty staying injury-free).

That said, your values will most likely come into play; Alaya often has her athletes integrate what matters most to them as they analyze their matrix. My personal values include trust, authenticity, and being part of the greater good. As I kept charging through chronic injury cycles, I eroded my trust with my body, the only one I'll have my whole life. Continuing to run would continue to wear down that relationship and doesn't honor that value. On the authenticity front, I was fully myself at Another Mother Runner. I talked openly about having postpartum depression and suicidal ideation. Telling the community that I was going to stop running, though difficult, wasn't as big a deal as I was making it in my head. I could still be authentic as my postrunning self. And being part of the greater good? I could continue to encourage women to run, walk, or move forward at Another Mother Runner as long as I was moving forward myself.

AID STATION

Permission to Quit

You have tried. I know you have. You've done the clamshells and glute bridges, the monster walks and single-leg deadlifts. You've stretched your hamstrings, foam-rolled your calves, worked on your ankle mobility, focused on your foot strike. You've visited physical therapists, the other kind of therapists, doctors, acupuncturists, masseuses. You've taken breaks and crossed your fingers. You've started back with run/walks, emphasis on the walk. So. Many. Times. You've fixated on the issue, ignored the issue, talked endlessly about the issue, and worked so very, very hard to alleviate the issue.

You're frustrated, overwhelmed, tired, and scared, but you're not willing to quit. It goes against everything running has instilled in you.

While running doesn't have an official motto, *Run when you can, walk if you have to, crawl if you must, just never give up* fits the bill. Running glorifies resilience, eking out one more mile when every cell in your body is screaming no. It celebrates discomfort: pushing your pace, taking on challenging routes, going longer distances. It revels in the commitment of setting a big goal, then reeling it in step by step, mile by mile. Running rewards pure effort: getting up in the dark, using your own power to cover miles, relying on your fortitude and discipline to keep moving forward.

Of course you want to hold onto the thing you have made happen all by yourself, the thing that reinforces your resilience, mental toughness, and courage with every workout. And of course you also don't want to think of yourself as a quitter; after all, we cheer the loudest for the last-place finisher of the marathon, not the person who dropped out at mile 17. Quitting oozes shame and weakness. Like you're giving up.

But I know you didn't give up. The mental energy you have expended on the question of whether you should step back from running, could power the state of California for a year. Still, if you're like most of the women I interviewed for this book, you have struggled alone. You haven't really talked to anybody about how truly hard this is. How conflicted you feel. How deeply personal the idea of quitting running feels.

I'm here to witness and validate your struggle, and if you, reader, need somebody else to give you permission to quit, consider it given.

If you no longer want to wonder whether your body will feel good enough to run today, you have permission to quit. If aches and pains ricochet through your limbs days after a run, you have permission to quit. If trying to sustain your running is draining your emotional or financial resources, you have permission to quit. If running is compromising your future self's ability to move through this world in a healthy way, you have permission to quit. If running no longer offers you the joy, release, and energy it predictably gave you for years, you have permission to quit.

I attach no judgment to your permission, but I do have a wish: Give yourself plenty of grace. Although it will feel like it, quitting is not a commentary on your ability as a runner or the depth of your commitment to the sport; it is also not an indictment of your personality. You are not making a decision out of weakness; you are making a choice that demonstrates the depth of your courage, resilience, and mental toughness. I am confident you are choosing the route that is now the best one for you, just like you have thousands of times before.

CHAPTER 3

The Calling-It-Quits Marathon

26 Miles to the End

I wish the process of stopping running would be like those race pace bands you wear on your wrist. Instead of it offering pace- and mile-related stats, it would offer time- and emotion-related guideposts: At two months out, your anger drops off, but your tears stay steady. Then, when you're unexpectedly crying in the elevator on your way to a dentist appointment, you could look at your wrist and think "Oh, this checks. I haven't run in nine weeks and I'm still in a particularly teary stage."

I tried multiple ways to put together a straightforward chronological timeline to chart your progress toward and emotions around the end of your running days, but that proved to be futile. Unless you've suffered a traumatic accident or experienced another hard-stop event, very little in this process is streamlined or straightforward. The slow descent typically happens random ache by consistent twinge, knee pain by bulging disc, stress fracture by torn labrum. Along the way, your emotions waver from acceptance to anger, regret to depression, envy to relief, and back again.

In other words, the needle tipping toward Empty is a long, wavering process that looks a little different for each runner. Think about how long it took you to get comfortable in the sport, both physically and socially. "You had to learn how to pace yourself, learn the norms at a race, trust that you could run for miles and miles," says sports psychologist Kim Dawson. "You're not going to back out of that overnight." My unscientific observation is that it takes at least twelve months to accept that your running days are numbered and to find a suitable replacement—and it can be much longer. "It's not something you can process in a month or even a year," says Jana Resch, who battled two rounds of COVID and the onset of menopause as she tried to maintain her regular routine of 20 weekly miles. "It's something you slowly come to terms with."

For runners who thrive on the cut-and-dry structure of a training program, the path toward the end can be as infuriating as the transition itself. "I drove myself crazy trying to get back to regular, healthy running for over a year before deciding to stop," says Jennifer Moynihan, whose plantar fasciitis topped off a cascade of injuries and finally forced her to retire from the sport. "It sounds ridiculous now."

Jennifer's year of yearning for a return to normal is far from ridiculous. To prove it, I finally figured out a timeline that best represents this gradual unfolding: the Calling-It-Quits (CIQ) Marathon.

This special, slightly twisted race is all about loops, but not the ones you might expect. Although the CIQ Marathon is presented as 26 miles, you'll likely cover more like 38, 47, or even 73 miles: You will circle back to visit certain miles repeatedly. Maybe you're at mile 17 feeling physically strong and emotionally stable in a strength class today, but tomorrow you'll be back at mile 7 debating whether a run/walk pattern is a viable long-term solution. Or maybe you run continuous laps of miles 13 and 14 for a few months as you try new activities and (inevitably) compare them to running.

There is no cutoff time for the CIQ Marathon and, more importantly, no prize for winning or for getting through it as quickly as you can. In fact, I encourage you not to aim for a PR; rushing it will make grief linger.

Jennifer also recommends taking your time. "I needed to do everything I thought I could do to get back to running before I could actually let go," she says. "There's no hurrying this process. You have to come to the realization yourself that running isn't serving you anymore."

Although the CIQ Marathon might sound like a bummer, it's quite the opposite. As you move through each mile, your feelings, thoughts, and actions will be validated. You won't wonder whether feeling discombobulated, crying in the elevator, or heading out for a run/walk for the nineteenth time hoping something will feel better is a normal part of this process.

Rest assured; it all is.

Mile 1: Notice Something Is Off

Something makes you realize this injury or this stretch of time with running feels markedly unlike anything else you've experienced.

Maybe the cortisone injection in your hip didn't work as well as it used to or the frequency of your postrun ice sessions has gone from weekly to daily. Maybe you surprise yourself when you turn down a half-marathon invite from a friend and say the 10K may feel better. Maybe your current energy levels don't match your regular mileage. "I was constantly overwhelmed, tired, achy, and overstressed," says Jana, now fifty-three. "It felt like I had overtraining syndrome, but I was barely doing anything."

Mile 2: Go for a Run

Hitting the road is the obvious next step if, like a typical runner, you use your miles to sort through emotions not easily accessible while standing still.

I belong to the pack of emotionally numb runners, and I usually laced up for an easy, short run when I knew I was going to be sidelined. I ran to let the tears flow and from a space of pure gratitude: I paid extra attention to flowers and sky, my (mostly) capable body and how it moved through the world.

Mile 3: Think Only About Running

The idea of losing running becomes an earworm, a relentless thought that bounces around as you read the news, feed the dogs, fill out a spreadsheet, call your dad.

As you fixate on the situation for hours, days, weeks, you may get nauseated, teary, or angry—usually a combination of all three—but you keep your feelings to yourself, lest you be judged for caring so much about something that most people consider a hobby.

"It feels silly to have this amount of grief when there are other more important things going on in the world, but when you lose a thirty-plus year habit, it's disorienting," says Becca Dinsdale, who ran five to six days per week for most of her adult life before a bulging disc in her back forced her to stop.

Mile 4: Feel Unmoored

As you sleep through your morning alarm, skip group runs, or otherwise cut back on your regular routine, a sense of unease creeps through your being, making you feel less grounded and more irritable.

"I loved the certainty of knowing I would go for a run in the morning and feel good for the rest of the day," says Debra Helfand, who ran for thirteen years before slowing down because of a diagnosis of follicular lymphoma, a slow-growing blood cancer that is usually very treatable.

Mile 5: Notice Runners Everywhere

Count four on your commute to work. Another two on your lunch break. A whole pack in a random park you have passed hundreds of times but barely noticed until now. They're running in a Netflix sitcom you're watching at night and a few more are in front of your house as you brew your coffee the next morning.

When you were blissfully unaware that your running career had an expiration date, you hardly registered a fellow runner unless you passed one on foot. Now it feels like there's an infestation of them swarming around you.

Mile 6: Judge

Judge every runner you see. They all seem to be running so easily, so smoothly. Have they ever been injured? Probably not, you tell yourself.* They have no idea how good they have it.

Mile 7: Feel Alone

If you're part of a running group, miss the camaraderie as much as the workout. If you had a dear running friend, miss the time chatting with her. (Lunch plans never work out.) If you're a solo runner, miss the time connecting with yourself. Regardless of the circumstances, feel very confident nobody has ever gone through what you're going through.

"I'm not looking for a meal train or even cards to cheer me up," Heidi Gillenwater, who tore her ACL and meniscus during a skiing accident, said. "But nonrunners don't get how emotionally hard this is and can't offer anything that resembles meaningful empathy."

Mile 8: Break Out the Tissues

If you haven't yet shed a tear or felt much sorrow, get ready for the floodgates to open. "I could fill orange Home Depot buckets with the tears that I've shed," says Lisa Payne Kirker, who ran for over twenty years before, at age forty-five, suffering a spontaneous coronary artery dissection (SCAD), a type of heart attack most prevalent in women in their forties and fifties with few or no risk factors.

Mile 9: Consider Other Options

Think about your bike sitting unused in your garage. Google the cost of a gym membership. Ask your friend how she likes her Peloton. Recall that you wanted to stand-up paddleboard last summer. Remember how much you hate Pilates.

---

* This is, of course, not the truth, but you're forgiven for not thinking clearly. Multiple studies have found that anywhere from 27 percent to 70 percent of recreational and competitive runners are injured during any one-year period.

You're not ready to pull the trigger on anything new yet. Rather, you watch the ideas float through your head at random moments: as you're showering, chopping broccoli, or tossing and turning at 2 a.m.

Mile 10: Add in Walk Breaks

If walk breaks previously weren't your thing, you try them now to see if they can mitigate some pain and preserve your mileage.

The run/walk pattern is a staple in this transition; as such, you'll likely come back to mile 10 repeatedly. Jana, who raced as often as she could for fifteen years, now does run/walk intervals on her treadmill two or three times per week and limits the running sections to two minutes tops. She's not a fan of the short intervals, but she's also realistic about what her body can handle. "I keep thinking that maybe I'll work my way back to longer running, but I doubt that's going to happen." A few months ago, she ran a straight-up mile just to see how it would go. "It was awful. And I felt terrible."

Mile 11: Overreach

Decide enough time has passed for you to give it another spin.

After suffering a slipped disc while doing a deadlift at CrossFit that derailed both her CrossFit and her running career, Sarah Lightner, a runner for thirty-five years, signed up for one of her favorite races: the Twin Cities 10 Mile. A few weeks into training, her back flared up again. "I was like, this is not a good idea," she says. "I've got to learn to be happy with three-mile loops of run/walk. That's my limit."

Mile 12: Compare Yourself

Compare your run/walk times to your straight-up running times. Compare yourself today to the runner you were two, twelve, twenty years ago. Compare how it feels to huff through 3 miles today to the way it felt to breeze through 10 miles a decade ago. Compare your PRs to the times you see as you scroll social media. Compare your legs to a fellow runner's who is walking down the frozen foods aisle at the grocery store.

Mile 13: Diversify a Little

Decide to try a new thing. Sign up for a spinning class. Ask a friend to go on a walk. Follow a strength-training circuit on YouTube. Go for a hike with your dog.

Mile 14: Compare Again

Immediately compare the new thing to running. Spoiler alert: It will fall terribly short in all aspects. Deep in my transition, "it's not running" is how I classified pretty much every activity that was not, in fact, running.

Mile 15: Miss Everything About Running

"I miss the wind in my hair, my feet pounding on the pavement, my lungs breathing to the rhythm of my feet," says Valorie Plesha, who picked up running in her fifties before being drawn under by both knees needing partial replacements. "It felt like I was flying."

Her list goes way beyond the physical sensations: She misses the camaraderie, the routine, the support, the accountability, the way it managed her weight in a way like nothing else has. Plus, she just lit up at races. "The energy is exciting, electric, addictive."

Mile 16: Get Angry

You did all the right things.

You were committed to running, a hard, healthy activity that nearly everybody else in your life doesn't have the discipline and motivation to do. You got out there, day after day, and propelled yourself forward in all kinds of conditions: hot, humid, cold, snowy, windy. You set goals, challenged yourself to reach them, and when you did, you set higher ones.

When your body didn't cooperate anymore, you didn't just give up. You searched high and low for a way to keep yourself moving forward: time off, physical therapy, acupuncture, foam rolling, surgery. Nothing clicked the way you needed it to, and now you're justifiably pissed. You're angry at your body, angry at your sport, angry at your world.

"It makes me extra mad that I can't run because I was always grateful every time I went out," says Cathy Annetta, who ran for seventeen years before degenerative arthritis and stiffness in her big toe took her out. "It's not like I ever took it for granted."

Mile 17: Feel Uncomfortable in Your Own Skin

"I do not feel good in my body right now," says Cathy, echoing a sentiment I heard—and felt myself—repeatedly.

At the end of a run, I always felt empty and clean, like my insides were sparkling. I loved that vast space, something I could back up with math.* Run 6 miles in an hour, burn 667 calories. Run 7 miles in an hour, add another 100 calories. Long before GPS watches calculated every calorie burned, I had a DIY calculator whirring in my head. I used my miles to metabolically cancel the massive bagel sandwich I had at lunch or a big bag of chocolate-covered pretzels I ate while watching *Saturday Night Live*.†

Running made my six-foot-four body, which, in my mind, failed to meet the acceptable standards for femininity, feel sleek and streamlined. It carved my calf muscles and made the bottom edges of my quads bulge ever so slightly. It gave me a thigh gap decades before it was a thing. When I stopped running, my body image shifted from that of a greyhound to that of a Saint Bernard.

I'm not the only one: Dual hip replacements forced Pamela Wakeman to mentally recalibrate how to view her physical body. "I have had to reimagine my idea of empowerment, strength, and frankly, beauty," Pamela, now fifty-five, says.

---

* One of my first jobs was as an editorial assistant in the fitness department at *Self* magazine, and one of my regular tasks was to confirm the calories a specific activity burned. In my top desk drawer, I had a well-worn copy of a scientific paper that listed the MET (metabolic equivalent of task) for every activity from sitting to recreational badminton to vigorous sex to running at 6 mph.
† Looking back, I'm not proud of my "balance it out" mentality, but it was my truth in my twenties and thirties.

Mile 18: Mourn Some More

Even as you approach the last third of the CIQ Marathon, the weight of your grief can sweep you away at times.

When Heather Escaravage, a runner for fourteen years, was in a couples counseling session with her husband, her running came up when they were talking about family time on the weekend; he was a little prickly about her spending Sundays doing long workouts. She reminded him that, because of patellofemoral pain syndrome in her knee, she wasn't really running anymore. And then she totally broke down.

The therapist asked her what she was feeling. "I don't know that I'm going to ever be able to run the way I used to," she explained, adding that running was how she identified herself and was the only way she, as a working mom, saw her friends. "Saying that out loud felt like I had just literally cleaved off a leg," she says.

Heidi, a self-described serial marathon runner, can relate. She started a new job after her knee surgery and doesn't like that her new coworkers know her only as a person who has trouble walking. "If I mention I have run fifteen marathons," she says, "I don't feel like they'll believe me."

Mile 19: Scurry Back Down the Research Rabbit Hole

If your situation has multiple potential cures, continually wonder whether there's a treatment, a magic exercise, or a medical method you might have missed.*

Kristin Zosa Puleo's stabbing piriformis pain confounded all the experts; having multiple MRIs, platelet-rich plasma therapy, and a cortisone shot brought no clarity or relief. The pain ultimately caused her to scale down to an occasional 5K, but she's not convinced there isn't a more permanent fix. "I search 'piriformis tight still flexible' once in a while," she says, even though she's pretty confident it won't lead to any new solutions.

---

* If you're on social media and have talked about your condition near your phone or searched your condition on the phone, you will be served up advertisements offering relief, a better method, a new expert, new supplements. It's exhausting.

"It's still helpful to hear from other people who are in the same situation I am."

Mile 20: Get Angry Again

Even though our day-to-day lives are constantly in transition, running feels like it should be immune. After all, you see four-year-olds running. You see seventy-four-year-olds running. "I thought I was going to be that eighty-year-old you see on social media doing the one-hundred-yard shuffle," says Kara Neuse, whose total knee replacement ended her running years.

Mile 21: Doomscroll

Scroll through running-related posts on social media as if you're inching by a car accident on the freeway: You have no option but to slow down and examine as many details as possible. Where did they run? What were their stats? What did they say in the caption? What are they wearing? What are they training for?

"I definitely feel the FOMO," admits Jill Passarelli, who has been sidelined by lower-back pain. "It's hard not to feel like you're missing out when your social media feed and inbox are filled with marathon training advice and pictures of friends at races."

Morgan M., who suffers from the effects of a partially torn Achilles tendon and other foot issues, limits her time on Strava. "I get down on myself for wishing I could still run. It's best for the time being to have some boundaries up around how much I engage with the running community."

Mile 22: Try Something New, Version 2.0

Ride a mountain bike. Take an adult swimming lesson. Try Pilates again. Go cross-country skiing. Walk with a non-running-related friend in a new-to-you spot.

Allow yourself to feel a small glimmer of hope.

Mile 23: Stop Comparing Quite So Much

True, the new activity is not running, but also true: It may not be as pain-ful on your body as running was. "I didn't realize how much pain I was in until the aching stopped," says Chris Cesena, who ran for thirty-seven years before extensive surgery on her big toe sidelined her permanently.

Also true: You might be so mentally engaged in this new activity, you don't even have time to play the comparison game. As she phased out of running, Paige Sato joined a women's dragon boating team; the intricacies of the stroke and the sport keep her mind whirring. "I can't think about anything but what I'm doing in the boat."

Mile 24: Keep the Running Door Slightly Ajar

The morning after a presidential election that didn't go the way she hoped, Kristin went out for a run. She craved the mental release she knew only pounding the pavement could provide. "It flared up all my piriformis pain, but my mind really needed it." She popped a couple of Advil, knew she wouldn't run again anytime soon, and had no regrets.

Jana also hasn't closed off all her options. "I always say I'll run one more half-marathon, but I probably won't," she says. "I don't beat myself up about it anymore though. Even if I never run another race, it just feels better to keep the door open."

Mile 25: Soften a Little

Seeing runners, either in real life or on social media, doesn't immediately send you into a mental tailspin you're not sure how to stop. "Even though the loss of running is really big, I try to focus on the fact that I can get through each day pain-free, which was not the case when I was running," says Maureen Powers, who weathered a broken foot, significant patellofem-oral pain, and plantar fasciitis before stepping away. Running delivered her highest highs and lowest lows, she says. "I exist more in the middle now."

Still, you're human, and you miss this thing you loved. "I'm not going to lie," says Chris, who felt restless and impatient as she went through the CIQ Marathon. "I still get a little jelly when I see others post about some badass run they did. I try to stay positive. Some days are easier than others."

Mile 26: Be Fine

Although *fine* feels like a milquetoast adjective to attach to the final mile of this marathon, it's also the most accurate. There's no announcer or arms-up finish-line pose to celebrate your arrival, but there is something more important: acceptance.

"It's fine. It's not awesome. I still really miss it, and I still don't have a thing that has totally replaced it," says Jennifer, age forty-six, the runner who thought that taking a year to get through the CIQ Marathon was ridiculous. "I wish I could tie it up in a pretty little bow, but I can't. I got to the other side, and it's fine."

AID STATION

What I Miss About Running: An Incomplete List

Accessibility: Most every road, minus the freeway, was runnable. In Cincinnati for work, I ran on dreary frontage roads lined with empty Red Bull cans and budget hotels. In Nebraska for my daughter's volleyball tournaments, I ran on wide gravel roads. In Florida on spring break, I ran on roads with minimal shoulders while rental cars buzzed by me. Not ideal, but better than the alternative: no run at all.

Agency: So much of life is dictated by others: a boss setting deadlines, kids needing dinner *again*, a partner feeling frisky. Running was all me. I decided the route, the pace, the musical accompaniment. Nobody else got to touch it.

Aid Stations: A much more satisfying way to mark progress in a race than simple mile markers. Slow my pace, grab a drink, thank the volunteers whose encouragement often made me feel like I could win the whole race.

Anticipation: I dreaded long, hard workouts, and I also loved them. They gave me a purpose that felt admirable, more important than writing an article, driving carpool, or filling a grocery cart. Come Wednesday, I'd start obsessing about Saturday's scheduled 14-miler with 4 miles of tempo thrown in. *Are my favorite mint-green shorts washed? Do I have a good playlist? Where should I go?* Moving through mundane daily tasks, I knew Saturday would make me feel special and strong, two feelings I didn't encounter on the regular.

Antidepressant Effect: I never feel elated when leaving a therapy session. I don't feel elated when I swallow my nightly generic Effexor. I always felt elated after any run. Everything was lighter, including the intensity of my thoughts. Yes, our planet is still melting; yes, politicians still make me froth at the mouth; yes, our dishwasher is on the fritz (again); yes, I owe a late fee on my credit card. Reality hasn't changed, but my perspective, now filled with buoyancy and possibility, has.

Best Running Dog (BRD): A dog trotting next to me on the trails is my version of heaven. Dharma, my first BRD, loped up arroyos with me in Santa Fe. A shy and neurotic Weimaraner rescue, she stayed by my side most of the time. Meanwhile, Mason, a Weimaraner / chocolate Lab mix who was also a rescue, took off as soon as I opened the car door and galloped through Colorado pine forests, easily covering twice the miles I did. Just pure joy.

Best Running Friends (BRFs): I've had a handful of girlfriends who ran next to me through countless miles. When our paces were synced and our eyes were on the road, no conversation was off-limits: tough patches in marriage, even harder spells of parenting, teary life regrets, scary thoughts I couldn't believe I was saying out loud. The miles together created a connection that I thought would last forever. Some friendships are still alive, albeit not at the intensity they were when we were running together, and others ended after our last mile together. Even though it's been over a decade since I've sweated next to—or even contacted—some of them, I keep their contacts in my phone and hold our shared miles as some of the most meaningful times in my life.

Corrals: Prerace pens were how I wish every social event I attended felt: I was in a "room" full of strangers but wasn't afraid to initiate a conversation with anybody standing close by. I knew we'd have an immediate connection, not awkward pauses as we fumbled for common ground.

Endorphins: Yes, they are real. And, yes, they are magic.

Farewell Runs: A last run before an injury required me to take time off running. I consciously soaked up as much as I could: tiny gravel rocks skittering away from my foot strike, morning sun slotting through massive oak trees, musical lyrics taking on a poignancy I never sensed before. ("*Leave all your love and your longing behind / You can't carry it with you if you want to survive*." Preach it, Florence and the Machine!) Farewell runs were like having a long conversation with an aging parent or rocking a baby to sleep: Presence and gratitude come naturally.

Feeling Clean: Running unclogged all my pipes, both metaphorical and intestinal. Mile by mile, anger dissipated, self-compassion blossomed, and the remnants of the Chipotle burrito I ate last night for dinner readied itself for expulsion.

The Final Hill: For most of my routes around my house, I climbed a short hill before I took a left onto my street. My legs were wiped; my spirit was soaring. I had done it again.

Friday Nights: On the night before a typical Saturday long run, I carb-loaded with pizza, then watched bad television with my kids before heading to bed, usually before nine. Although Friday nights connote socializing and staying up late, I loved that the upcoming workout gave me a valid excuse to bypass both.

Getting a Medal: The finish line was in my rearview mirror, my sports bra and shirt were soaked with sweat, the smile on my face felt like it would never disappear. A volunteer handed me a medal and, even though I'm rarely on trend, fashion-wise, I was an owner of the current *it* accessory. Other runners, similarly bejeweled, smiled at me; random strangers congratulated me; and every time somebody saw a picture of me wearing it, they knew I was a runner.

Identity: I am a daughter, sister, wife, mother, desk jockey. Cool, but almost everybody I know is some variation of those. I am a runner. Very few people can say that, but most everybody knows what it means: I'm disciplined, self-motivated, strong, reliable.

Internal Conversations: My mind wandered as my feet pitter-pattered below me. I replayed previous interactions during which I wish I would've been wiser, cleverer, or more protective of myself. I imagined tough conversations I hoped I would have the courage to enact in real life. When I became weary of sorting through the current flotsam of my life, I talked to people no longer on this earth, including my dad and my favorite uncle.

Key Pockets and the Like: Wearing thoughtfully designed running gear made me feel legit no matter what pace I ran. I delighted in hidden pockets that held a gel, key, credit card, and lip balm but didn't feel overstuffed; thumbholes in a long sleeve that kept my wrists covered on chilly days; sticky grips on shirt hems so my belly button didn't make a surprise appearance; reflective hits where I didn't expect them.

New Shoes: A pair of new kicks held promise, bounce, youth. No matter when they arrived, I put them on right away and sprang around the kitchen island for a few joyous laps.

Possibilities: When I ran, I felt like I could enter a race of any distance, any difficulty. After all, I had the fundamental left foot / right foot skills and knew that training basically required patience and focus. (Oh, and an injury-free body. Ahem.) One of my favorite searches while procrastinating at work was "beginner-friendly ultras," which would predictably pull up the Ice Age Trail 50K in Wisconsin and the Way Too Cool 50K in California. (At one point, I was so obsessed, I could've recited their registration fees and elevation gains.) Other times, I'd ogle half-marathons in national parks and team relays across Montana, weekend-long trail festivals and island marathons.

Quads: During my peak running years, my quads were Chinook salmon swimming upstream: nothing but muscle and business.

Secret Playlists: Runs gave me a chance to indulge in music mixes I was confident would make others cringe. Long after my kids were over *Here Comes Science*, a children's album from They Might Be Giants, I remained obsessed. I also played the soundtrack from *Rent* approximately 589 times. "Bette Davis Eyes" followed by "Hot to Go" and then "You're So Vain"? Yep, DJ Dimity is spinning 'em now—and nobody else gets to listen.

Homemade Signs at Races: Neon posterboards with block letters, some glitter, and maybe even stickers. There were never enough. I'm not against oldies but goodies (*Worst Parade Ever!*), but I love a fresh sentiment, especially if it relates to current news or dogs. *Be the Runner Your Dog Thinks You Are*, which I spotted at mile 11 of the Philadelphia Half-Marathon, remains my all-time fave.

Stats: After nearly every workout, I'd spend an excessive amount of time scrolling through my numbers. I compared mile splits (*Did I start too fast? Likely*), admired the elevation profile, scrutinized my heart rate like it was an EKG readout, noted how many miles I covered that week, month, year. To be clear: Studying the numbers didn't mean I really applied them to my performance and, say, slowed down at the start. Their existence was enough to keep me entertained.

Track Workouts: I didn't run in high school or college, so speed workouts on the local middle school track was like a field trip. So bouncy underfoot! Such definitive lanes! So easy to track your times! The workouts were tough, but I didn't mind; the special setting demanded it.

Keeping things real, there are a few things I don't miss about running.

Chafing: In my armpits. Under my heart rate monitor. Between my thighs. It hurt while running, but the agony when water hits my raw skin in the postrun shower? I think scraping my knuckles on a cheese grater is preferable.

The Comparison Trap: With crisp splits and daily mileage so easy to track (and publicly display, if you're so inclined), running often felt like a constant competition with myself and others. Yes, I rationally understood my pace would vary based on fitness, stress, sleep, and weather, but my emotional, more critical side had a hard time accepting that.

Constant Craving: Running was my drug of choice, and being caught in endless injury cycles only intensified my craving for pure, uninterrupted miles. The more elusive they became, the more I wanted them. Chasing a high I couldn't quite reach. Just exhausting.

Summertime Training: Sure, I could—and often did—get up at 4 a.m. to complete a long run before the Colorado sun scorched my skin, but was it pleasant? No, not really. And if I slacked on my alarm, I'd have to summon all my mental toughness to get 'er done. Although consistent August miles made for fast October races, I don't miss that pressure one bit.

CHAPTER 4

Sweating, Crying, and Trying

Guidelines for the Transition

During the first few months of phasing out of running, prepare to feel like a newborn foal: shaky, unsure of yourself, constantly looking for your mom or another loving soul who will lead the way and comfort you.

Although I wish we could go for a hilly hike together so you could solidify those wobbly legs, these guidelines lay solid groundwork to help you gently explore your grief, keep moving forward in a healing, healthy way, and plant the seeds for your next athletic chapter.

Don't Go More Than Forty-Eight Hours Without a Good Sweat

If you are like every runner I've ever encountered, running isn't just exercise. It's how you cope with emails that cc ten of your coworkers, encounters with a toxic boss, the grief of a terminally ill parent. Even though your current exercise options may seem as appealing as ripping off a black toenail, it's worth it to figure out how you can work up a sweat. "Your body is accustomed to using movement to emotionally regulate itself," says Niamh Rawlins, a licensed professional counselor in Nashville, Tennessee, who helps clients through transitions.

What's more, even if you're convinced you've never had a runner's high, your physiology would like to differ: Endorphins, dopamine, serotonin, and other feel-good hormones are produced by aerobic exercise. In other words, getting your blood flowing boosts your mood. Although endorphin withdrawal specifically regarding running has not been scientifically researched, I am 100 percent sure it's a real thing. "I miss the endorphins," says Joan Machanic, who stepped away from running at age sixty in part because she didn't like comparing her current self with her former self. "I tend to get a little depressed, and running helped me boost my mood in a way I haven't found elsewhere."

If your body allows, sweat at least every other day doing something more vigorous than walking. As running was fading in my rearview mirror, my goal was to soak my sports bra and, in doing so, flood my system with those juicy endorphins. Here are things that worked for me:

- **Ride a Bike Inside:** Options include taking a spinning class, riding an exercise bike at the gym, and jumping on a friend's Peloton. I did workouts with intervals or a hill climb for two reasons: A preset workout relieved me of any decision making and gave me a sense of accomplishment when I was done. (Yes! I climbed to the top of the red-dotted mountain!) The low-impact motion of pedaling didn't hurt my body, and the alternating rhythm of the legs moving felt running-adjacent. I stayed inside so I could crank my music, let my mind run, and not have to worry about traffic.

- **Hike Hard:** I hit trails that featured uphill climbs or rolling terrain. Climbing invites a running-esque leg-burning effort, but being on trails, not pavement, didn't invite immediate pace comparisons.

- **Climb Stairs:** This is a variation on a hard hike. I am fortunate to live near Red Rocks Amphitheatre, which offers a quad-burning 380 steps from bottom to top.* I liked that I could see progress in real time, similar to climbing a huge hill running; just when I was about to cry uncle and walk, it flattened out. Plus, my legs after a Red Rocks workout felt both rubbery and crazy strong: my favorite combo.
- **Swim:** Admittedly, I don't soak a sports bra in the pool, but the consistent rhythm and steady effort of the freestyle stroke, combined with the sensory deprivation of the water, let me escape my whirling head and exhausted my body. Like with the bike, I went in with a preset workout. Writing down 2,000 meters' worth of reps and distances gave me a focus and purpose once I pulled on my suit, cap, and goggles.

Other options to get your heart rate up include walking on the treadmill at an incline (assuming, of course, you feel mentally okay with hopping on a treadmill); taking a dance class, like Zumba or hip-hop; and trying a vigorous yoga class.

Although I'll praise the health benefits of strength training all day long, it's not a great substitute workout when you first stop running. It requires rest between sets and lacks the meditative rhythm of a steady cardio. And even though holding a plank for a minute may make you shake, doing so doesn't exactly leave you emotionally lighter.

Tell Your Head to STFU

As you sweat, adamant voices in your brain are going to protest: "This is not running! This is not as good/hard/easy/simple as running! We don't like this! We don't like this!"

---

* A high school or college stadium is also a great call, as are longer flights of stairs outside.

When Ann Callarman moved to a rural town that wasn't super accessible for running, she switched from running to mountain biking and heard a chorus of dissenting voices. "No other activity seems like it's enough," she says. "I never feel like I'm working as hard on a bike as I did when I was running. That's probably not true, but it's automatically where my mind goes."

During the first few months, expect those voices. Their volume will naturally decrease with time, but realize they are initially loud, aggravating sirens because you're messing with their gold standard: running. If workouts got a grade, accessible, familiar, soothing running would get an A. If you can rate your sweat sessions during your transition with a grade of D or better, you're passing with flying colors.*

Meanwhile, talk back to those voices. You can tell them to STFU, or you can be a little gentler with yourself. "Yep, I know this isn't running," I told myself more than once while I hiked or biked. "I wish it were too. But I'm moving forward, and my body doesn't hurt, so this is our solution for now."

Get Outside

A big appeal of running is moving through the world without a windshield in front of you, going at a pace that allows you to digest your surroundings and your place among them. Don't let go of this important grounding practice.

Be sure to make time to move forward in fresh air, ideally in vitamin D–rich sunshine. You can go for a walk, of course, or you could ride a bike, snowshoe, cross-country ski, or hike.

Walk and Talk with a Friend

Walking with a friend, ideally a chatty one, doesn't allow you to dwell on the fact that you're not running. Plus, if you've been having a tough time

---

* Over time, we're going to focus on raising that grade to a B–, but initially, a D is your goal.

motivating to move, a walking date creates accountability. While you're moving, if you want to talk about your running, you're in a good spot; conversations about emotional topics don't feel so intense when eye contact isn't involved. "Talking to somebody about it externalizes it in a way that helps you reorient what you're experiencing," says Rawlins.

One of my closest friends, who is not a runner, lives nearby. We have walked together once per week for years, and when I quit running, I was so grateful for our routine—and for her. When we walk, I never think about our pace or mileage. Instead, the whole point of the walk is to feel connected and to support each other as we catch up. (Yes, she's heard plenty about my frustrations and sadness about my running journey.)

Steer Clear of Your Running Route

If you have flexibility of where you can walk, my strong recommendation is not to walk on the route where you used to run. Inevitably, you're going to compare your running times to your walking times, and walking will never win. *It's taken you twenty minutes to get to a place that used to take you ten?* (You can tell this voice to STFU also.)

I live in a neighborhood with a few parks and plenty of streets that create variations for walks, so I consciously traced new routes, not the ones that I always ran with my friends. I also listened to podcasts and audiobooks to keep my mind occupied.

If your options for walking from home are limited, treat yourself to novelty: Drive to a local park or a new spot and walk there.

Preserve Your (Running) Time

Do your best not to let life—work, chores, family matters—absorb the time you typically spent running.

If you usually ran for three hours per week, fill those three hours with things that are focused on you and your well-being: workouts, likely, but you can also include long baths, art projects, a great book, or anything else that feels good.

If you typically worked out in the morning, stick to that routine as best you can for the time being. "I really counted on my morning run to set my day," says Paige Sato, who pulled back on her running after she had a few serious falls. "When I stopped, it felt like adult-onset ADHD took over." When she was running most days of the week, she could run 5 miles, get home, walk the dog, make a few lunches, drop her kids off at school and her husband at the train station before 8 a.m. "Now, for the life of me, I am late to 10 a.m. appointments."

I get it. Even though I know my lightest, most positive days happen after a morning workout, I'm more prone to hit snooze and tell myself I'll work out later since I no longer have kids to shuttle out the door. Signing up for an early-morning strength-training class and committing to teaching spinning twice per week at 6 a.m. helped me find my morning groove again. Sure, I often question my life choices when the alarm goes off at 5:15 a.m., but by 5:15 p.m., when I'm pleasantly tired after a calm, productive day, I never regret it.

Let It Flow and Let's Go

These are the names of two playlists I want you to assemble.

"Let It Flow" is a playlist of your favorite songs that make you reach inside and feel all the feels. Use this whenever you are feeling sad, resentful, angry, or just need a good cathartic cry. Even though I am five years without running, I still have my moments. This fall, I listened to my Let It Flow playlist as I drove to volunteer with Girls on the Run at my third-grade niece's school. The tears weren't just because my body no longer allowed me to trot around the playground track with the kids; they were also because I used to volunteer at my daughter's Girls on the Run, and she is now a college senior. A landslide of tears, thanks to Stevie Nicks: "But time makes you bolder / Even children get older / And I'm gettin' older, too."

The second playlist I want you to create is "Let's Go," which is for bringing the motivation when you need a nudge. Load it up with songs that push a little pep into your step and make you feel powerful and strong. Hit play on this one when you want to rally for a workout or need a boost when you're feeling low; you'll be amazed at what dancing to a single song can do for your mood. My power song right now is "Throw Some Ass," by Sofi Tukker, a bawdy little tune about getting out of chronic pain and celebrating with your booty. (Don't judge it until you hear it. In fact, go to the27thmile.net to access my Let It Flow and Let's Go lists.)

Grieve Deeply, but Not All Day

There is no specific timeline on how long you will grieve running, but designated cry-it-out sessions, especially at the beginning, help your emotions flow through your body so they don't get stuck. Clock your sad sessions by minutes or sad songs and tell yourself that you're going to feel really, really crappy during the time. Whether you cry for ten minutes or two melancholy ballads, the key is to let it out and lean into the sadness.

When time's up, shift gears and put your focus somewhere else. Emotional release will have happened, even if it was brief. "It's a good way to give space to the emotions without allowing yourself to turn in circles," Rawlins says.

This doesn't mean sadness won't catch you off guard at other times. It will. When that happens, acknowledge the sadness and, if you can, let the tears flow then too.

Write a To-Try List

A to-try list is your forgiving launch pad that catches ideas to fill the space that running held. Nothing is off-limits, so think far and wide. What other things are potentially interesting to you besides running? Running may be so ingrained in your routine that you have a hard time picturing yourself doing anything else, but I have confidence you can come up with at least a few options.

One place to start: What did you like to do as a kid? I wandered in the woods on my cross-country skis. I liked to walk on stilts. I played tennis. I loved to roller skate. I won't ever pull out the stilts or roller skates again, but the thought of taking up tennis and cross-country skiing again made me excited.

Activities on your to-try list don't necessarily need to be aerobic exercise. Maybe you want to volunteer at the humane society walking dogs or try a sailing class. Perfect. Write them down. We'll get back to this list in Chapter 10, but if you feel a spark from anything right now, feel free to grab a racket or a dog leash and jump in ASAP.

Write a (Kind of Want)-To-Do List

Even though the act of running is efficient, the preparation around running—endless loads of laundry, traveling to races, staying up to date on social media—gobbled up more time than you might have realized. Now that some of it has opened up, what have you been putting off? Make a list of at least five things you've been meaning to do. These can be small, medium, or large: anything from catching up monthly with an old friend to finally reading that novel on your nightstand, decluttering the garage, or updating your résumé.

Then create a schedule for four, eight, or twelve weeks, depending on the time needed for each task, and give yourself deadlines for these things. You can even break down large projects into smaller tasks, much like you would break down training for a long race into shorter runs. As you complete each task or project, cross them off, just like you would if you were on a training program. It's satisfying, productive, and gives you a sense of progress, even if you're not logging miles.

"We're filling your schedule just enough so you're not completely floored by the change," says Rawlins. She emphasizes this tactic isn't about avoiding your emotions but rather about easing into them. If movement was your go-to way of processing things, this list becomes another gentle structure to help you navigate what's next.

Other Athletes Sound Off

Don't just take it from me; take it from other long-time former runners. I asked them: "What is the best thing you did for yourself as you phased out of running?"

I stayed open to other forms of exercise, like weightlifting, rowing, and the exercise bike. I made sure those opportunities were easily accessible. While it was hard to do, I tried to remind myself that I was doing the exercise that my body, at this moment, could do.

—*Mariah Gianakouros*

It was really tempting to jump headfirst into competition in another sport to fill the gap left by running and racing. Instead, I kept things low-key. I swam, I biked, I hiked, I kept doing tae kwon do. My only goal was to have fun and not turn myself inside out. I really needed that break.

—*Amy Csizmar Dalal*

I worked to let go of my expectations around my identity, my body, my progress (or lack thereof), and my journey. It was so hard, but reminding myself each day—and sometimes repeatedly during the day—to hold things loosely slowly worked to relax my expectations.

—*Ellen Ewing*

I kept running a few races each year. It still feels ecstatic to cross a finish line even if/when I'm walking, jogging, or wobbling. The endorphins are still there, the cheers are still there, the bling is still there, and most importantly, I am still there.

—*Joanne Godfrey*

I started strength training because I knew lifting weights was going to be important to succeed at any activity I decided to try next.

—*Pamela Wakeman*

I kept moving. I started doing high-intensity step workouts and lifting weights and I did them hard.

—*Sister Michaelanne Marie*

I talked to a counselor about it.

—*Heather Escaravage*

I tried hard to have patience and grace with myself. I had been a runner for more than thirty years and knew it would take time to find something to fill that void.

—*Sarah Lightner*

I kept waking up and going outside on my same schedule, even if I'm only walking briskly. Doing so allows me to keep the shape of my days and not feel quite so adrift.

—*Jeanne Hanisko*

AID STATION

Ellen Calls It (the Good Kind of) Quits

Ellen Ewing wasn't sure she had it in her. After all, the thirty-five-year-old had two young kids and was feeling, in her own words, "very lost, overweight, and sedentary." Eyeing a small track in her St. Louis, Missouri, neighborhood, she challenged herself to run one lap. "I didn't tell anybody, including my husband," she says. "If anybody knew and I failed, I would be super embarrassed." She covered the paved surface, a little over two-tenths of a mile, in about five minutes. "It was horrible—I was sucking in air like I was drowning and my legs felt like concrete—but I was so proud of myself."

One lap turned into two laps turned into three, and feeling emboldened, she asked a friend to help her train for a turkey trot a few months away. "I was smitten after that," she says. "The endorphins hooked me."

Also appealing: the fact that the more Ellen ran, the more weight she lost. People were complimenting her body, something she hadn't experienced before. The external praise was validating, but even more empowering was how her athletic body changed the way she looked at herself. "It was 100 percent a dangerous mind-body connection, but it felt really good," she admits. To her, races were "the most magical gatherings" ever, and within two years she completed twelve races in twelve months, culminating in a 5K PR while wearing a red and green tutu at a holiday race.

Running gave her peace of mind, an identity outside of wife and stay-at-home mom, and it helped her cope with then undiagnosed anxiety and depression. The only problem? Her feet weren't on board. Ellen couldn't string together a few months of training without plantar fasciitis flaring up; it ping-ponged between both her feet. When her feet acted up, her anxiety kicked in. "I was like, running is my one healthy way of coping, please don't take that away," says Ellen, who tried everything from cortisone shots to multiple pairs of custom orthotics. She'd run in bliss for a bit, get a little too relaxed on her stretching and cross-training routine, and her plantar fasciitis would come roaring back.

Still, her feet cooperated enough to take on a 10-mile trail race, her celebration of a decade of running. A trail newbie, Ellen tripped on a tree root at mile 7 and fell hard, landing on her hand. Until then, the race had aid stations every 2 miles, so she was expecting to find first aid and a ride back to the start at mile 8. No such luck. She had to run to the end, crossing the finish line with a broken pinky and the knowledge that she was dead last. "What the actual fuck?" she asked herself as she saw volunteers breaking down the finishing chute and tables emptied of postrace food and drink.

Feeling invisible at the trail race made her face something bigger she'd been wrestling with: Running was no longer serving her. Mentally, she was exhausted by riding the ups and downs of injury and recovery, and physically, she was gaining weight thanks to embracing a healthier relationship with food, exercise, and her body. Fatigue also played a pivotal role in the shift. "I was tired—and I mean really tired—of thinking about my body and food and exercise and if I had done enough or not enough or if I was good or bad because of what I weighed or looked like." She opened her mind to the possibility that she didn't have to feel like that anymore. "The validation I had been getting from being thin or a successful runner was feeding something that actually wasn't good for me," she says. "I wanted to find my value and worth outside of those two things." What's more, she was in her sandwich generation era: Her kids were now teenagers with needs more complicated than they used to be, and her mother was diagnosed with Alzheimer's.

The awful trail race was the last time she pinned on a bib, but Ellen kept running for two more years as she explored other ways to move her body. Her feet were "still jerks," and her joints didn't respond well to her weight gain. She knew she had to break up with running for good, despite feeling internal pressure to keep going. "Nobody likes a quitting story," she says. "But I decided to reframe that. Instead of saying I'm quitting, I'm saying I'm finding a different way that honors my body."

These days, Ellen walks for miles outside. "One of the things running gave me that I didn't know about myself was that I really thrive when I'm outside," she says, adding that her mom used to say Ellen's idea of camp-ing was a Holiday Inn with a broken air conditioner. She hits the yoga mat almost daily ("great for my soul") and recently took up swimming again. She still misses the fog-burning abilities of a good run, hangs on every word of a race report from her best running friend, and gets very tempted to pound the pavement when she wakes up on a fall day and temperatures are a crisp 45 degrees. "I'll run for maybe half a block and am immediately like, 'No, no.'"

For a dozen years, Ellen defined success by her miles, floating on the physical accomplishment and mental peace they brought her. Today, she's focused on staying out of pain and feeling comfortable in her own skin. "I've gained weight, but I don't view that as a negative," she says. "I've learned to love my body just as she is. She let me run when I needed to, and now she's carrying me though other pursuits."

CHAPTER 5

Feeling the Grief

Yes, It's Real

"Losing running was like the death of a parent," writes Kim Harland, a runner for two decades. "I grieved it. There are no other words for it."

As I read through the surveys that form the foundation for this book, that line took my breath away. Kim had recently lost her father, so she knew intimately how devastating that kind of loss can be. Could the end of running truly compare to the loss of a loved one?

I got my answer a few surveys later. When Cathy Nickels tore both of her Achilles tendons in a marathon, she was reminded of losing her sister in a car accident. "Both situations were sudden, horrible breaks," she says. "There were days when I thought my sister would just walk through the door again. And there were days I thought I would be able to run again. Running would feel like euphoria, just like seeing my sister would."

Those gutting comparisons took me back to the time I was sitting in a psychiatrist's office for what was supposed to be a short appointment to adjust my meds, antidepressants that I'd been on for over nine years. After explaining something about dopamine receptors, the psychiatrist asked me what I like to do in my free time. I said something like, I'm not able to run as much as I want to.

The tears started to flow as soon as the words left my mouth. I was mortified. This wasn't my normal therapist, who knew how sensitive I was and how much I relied on running for my mental health. This was a psychiatrist, a medical doctor who cared for people with serious issues like schizophrenia and personality disorders, not for somebody like me: a middle-aged, middle-of-the-pack runner who needed a prescription tune-up for mild to moderate depression.

As I emptied her Kleenex box, my thoughts spilled out as quickly as my nose was running. "I mean, I'm not sick," I said. "I haven't lost a parent recently. My mortgage isn't underwater." I continued to list all the reasons why I shouldn't be this despondent: I had two thriving kids, a lovely husband, and a body that was so healthy my only non-running-related visit to the doctor was my yearly annual. In my mind, losing running was the definition of a first-world problem, and I hated how fragile and self-absorbed I felt for caring so much.

The thoughtful, kind psychiatrist gently set me straight. "This is real grief," she said, encouraging me to treat my dwindling miles like I would treat the end of a relationship with any important person in my life. In other words: Losing running is losing a dear friend. That simple comparison changed everything, shifting my perspective from self-criticism to acceptance. It validated my tears, my mood swings, my inability to focus on anything but the looming end of my running years.

For thirty years, running *was* one of my best friends. She was always ready to rally. She was my confidante and my antidepressant, my kick in the butt and my place to relax, my connector to a higher power and my path to peer inward. She was my cool side of the pillow and my reality check when I needed one. She could create and dry tears (sometimes in the same workout); make me second-guess my devotion to her with two minutes of speed work; elicit a burning muscle pain that I both loved and hated; and summon feelings of confidence, gratitude, strength, and ownership I've never felt standing still.

Even if your relationship with running doesn't feel as pivotal as mine did, it likely delineated your daily schedule, personal goals, and overall lifestyle for years. "Running helps you access a deeper, richer life and greater relationship with yourself," says counselor Niamh Rawlins. "It's a gift."

Whether you frame running as a gift, a friendship, your primary sport, or some combination of the three, when you are no longer able to run, it's a true loss, which initially might not jibe with your definition of grief. We typically associate grief with death, but the reality is, it can occur with any kind of loss, from losing your faith to being fired, facing divorce, and watching a long-held dream slip away. "Grief is a reflection of your relationship with what has been lost," write Eleanor Haley and Litsa Williams in *What's Your Grief? Lists to Help You Through Any Loss.* "At its most basic, grief is love with nowhere to go," adds Rawlins, another line that took my breath away. I picture myself wearing my running clothes, standing in front of a dead-end sign where the road stops abruptly at the edge of a thick forest. There was nowhere else I could go.

Haley and Williams document various kinds of grief in their book, including disenfranchised grief, a type of grief that is not openly acknowledged, socially sanctioned, or publicly mourned. Because the loss doesn't seem legitimate or the relationship with the deceased wasn't "official," people often minimize it. Losing running falls under this disenfranchised grief umbrella; you don't get bereavement leave, bouquets of flowers, or even much sympathy when you can't run half-marathons anymore.

"Whether you have a cancer diagnosis or are losing running, here's the thing: Both are equally probable to set us off course in our life," says Kim Dawson, a professor of sport and exercise psychology. She's quick to clarify: Cancer and losing running obviously don't have the same outcome, but they can be similarly disruptive. When you can't run anymore, you miss your regular routine, the momentum a run brings to your day, the opportunity to connect with yourself and friends.

On an emotional level, you may feel everything from resentment to relief, anger to overwhelm. "Every emotion is welcome, and should be accepted and listened to," says Kristin Armstrong, a long-time runner and transition counselor in Austin, Texas. "Nothing is off-limits."

Saying nothing is off-limits and believing it, especially when it comes to grief, are two different things. "Our culture rarely flexes to accommodate the needs of grief," write Haley and Williams. "People sing the praises of those who are 'brave' and 'strong' in times of crisis."

Your cumulative miles have tattooed bravery and strength on your identity; those personality traits, coupled with the fact that running isn't a typical loss, mean you may be tempted to minimize things. Not a great idea. "If you skip over or rush the grieving process, your grief will get bottled up," Armstrong says, adding that unprocessed grief can morph into anxiety or depression, isolation, emotional outbursts, or rumination, among other things. What's more, don't trivialize your loss by thinking to yourself, *At least I can still...* (walk, do yoga, move forward). "That's rushing a kind of positivity that invalidates the grief," she adds.

Healing from any loss can happen in myriad ways, but there are certain elements—acknowledgment, expression, support, moving forward—that reliably transport you from one side of grief to the other. Here's a deeper look at those.

Don't Run Away from Your Feelings

Acknowledging your grief means allowing yourself to feel the loss, the breadth of your emotions, and not judging yourself for being preoccupied by them. You're not being selfish if California is on fire and your child is contemplating dropping out of college, yet the thought that courses through your mind all day long is this: I can't run anymore. "Thinking you shouldn't be upset over something that shaped how you see yourself and the world: That's shaming yourself out of your feelings, and it's not helpful," says Armstrong. She adds that multiple studies show that feeling shame keeps your nervous system in fight-or-flight mode, so prevents your body and mind from relaxing and delays healing.

During this transition, think of your emotions as a playlist on shuffle; you won't be able to predict what's coming next, but do your best to listen closely to each track. Megan Hinckley, who PR'ed by five minutes in her final 10K before surgery for hip dysplasia stopped her running, has experienced a mix of envy and anger. "I've seen people who had the same surgery as I did and they're out there running marathons," she says. "It's hard not to be jealous. I feel left out and can berate my body for things that are outside of my control." Arlene Barr, who ran for nearly a half century, teaches PE, and coaches track and cross-country at a high school, echoes the feeling of betrayal. "I am disappointed in this body that I thought I had always taken care of," says Arlene, who needed to have both hips replaced. "It feels like a death of a part of me."

After arthritis and stiffness in Cathy Annetta's big toe sidelined her, her anger flared up when other people started telling her about their runs. "I know it's not rational, because they're not connecting the dots of their life to what I'm going through," she says. "But I think to myself, 'Why aren't they at least toning it down a bit?'" Jennifer Moynihan, who ran the 1500 in college, loved doing speed work over her thirty-three-year span as a runner; that aspect of her loss, due to plantar fasciitis and other cascading injuries, feels acute. "The knowledge that I can only run in a limited way now—and will never get to run as fast as I used to—makes me really sad."

Shame can also sneak in through the back door of recovery, as Heather Escaravage found while working through patellofemoral pain syndrome. "Even though I have the physical therapy bills to prove I put in the work, I feel like I didn't try hard enough at recovery," she says. "I felt like I abandoned the process, even though I rationally know I didn't."

And sometimes, surprisingly, relief is also part of the emotional playlist. For college professor Amy Csizmar Dalal, repeated attempts to return to running left her anxious, frantic, and at odds with her body. "Allowing myself to stop," she says, "gives me relief."

Express Yourself

I asked everybody I interviewed for this book whether they had talked to anybody about leaving running, and with only a handful of exceptions, the answer was a consistent no. At least not until they'd had a detailed and healing conversation with me. "It's like free therapy," Michelle Bingham said, echoing a thought I heard multiple times. "I truly appreciate this discussion about the loss of running," Mariah Gianakouros said. "I didn't realize how much running did for me until I could no longer do it."

I am not a therapist, but talking to a trained one can expedite your healing. "At its most basic, therapy is a safe space being held just for you," says Amy Ebeid, a runner and clinical psychologist in Fairfax, Virginia, who has also grappled with the loss of running. "You're not responsible for anybody but yourself, and you're allowed to be as messy as you need to be." If you're like me, who naturally bottles unwelcome emotions, verbalizing your situation is key; my saying the words "I can't run as much as I want to" out loud in that psychiatrist's office made me feel about fifty pounds lighter. "The world moves on even when you're grieving," says Ebeid, who often takes her clients on healing walks during their appointments. "In a therapist's office, there's no timeline on your grief, so you can talk about running for as long as you need to."

Therapy can be helpful at any stage of the process. After finishing a 50-miler in 2019, Leah Wiesner didn't feel the validation and fulfillment she hoped she would after such a monumental achievement, so she spent a therapy session talking about why she identified so much as a runner. "I didn't know what else I had in my life," she says. In 2022, when she got a diagnosis of arthritis in both knees and Hashimoto's, an autoimmune disease, that earlier session she'd spent unpacking running three years prior eased her transition out of the sport. "It didn't feel as abrupt," Leah, who is thirty-nine, says. Similarly, Amy Csizmar Dalal found relief in her therapist's office. "He helped me figure out what running did for me," she says. "When I decided to stop, he was helpful in reminding me all the different ways that movement could occur."

Talking to a friend is also a valid option; just make sure you pick somebody who understands your connection to running and doesn't view your transition as a temporary leave of absence or a speed bump to be overcome within weeks. When Leah was walking with a former running friend, the conversation turned to her situation. The friend commented that, if a doctor ever told *her* she was done running, she would find a new doctor or simply ignore the advice. Leah was taken aback. "I think people don't realize it's my body, not my mind, that's holding me back," she says. This wasn't the compassionate shoulder she was hoping for. "You want to be able to express your feelings, be validated, and be seen," says counselor Armstrong. "You don't need the person to solve things for you. You just need to feel connected and not so alone."

Finally, if you have a partner or close friend who has been present and supportive during a prolonged stint with injury, realize that compassion fatigue is a real thing. Case in point: I know my husband loves me and wants to support me through adversity, but I also have seen him become weary of hearing about my same issues again and again. (Even *I* am weary of hearing about my same issues again and again.) Finding a set of fresh, compassionate ears is valuable and healthy for both of you.

It bears repeating: Don't go through this alone. You might feel tempted to downplay your pain—out of shame or because it feels too insignificant—but the loss of running is real, and pretending it's not or isolating yourself only deepens the hurt. If nothing else, that's why you're here: to be among people who understand what it means to miss something that moves you.

Commemorate Your Running Years

We hold funerals for people who die. Getting a divorce requires multiple steps and a final signature. Same for leaving a job: There's a clear finality to it. Stopping running doesn't have any protocol that marks the end. Until now.

Celebrate your running years—and cross a final virtual finish line—by writing your running obituary. As I wrote mine, my tears streamed like

I was watching the movie *Beaches* for the seventeenth time: so cathartic. If you'd like, use the following questions to get you started, but just know that there is no need to follow my or any standard format; like a good run, let it flow.

- Why did you start running? What kept you going?
- What were the biggest benefits running brought to your life?
- What are the most memorable highlights, racing or otherwise, of your running years?
- What did you learn about yourself through running?

Dimity's RIP Running (1990–2020)

Dimity has two distinct memories of running prior to actually choosing to run: one, in middle school gym class, when her gym teacher, whistle and stopwatch around his neck, chastised her to "use those long legs for something," as he stood at the end of the 100-meter dash. She was easily three seconds slower than her competition, a top gymnast. The other happened a few years later in high school, when she accidentally left her shiny marching band hat, which she needed for a football game, in the back of her mom's minivan at school drop-off. She sprinted across the parking lot to stop her mom from driving away. "I've never seen you run so fast," her mom said as she handed Dimity her hat.

Dimity's first real run was in college, likely a slog past the frat houses of Colgate University and up and down the hills of tiny Hamilton, New York. Truthfully, she doesn't remember her inaugural run. Rowing was her main sport, although the lake froze over in winter and the roads of upstate New York did not. ("Line your sweatshirts with newspaper," one crew coach told the team when a few members complained of being cold on a 3-miler.)

Dimity's first spark to train and run in a race happened when she was watching the 1996 New York City Marathon. She and her friend Kathy stood in Central Park, about a mile from the finish line, and just couldn't get enough of it: the energy, the variety of runners, the way participants smiled and picked up their shuffle when she cheered for them. When the duo, interns at Sports Illustrated for Kids, *arrived at work the following day neither of them had a voice.*

Dimity mailed in a paper application to enter the New York City Marathon in 1997—way before it became ridiculously hard to get into—and followed a New York Road Runners paper training plan she tacked to her bedroom wall. She'd rise early on Sunday mornings and run all over the city to get in her miles: across the Brooklyn Bridge, through Chinatown, to the World Trade Center when the Twin Towers were still standing. Calling home to Minnesota to report on her training, she mostly remembers her mother being concerned that she was running for two or three hours at a time. Is that safe for your body?

Dimity bought her first pair of running shorts—royal blue, made by Moving Comfort—at Lady Foot Locker at the Ridgedale Mall outside of Minneapolis. The first few times she put on shorts with liners, she couldn't believe she didn't need to wear underwear—such a change from her Umbros, those trendy soccer shorts and the only sporty shorts she owned previously. She wasn't loyal to any shoe brand: She wore everything from Adidas to Altras and loved when the spring and fall editions of Runner's World Shoe Reviews *landed in her mailbox.*

Dimity especially loved a few routes: the Big Block (about 3.5 miles, near her Minnesota childhood home); the Big Loop No. 1 (6-ish miles, Central Park, including the hills at the north end); the Big Loop No. 2 (5 or so miles, hilly, in Santa Fe); and the Highline Loop (a crisp 10 miles, in Denver). She preferred hills over flats, loops over out-and-backs, and an easy run over one with speed elements. One trail in Winter Park, Colorado, was her nirvana. Her dog Mason would often cover 10 miles to her 5 as they loped together through pine forests and by a rushing river, where Mason would stop to rehydrate. She often fantasized about taking the final run of her life on that loamy, quiet trail under a blue Colorado sky. Alas, that didn't happen.

Dimity loved two things about running more than the actual act itself: completing a run and writing about running. The former set up the rest of her day as a downhill coast: Endorphins coursing through her system, she could step in the house and knock out breakfast for two kids, empty the garbage and get the cans to the curb, and answer a few emails from editors. Four or five miles in the morning air, *she'd think,* and I'm set to handle whatever the day throws my way.

Writing about running was the impetus for many of her miles; she was fortunate enough to build a professional career around her running, even though she never stood on a race podium and she sustained injuries as frequently as her off-the-height-chart kids outgrew their shoes. While her feet ran beneath her, her mind bloomed with creativity and possibility, and she dreamed and wondered without reservations or apology. Running connected her to her emotional and spiritual sides, perspectives she was unable to access as deeply, if at all, standing still.

Highlights of her running career, marked by participation medals that now hang above the dog food bin in the garage, include 2007 Nike Women's Marathon, where she and her business partner Sarah Bowen Shea fortuitously planted the seeds for Another Mother Runner; and the 2014 Coeur d'Alene Ironman, which felt like her wedding day: an extra-long day that goes by so quickly! She also adored Ragnar races—twelve teammates taking on 200 miles—even if the actual event depleted her for weeks afterward. (Nine miles at 2 a.m., chased by Chipotle and Twizzlers? What's the problem?)

Her final race was the 2018 Casco Bay SwimRun, which she did with her beloved friend Katie, an ultrarunner who always encouraged Dimity to chase after her adventures. Her final true run—actually, it was a run/walk—was on January 18, 2020. A lunch run: 2.93 miles, 10:30 average pace. Nothing extraordinary about it, except that it was the culmination of three decades of running and three years of trying to manage pain in her right hamstring, lower back, and glute so she could continue to do what she loved. The salve of time, combined with relentless support from the Another Mother Runner community and acceptance of prioritizing her physical health, allowed her to finally come to terms with the end of her running days.

Dimity's running career is preceded by stints in various youth sports, four years of high school tennis, zero years of basketball despite being pestered almost hourly by the high school coach, and an unexpectedly successful rowing career that she has no interest in revisiting even if her husband loves his current masters rowing club. Her running career is survived by hiking adventures with good friends, cycling for miles soaking up sun and fresh air, and cheering for and encouraging everybody around her to go for it, no matter what that looks like for them.

Keep Moving

If you're tempted to have a Netflix marathon as you process your grief around running, go ahead: Rewatch all twenty-two seasons of *Grey's Anatomy*. But also make space for daily (or near daily) physical movement. As you well know, it eases tension, provides some mental clarity, and gets feel-good endorphins flowing. It may feel awkward or unfulfilling to go for a walk, ride a bike, or join a strength-training class, especially if you're mentally comparing it to a tempo run or trail run. But the healing benefits of physical exertion far outweigh the judgment you may cast on the activity. If your body allows it, get your heart rate up with kickboxing, cycling, or another blood-pumping exercise. In fact, a meta-analysis of over four hundred studies on aerobic exercise and mood found that aerobic movement significantly improves emotional resilience and reduces symptoms of depression, anxiety, and stress across all age groups. Those are exactly the kinds of results we're aiming for right now.

Chapters 9 and 10 dive into finding your next athletic chapter, but for now, look for an activity that is accessible and that feels safe, both mentally and physically. (Read: Don't go walk on a track.) Counselor Rawlins, a former collegiate soccer player, suffered major knee injuries during her athletic career and is no longer able to play soccer or run. She realized that working out around other people brings out her competitive side, the side that ignores her physical pain in favor of being the best. To intentionally disrupt that perspective, she bought a used Peloton bike and uses it in her basement for rides and strength-training sessions that don't hurt her knees and that cannot be directly compared to soccer. "I'm able to tune in to my body," she says, "instead of listening to my preset idea of what a workout should be."

AID STATION

Rage at the Richmond Marathon

I'm weary of booths selling half-zips with race logos stitched on the left breast, $280 Nike Vaporfly super shoes, and plastic teal Goodr sunglasses.

The taper energy thick in the air—anticipation for tomorrow's race—grates on me.

I glare and move past the guy who walks too close to me again offering a discount card for an upcoming local marathon. I've said *no thanks* twice already; the third time, I don't have it in me to be polite.

Although it doesn't seem rational, I think I'm actually angry at the empty Gatorade bottles and silver sports-chew wrappers piled on top of trash cans. Yep, the carbs being consumed in earnest today so they can be burned off tomorrow definitely annoy me.

When a friend tells me her coach thinks she can pull off a sub-two-hour half-marathon, I'm happy for her—and very jealous. I used to be able to do that.

Tomorrow, most everybody here will have a finisher's medal and the pink cheeks and tired legs of exhilaration. I will not.

A sixty-three-year-old runner tells me she's running more miles than ever, that her secret is protein and strength training. "That's really cool," I say, while my inner brat thinks, *Good for you*.

When somebody asks which race I'm running, "I'm not running tomorrow," I say quickly, trying to keep it light. I'm not in the mood to elaborate.

Even if I did elaborate—that I haven't run in four years because of a lower-back and hamstring issue I spent over a year trying to fix—I wouldn't get a response that calms me down. The anger I'm feeling is not true fury; I don't want to punch anybody, except for maybe Mr. Handout.

I think back to what counselor Niamh Rawlins told me about anger: It functions as a Check Engine light. "Anger is a sign when something feels unfair," she said. Yep, this all feels unfair to me today. I feel isolated and disconnected, like everybody else is going to a big party tomorrow, and I didn't get an invite.

Plus, I am in survival mode. Lately, I've been nursing a bad case of sciatica, nerve pain radiating down both of my calves, which is exacerbated by standing and walking, two things I can't avoid today. When I start to judge myself for being such a Debbie Downer, it dawns on me that being at a race expo when I'm physically fragile is like spending a weekend in my childhood home as grown adult: My default setting is petty, juvenile behavior.

Midafternoon, a woman walks over and introduces herself to me as Heather. I envelop her in a huge hug. Her hair is a cute, gray bob, and she's wearing an Oiselle Volee shirt. I immediately ask how she's feeling. "Detached," she says. "Like I'm not really a part of this." I hug her again.

Heather and I talked two months ago over Zoom. That's when she told me her running story. A collegiate cross-country runner, Heather ran mostly injury-free for a whopping thirty-three years. Eighteen months ago, she suffered a pinched nerve in her neck; it was so debilitating, she couldn't hold a pen or drive for nearly six months. As her neck healed, she started walking, slowly building up to a run/walk pattern so she could do a 5K while on a family vacation in Wisconsin. Her neck survived the race, but one knee, which swelled up considerably, did not. For the rest of their two-week trip, it ached, and she limped.

Her husband is standing nearby, listening. He's running the half-marathon tomorrow. I ask her whether she has attempted to run since we talked. She hasn't; she's scared to try in case it doesn't go well. We talk about the Another Mother Runner shirts on the table; she's eyeing a long sleeve that says "Virginia is for Runners," but she's not sure she can justify wearing it these days. "I get it," I say.

I am swept up into another conversation before I can say goodbye, but I am thankful for our short chat. Talking to her reminds me that I'm seeing things in black and white. I'm out, they're in. I'm hurt, they're not. In fact, not everybody here is on the verge of a PR or running more miles than ever. Not everybody here is as healthy and excited as I tell myself they are. Not everybody here is confident they'll even make it to the finish line tomorrow.

Heather stops by on the way out; she wants to take a picture with me to send to a running friend who has recently been diagnosed with breast cancer. Thanks, Universe, for the reality check.

The morning of the race, I roll my suitcase through the hotel lobby at 6:15 a.m. to catch my ride to the airport. I'm grateful I need to get home for a family commitment. Runners stand in clumps, their nervous chatter and laughter bouncing off the high ceilings. Millennial women are wearing bike shorts and matching sports bras; millennial men don shorts with smiling yellow emojis on them. Hydration belts sit on faux marble tables, their owners likely in the bathroom.

"I can't do a clementine before a race," one runner says as she picks through a fruit basket. "Where are the bananas?" The line at Starbucks features a handful of runners in bathrobes, which will be shed in the starting corrals.

Thanks to a good night's sleep, my Check Engine light is off. I smile at one runner waiting on the curb as I step into my Uber. "Have a great race," I tell her. And I mean it.

CHAPTER 6

Processing Your Grief

Four Paths Forward

We runners like our details: mileage, pace, heart rate average, training score, elevation change. We plan where we're going, then we ground ourselves along the way. ("I'm at mile 3.8 of my 6.4-mile loop.") Weeks before a race, we study course maps and elevation profiles like we're cramming for the SAT. Days before the starting line, we refresh forecasts for temperature, humidity, wind speed, and dew point as if we're expecting to flee from an incoming hurricane, not run a race.

Grief doesn't come with that kind of data. But just like tracking your miles helps you gauge your fitness, tracking the emotional terrain of loss, however murky, can help you find your footing. Although these emotional mile markers won't be as clear or satisfying as last year's cumulative mileage, they can offer a framework for navigating the months ahead.

With that in mind, I've laid out four common models of grief, paired with stories from athletes who've lived through them. Connecting theory to real-life experience is like filling in a jumbo paint-by-numbers scene: What starts as a jumbled mess gradually takes shape.

A quick reminder: Like everything else tied to losing running, grief doesn't unfold in tidy stages like a well-executed progression run. One day, you'll feel solid in your identity as a hiker. Then, on the drive home from a few calming hours in the woods, Beyoncé's "Run the World (Girls)" pops up on a playlist, and you're back at the finish line of a 10K where the song blared as you raced to your PR. A wave of longing for that strong, exhausted, invincible feeling rolls in.

Do your best to take these emotional shifts in stride. Trust that, eventually, the weight you're carrying will feel lighter. "The hardest part is when you're shrouded in and weighed down by grief," says Ellen Ewing, who ran for a dozen years, before her problematic feet forced her to stop. "It sucks, but I promise it won't always feel like that."

The Five Stages of Grief

What It Is

In the 1960s, the Swiss American psychiatrist Elizabeth Kübler-Ross identified the five hallmark emotions commonly felt by terminally ill patients. She initially created the stages of grief model to help doctors and nurses understand how patients diagnosed with imminent death are feeling; over time, the model has expanded to apply to people feeling all types of grief.

Stage 1: Denial

The ability to deny pain is a prerequisite of being a runner. But there's a big difference between tuning out your aching legs during 800-meter repeats and selectively ignoring a deep hip ache that has been lingering for months. In this early stage of grief, we cling to the past, unwilling or unable to fully process what's changing.

Julie Baker's first run was 0.3 miles, one lap around her block. In 1977, she and her neighbor, who wanted to lose weight, started running in the summer evenings. Once they reliably conquered the block, they added distance. Nearly fifty years—and twenty marathons—later, Julie was still at it, albeit not comfortably. She gritted her teeth through a couple of awful half-marathons. "Around mile nine or ten, the wheels just came off the bus," the sixty-nine-year-old says. "I limped my way to the finish lines." The physical evidence to support weaning off was there, but her mind wasn't on board.

Despite a diagnosis of osteoporosis and a history of not picking up her feet, a risky combination that had already led to multiple fractures, Julie kept signing up for races. Instead of acknowledging her limitations, she shifted into mental cruise control. "I was imagining myself five years ago," she says. "I wasn't imagining myself potentially tripping and having a tough time finishing races."

Stage 2: Anger

Anger is a sign your brain is trying to reconcile the unfairness of losing something that once defined you. As the reality of no more running sinks in, a race-day photo, the smell of your running shoes, or pretty much anything can tip off feelings of injustice.

Fellow runners can easily ignite the flames of anger. "When I'm out hiking and runners pass me, I want to say, 'Hey, I was a runner too. I did big things too,'" says Cathy Engstrom, who ran for thirty years before her right knee, with a torn meniscus and little cartilage, sidelined her. "I'm not angry at them, but I'm angry at the whole situation. One of the most empowering things I've ever done is spend whole days solo on the trails, and I can't do that anymore."

For Jenny Davies, social media became a painful trigger. The research scientist had a marathon on her life's bucket list. Despite signing up for the Los Angeles Marathon three times, she was never able to put together a full training cycle and get to the start line. Although her injury-prone body frustrated her, so did the smiling faces of her teammates popping up after successful long runs. "Just watching everybody prepare for a marathon made me feel hurt and angry," she says. "I mean, I'm happy for them, but it's still really hard for me to watch." She deleted social media after her second marathon attempt, reinstated it before her third, but knows now to proceed with caution. "I don't think I want to open Instagram right now," she says, weeks before the LA Marathon, which she will (once again) not be running.

Stage 3: Bargaining
Bargaining can be disguised as discipline: I promise to do my physical therapy exercises; I'll never run another marathon; I'll only run three times per week. Although it has a hopeful tone, it's really a distraction from the bigger situation: trying to control the uncontrollable.

Arielle Rosson, who started running at age six, has often offered up the gratitude bargaining chip to salvage her ability to run. "I often think, 'If only I could run again, I would never complain about anything in life ever again,'" says the thirty-eight-year-old, who has undergone three unsuccessful knee surgeries.

Arlene Barr's version of bargaining showed up during her recovery from a right-hip replacement, while she was awaiting surgery to replace her left. When the 125th Boston Marathon was moved to October 2021 because of COVID, organizers announced a virtual edition open to all: no qualifying time, no time limit. All you had to do was complete 26.2 miles in a single, continuous effort.

Arlene was elated. She'd run the 100th Boston and was eager to claim another unicorn medal—and control of her body as she came closer to the end of her forty-seven-year running career. With a virtual Boston in mind, she tried running outside. No good. She tried the treadmill. Ditto. The pain was too much, something her doctor, physical therapist, and chiropractor all warned about.

Still, Arlene wasn't ready to let go. She combed through the virtual race rules. Treadmills were allowed. Steppers were not. There was no mention of an elliptical though. The motion mimicked running, didn't aggravate her hips, and allowed her to finish 26.2 miles in one effort. "Plus, an elliptical requires your own momentum; it doesn't have a motor, like a treadmill," she explained. She emailed the Boston Athletic Association

(BAA) multiple times to ask whether she could use the elliptical, but never got a reply. In her mind, earning 26.2 miles—and continuing to feel like a vital member of the running community—was the goal. She completed the distance on her elliptical and submitted her results with a note explaining the situation. The BAA wrote back this time: She was disqualified. No medal. No name listed on the 2021 results.

"I was absolutely devastated," Arlene says. "I felt nauseous for weeks. It was like I'd been officially disqualified from the running world."

Stage 4: Depression
In this stage, you're as low emotionally as you're going to go. For some, this stage may feel like a partly cloudy day; others may feel like they've been in a downpour for months.

Knowing a time-related goal would keep her motivated as she rehabbed from both a hip and a knee replacement, Gretchen Gibson told herself she just needed two more months before she could run again. When that didn't happen, she thought she'd be ready in two *more* months. Ten months full of two-month goals later, she put Miles, her dog, on his leash and gave it a go. Within a quarter mile, she knew she had to abort mission. "All my optimism came crashing down," she says. "I've been fighting darkness and depression ever since."

Starting with track as a freshman in high school, Christina Smith took up half-marathons in her thirties when she realized how much training for the longer races helped her cope with her day-to-day life. She ran for forty-two years before a hip drop, when one side of the pelvis drops during a stride, became too pronounced and painful.

The end of her running days ushered in a long spell of depression. "Everybody has down days, bad days, but I did not come out of it," she says. "I live in the Northeast, where the winter blues are common, and then in the spring we all perk up and feel better. But I just felt nonstop doom and gloom." A year of therapy, which focused on her leaning into her emotions, helped her dig out of the hole. "My therapist told me the only coping mechanism I had was running," she says. "Learning how to feel my emotions and sit with them is a new skill and way to cope. I feel much lighter now."

Stage 5: Acceptance
Although this final stage feels like it should be a finish line, it's more of a state of mind that can wax and wane depending on your mood, surroundings, and stress level. Still, as time passes, you find more peace with the situation and this version of yourself.

Around the time Chris Cesena's foot, which had bone marrow lesions, couldn't withstand her running anymore—it ached for three days after a 3-mile run—her life was hit with a one-two punch. Her mom was diagnosed with metastatic lung cancer and, six months later, her dad with Stage IV pancreatic cancer. "I went through a time where it was hard to find the hope in anything," she says. "And I wasn't able to use running to soothe my grief."

A year out from her foot surgery, Chris feels much more optimistic about life—and losing running. "I realized I had to find another way to move my body," she says, "and it's okay if it looks different than I did before."

She does yoga three times per week, takes Pilates with her daughter, likes to mountain bike, and has paddleboarding on her list of things to try. She also takes nightly walks with her husband. "They're not power walks," she clarifies, noting that he gets annoyed when she picks up the pace. Still, she's a runner at heart and wants all her miles to count. "Don't get me wrong," she says, "I still turn on Strava during our walks."

The Four Tasks of Mourning

What It Is
The Four Tasks of Mourning is a proactive, practical approach to grief created in the 1980s by William Worden, a psychologist and grief expert. Flexibility is a hallmark; you can revisit or combine tasks as necessary.

Task 1: Accept the Reality of the Loss
Acknowledgment is the first task; by acknowledging the loss first, you can take action in the next steps.

When Kim Harland had surgery on a torn labrum in her hip, her surgeon assured her she'd be back to her regular routine in three months. That wasn't the case. "I never really ran properly after that," the Australian says. "Instead of getting functionality back, I lost it."

Although Kim ran both the Melbourne and the New York City Marathons, her favorite part of the sport wasn't the finish line. It was a long run on Saturday mornings with four friends, followed by coffee. Their conversations were so engaging, their friendships so tight that "the coffee was sometimes longer than the long run," says Kim, now fifty-seven years old.

Because of her hip and a stress fracture in her foot, Kim occasionally thought about who would be the first in her group to have to stop. "I knew nothing goes on forever," she says, "but I didn't think it would be me."

Unwilling to let go of her well-carved routine and deep friendships, she tried desperately—"and I mean desperately"—to hold on for three years after her hip surgery. She threw herself into physical therapy and limited her running to three runs per week, 5K max.

It wasn't enough. After her short runs, she would limp for about two days, which her colleagues noticed—and asked her about. "That bothered me terribly because I was in my mid-fifties," she says. "I don't need to be seen as ten years older than I actually am."

Even her beloved postrun coffee went bitter. She skipped the endorphin- and chatter-filled miles but still met her friends at the café afterward. She left feeling disconnected and hollow. Admitting just how deep the void ran ushered in true acceptance and allowed her to move onto something entirely new. "I knew I really had to find something else," she says.

Task 2: Process the Pain of Grief
This step encourages you to lean into the emotional, physical, and spiritual pain associated with the loss.

Kim realized she needed professional help. "It seemed so irrational that losing friends like that could bother me so much." She sought out a sports psychologist for a handful of sessions. The therapist helped her see how running dominated her identity; it was how she saw herself physically, mentally, and in community. The therapist encouraged Kim to look forward, not back, and recommended she challenge herself with cycling, which she had recently picked up. "It was lovely to be able to debrief with somebody who could objectively see the situation," says Kim. "I would recommend it to anybody."

Task 3: Adjust to a World Without the Deceased (or Thing You Are Grieving)

Fill in the holes of the loss by reshaping your identity, adjusting your routine, finding a new community, and otherwise moving forward.

The metatarsal stress fracture Kim suffered while training for the New York City Marathon made her recognize that she needed to do some low-impact workouts to complement her running. She grew up, as many Australians do, in the water. After a few months of doing laps solo, she joined a team. She loved the momentum of the group but found the structure of the workouts didn't promote the community vibe she was craving. "You've got a few seconds at the end of a lane before you push off again," she says. "Not a lot of time for socializing."

A few years later, as her 5Ks were dwindling, she took up road cycling. As with swimming, she rode by herself for a few months, then joined a women's group that taught skills like how to be road aware and ride in a peloton. She loved how competent she felt on her bike, but the best part? Her bike group goes out for coffee *and* breakfast after a ride. "I think my cycling group is even more social than my running group." Kim currently rotates between cycling and swimming six days per week; her cup is overflowing with activity and community.

Task 4: Find a Way to Maintain a Connection While Moving Forward

Don't bury running; rather, honor it as an important chapter of your life.

Turns out, once Kim found her own groove, she had plenty of emotional space for her Saturday morning run friends. She catches up with them over coffee or lunch every two to three months, and they celebrate each other's milestone birthdays. "If life went to hell in a hand basket," she says, "those are the people I'd pick up the phone and speak to straightaway."

The Dual Process Model of Coping with Bereavement

What It Is

European psychologists Margaret Stroebe and Henk Schut developed a dynamic framework called the Dual Process Model of Coping with Bereavement in the late 1990s. It classifies the stressors of grief into two categories: loss-oriented tasks, which involve confronting the grief head-on; and restoration-oriented tasks, which focus on adjusting to life after the loss. The griever oscillates between the two types of tasks. This model neatly overlays the loss of running in that the restoration tasks—namely, finding a substitute for running—seem to soothe the direct loss.

Loss-Oriented Process: Directly Grieving the Loss

When Lisa Payne Kirker suffered a heart attack, she didn't just lose running; she lost faith in her otherwise healthy forty-five-year-old body. "I felt like there was a time bomb inside of me, so for the first year, running was the least of my worries," she says, adding that she lives in rural Michigan, so the thought of another incident happening while she was alone, miles from home, was terrifying.

Still, she missed everything about running: the freedom, the time to herself, the pride of knocking out a marathon training run in summer heat and humidity, the sculpted legs running gave her ("kind of not kidding"). Plus, she missed running's metabolic efficiency. "I gained about twenty pounds that first year," she says. "It was really, really, *really* hard for my brain to be okay with it."

Restoration-Oriented Process: Adapting to Life After the Loss

Lisa's cardiologist said she could keep running if she kept her heart rate under 130 beats per minute. That requirement translated to a very slow pace for Lisa, but she was game to try it. She decided to train by heart rate for the Grand Rapids Marathon, her second. "I loved coming home and highlighting the workout I just finished," she says. "So satisfying."

The race itself was a disappointment; shuffling along at fifteen-minute miles did not bring the sense of accomplishment she was expecting. "Training has the promise that you can go faster, and I can never do that." The only bright spot on race day? She managed to clock a negative split and won a prize for doing so: a pair of New Balance kicks.

Loss-Oriented Process

Deciding that running with a low heart rate wasn't how she connected to the sport, Lisa grieved all over again as she made peace with the new shape of her body and a future that didn't include the numbers 13.1 or 26.2. "I lost ten of the pounds, but I also realized my body will never be as strong as it was when I was a runner."

Restoration-Oriented Process

Lisa embraced new ways to move. Five months after her heart attack, her family gave her a bike for Christmas. "Riding it gives me those quiet brain feelings that running brought me," she says. "It's not quite the same, but it does the trick." She rekindled a friendship with a fellow former runner, and they hike or walk together on Sunday mornings. On weekdays, she rides her stationary bike and strength trains when she has the energy. "I can't really sweat anymore," she says, "so finding motivation can be a challenge."

Loss-Oriented Process

Grief still visits. On fall days, when the temperature is a brisk 45 degrees, Lisa gets a little melancholy remembering she'll never have one of those perfect runs again. "You know," she says, "the unicorn ones when your legs feel so good, the pace comes easy, everything just clicks."

Restoration-Oriented Process

Knitting has become a gratifying stand-in for the training process. "I love following a complicated pattern," says Lisa, who taught herself to knit via YouTube videos. "It's hours of repetitive movement toward a final goal that gives me a satisfying sense of accomplishment."

Growing Around Grief

What It Is

American grief counselor Lois Tonkin developed this simple model that posits your grief doesn't diminish or shrink with time, but your life becomes larger and richer around it, thus making it feel not so acute. It's sometimes referred to as the fried egg theory: Grief is the yolk, and the egg white is life.

In high school, Angie Melton was in a car accident that broke one of her legs, required multiple surgeries, and created chronic osteoarthritis in both knees. Despite her compromised joints, she started running to get back in shape after having three kids. "It was my solo time to process things, so I kept it up as long as I could," she says. "But I felt like I was running on borrowed time."

Angie finished a couple half-marathons, including the Disney Princess when she was twenty-five weeks pregnant with her fourth child. The Cherry Blossom 10-miler was the final race of her career; one knee swelled significantly, and she struggled to finish because of the pain. "Honestly, I'm surprised my orthopedist let me go as long as I did," the fifty-three-year-old says.

A swimmer in high school, Angie dabbled in a few triathlons before her running stopped for good; when it did, she ramped up her swimming. A member of her masters team encouraged her to do a 2-mile open-water swim, which led her to embrace long-distance swimming, including the 4.4-mile Chesapeake Bay Swim and a 10K river swim. Swimming soon became the "white" to her running yolk, allowing her to transfer her athleticism from the pavement to the water. She's now in the pool year-round and has multiple distance events on her annual calendar.

Although she misses how accessible running is, she is grateful for her ten years in the sport. Running taught her that she requires regular movement to be her best self and that she loves to compete. "I never would have thought I could do open-water swimming if I hadn't started running," she says. "Running gave me the initial confidence in myself as an athlete."

Good to Know: Secondary Losses

The physical act of running is hard enough to lose, but unfortunately, that's not where the grief ends. "An immense loss [is] followed by a series of smaller losses in its aftermath," write grief experts Haley and Williams in *What's Your Grief? Lists to Help You Through Any Loss.* These secondary losses include shattered beliefs, dashed hopes, and shifts in identity. "Grieving people are often caught off guard by the ongoing losses and how they compound grief."

So that you aren't caught (too) off guard by these ongoing losses, here's a look at two examples of secondary losses.

Mourning the Dreams

Running makes you feel like almost anything is possible; all you need to do is channel your discipline and commit to it. Losing running pulls a curtain on that feeling, as Chris Cesena knows. She was watching television, and there were some firemen doing drills that involved running. She thought, *I can't ever be a fireman now.* To be clear: She never wanted to be a fireman, nor was she interested in a career change at age fifty. "But there was something really final about it," she says. "I always felt like I could do something because I chose to do it. That's not the case anymore. My world got a little smaller."

Sometimes the dreams are very specific. After Debra Helfand ran the New York City, Chicago, and Berlin Marathons, she fantasized about running the other three major marathons (Tokyo, Boston, and London). "My body can't handle a marathon anymore," she says. "I'm struggling to let go of the Six Majors dream." Heather Escaravage's goals involved being a role model. "I had so much pride when my daughter came to my triathlons and would run in with me. She got to see me being strong, doing something for myself," she says. "I feel like I've lost the opportunity to lead by example with my running."

Sports psychologist Kim Dawson acknowledges that unfinished goals—and the loss of opportunity—can be deeply frustrating and disappointing. "The brain naturally defaults to what we didn't do rather than what we accomplished," she says. Over time, though, you may begin to feel pride in what you did achieve and gain some hard-won perspective. "Perspective" might sound like a bucket of BS right now, but Dawson encourages you to keep trying: "When you can, step back and ask yourself, What did I do?"

The accomplishments of this trio of runners likely mirrors some of your highlights; they are worthy of reflection and recognition. A cross-country runner in high school and a triathlete in college, Chris ran off and on for thirty-seven years and thrived on trail running. "There is nothing like running down a trail, feeling strong and unstoppable."

Debra started running in her forties and, in addition to her three marathons, ran countless other races, including an unexpected victory in the 40+ division of a 5K. ("I had no idea what a masters category even was.") Beyond the races, running helped Debra break out of her introverted shell. She reached out to Kim, a Strava-only friend who was passing through New York City, and asked her to run together. That day, Kim invited Debra to run a half-marathon in the Swiss Alps, where she lives. Debra's first thought: "Wow, I can't do that." Then she paused. "Actually, yes, I can." Her husband and friends were stunned she accepted an invitation to a foreign land with a friend she'd met once.

A runner for fourteen years, Heather completed a DIY marathon during COVID. "I ran with my training partners, and friends and family cheered for us on the route we designed." Conquering 26.2 miles with almost no support: the kind of story she'll proudly retell at family dinners, even as her daughters (likely) roll their eyes.

Shifting Your Identity

Nonrunners hear the word *runner* and think of a solitary person in the dark and cold, pounding out the miles. In other words, they think of someone like Heather Treptow, who took on her first half-marathon when she was in college. A collegiate cross-country runner, she chose the Frozen Half in St. Paul, Minnesota, in January, way before climate change made Minnesota winters more palatable. Her father drove behind her on dark, snowy mornings to light her route. "I was going to get in my eight miles no matter what," she says.

Over thirty-three years as a runner, she kept getting in her miles, solidifying her identity as a runner. "Everything I did was directed at running. In college, people knew me as the girl who ran around campus in the cold weather," she says. In Connecticut, where she had her three kids, people knew her as the woman always pushing the jogging stroller.

When her running slowed down, she asked herself, "Who am I now? What else is there about me?"

Losing your running identity is especially tough because it's got multiple layers: Running shaped how you saw yourself as well as the personality you projected into the world. "I was so proud of putting a 26.2 magnet on my car after running the New York City Marathon," says Mariah Gianakouros. "For so much of my life, I was 'Donna the runner,'" Donna Nash says. "It's even part of my email address and Instagram handle."

Ruthie McCartney, the president of her local running club, organized turkey trots and displays her trophies and medals in her sixth-grade classroom, where she also uses running to help her teach lessons. "We talk about rise over run with slope," she says. "I say, 'I have to rise up out of bed before I can run my miles.'"

"The more you identified as a runner, the more space that running took up in your day-to-day life," says sports psychologist Erin Alaya, "the more challenging the transition is going to be." As with other aspects of grief, do your best to treat yourself with compassion and grace, not shame or judgment. Alaya continually reminds her clients who are shifting away from their primary sport that, even though they're no longer running, bobsledding, or playing tennis, they are still a capable, strong athlete who possesses all the traits that brought them feelings of success and fulfillment.

I pictured my athletic identity shift this way: I held a huge box with the label RUNNER on it. I opened it, and in it were a bunch of smaller boxes. I pulled those smaller boxes out and set the big RUNNER box aside. Those smaller boxes contained all the personal traits that three decades of running gave to me: physical health, mental wellness, the ability to motivate myself, self-confidence, a fondness for structure and routine, power, strength, resilience, and a love of being outside. Running also gave me professionally related smaller boxes: my livelihood, the ability to write stories that resonate with everyday athletes, the opportunity to train people to achieve their personal goals. I will own all the small boxes for the rest of my life; I just needed to find another big box to be their home.

Over time, as I realized my next big box would be labeled CYCLIST AND HIKER, I had the courage to break down the RUNNER box for recycling. I piled all the smaller boxes in CYCLIST AND HIKER, and they fit perfectly. I changed my Instagram handle from "dimityontherun" to "dimityonthemove." I donated some of my race shirts to Goodwill. I registered for an email alert when XL gravel bikes come up on a secondhand bike website. I bought a pair of hiking poles and a hydration pack big enough to fit everything I need for an extra-long day hike. Everything just happened naturally; I didn't force anything.

Christina Smith pictured her shift as if she was standing in a doorway between two rooms. Behind her lay the familiar space of her running career and identity, while the room ahead was unknown and uncharted. She realized she had to move forward, but "everything looked different from what I knew, and I wasn't sure if I was ready to leave the past behind," she says. After a year of transition and weekly therapy, Christina grew comfortable exploring the new space. Now she's a golfer, a line dancer, and a gardener who proudly built her own fence around her raised beds. "I had never built anything before," she says. "It felt incredibly empowering."

AID STATION

The Nun That Said Yes

Andrea Brown was not looking forward to turning fifty. "I thought, it's just going to be getting fat and having hot sweats from here on out," she says. A healthcare administrator at the time, she dabbled in Jazzercise in her thirties and had an on-again, off-again relationship with fitness. For her milestone birthday, she wanted a reset, a way to start taking care of herself again. Hearing talk show icon Oprah Winfrey rave about Canyon Ranch, a luxury wellness retreat in Tucson, Arizona, Andrea was in: five days of exercise and pampering would be her gift to herself. "The trip cost the equivalent of two mortgage payments." Andrea, now sixty-six years old, laughs. "But it was worth it."

While there, Andrea wanted to see "how bad things really were," so she tested her VO_2 max, the gold standard of measuring how efficiently a body uses oxygen. It's a brutal workout: Wearing a plastic mask over your face, you increase a treadmill's speed and incline at regular intervals until you reach total exhaustion. Andrea aced it: Her VO_2 max was in the 99th percentile for fifty-year-old women, which equated her cardiac efficiency to that of a nineteen-year-old. The exercise physiologist delivering her results put it bluntly: "Your heart is a Ferrari engine pulling a tugboat body."

The day before she took the test, she considered herself a menopausal woman trying to stay in size 14 pants. "The day after," she says, "I was ready to train to be an athlete." Upon returning home, she did her first 5K: thirty-three minutes. Her immediate goal? Getting it under thirty minutes. Within months, Andrea was running 800 repeats at the track, registering for the Senior Olympics, and hiring a coach to oversee her training. "Running fixed nearly everything that was broken in my life," she says, "depression to high cholesterol, lack of confidence to loneliness." She ran almost daily for ten solid years and came within seconds of accomplishing a big goal: going under two hours in the half-marathon.

One thing that wasn't broken in Andrea's life was her relationship with God. At age fifty-nine, she decided to become a nun. "God gave me nearly sixty years of a fabulous life," she says. "I was ready to devote myself to him."

All nuns take vows of poverty, chastity, and obedience, but guidelines regarding lifestyle and societal integration vary by order. Now known as Sister Michaelanne Marie, she knew the traditional, conservative order she joined didn't condone running or other exercise besides slow, contemplative walks. "Modern sisters may run," she says, "but those of us in old-school Latin Mass full-traditional religious habits do not."

During five years of preparation for sisterhood, she had a few conversations with priests who reminded her that, once fully professed, she would need to let go of running. The sport was viewed as an exercise in vanity that could easily become an unhealthy obsession. There were also practical concerns. For modesty reasons, Sister Michaelanne Marie and her sisters are not permitted to wear secular clothes; they dress in floor-length habits even while on vacation. Andrea tried running in her habit when she was alone in the country, but the reams of fabric swishing around her were unwieldy.

She's now assigned to a convent in Los Angeles, a location that doesn't allow for any kind of privacy. "If I were running down the street in my habit, I'd stop traffic," she says. "I'd create a spectacle and the next thing you know, I'm on YouTube."

She slowly came to terms with losing running but wasn't willing to stop all exercise, a practice that made her feel reborn and brought a sustained vibrancy to her body, mind, and spirit. "I'm going to give you the rest of my years," she told God, "but I need to keep this body strong because I want to serve you properly." Similarly, she gently informed her priest of the belief that has blossomed in her ever since she stepped off the treadmill at Canyon Ranch: Bodies are not neutral. "If you are not pushing your body ahead, you lose ground every second you breathe."

When Sister Michaelanne Marie moved to LA for her first official assignment, her luggage included a few sets of dumbbells and a plastic step with risers. Most days, she gets up at 4 a.m., has coffee with God, then does a strength-training routine assigned by her coach. Sometimes she complements that with a high-intensity training circuit on the step using a Les Mills on Demand workout.* Her in-room workouts are not a secret, but because she does them during her free time and she's not putting herself on display, they're not a violation of the vows she has taken.

She aims for five days per week of squats, deadlifts, push-ups, and the like but admits the lack of flexibility in her schedule has been a little more challenging than she anticipated. Still, she's committed to both deepening her relationship with God and staying physically fit for the rest of her life. Given her resilient genes and ingrained habits, the latter will likely keep her on this earth for a few more decades.

Plus, the routine gives her daily benefits. "We genuflect in front of the altar in chapel several times a day," she says. "When I'm working out, I can go down and get back up like I'm twelve years old."

* "It's so unfun, but it's my only opportunity for hard cardio. It's either that or give in to the slow decline."

CHAPTER 7

Taking Action

Soothe Yourself and Quiet Your Ego

Grieving thoughts surrounding running often feel overwhelming, like a Ferris wheel that never lets you off. Small physical actions, however, can stop the wheel and make you feel like you can get off and try a new ride. Simple healing practices are tangible ways to calm your mind, soothe your nerves, and reframe how you see yourself. Ideally, you can create your own healing toolbox in the same way you approached running: one mile at a time.

I assembled my toolbox through a series of moments you may recognize. I'm standing in the shower, flexing my quads, scanning for definition I think should still be there. A wave of self-loathing rushes in. I'm in line at the grocery store, scrolling on my phone, and a flashback finish-line picture shows up: My smile is as wide as the medal around my neck. I'll never experience that feeling again, I'm sure of it. I overhear work colleagues chatting about their race plans this weekend. I feel invisible, left behind.

Rationally, I know my legs are still strong. I know joy and athletic fulfillment still exist for me. And I know my colleagues aren't trying to exclude me. But in those moments, I am not levelheaded. I feel stung and become critical, catastrophic, judgmental—and my actions, mood, and language follow suit. It's not pleasant for me or anybody around me. (I hope you don't know what I'm talking about, but I'm pretty sure you do.)

I think of the following tools like the staple items I keep within arm's reach in my car: Burt's Bees lip balm, high-quality hand cream, and a tin of Altoids. Even though they're for emergencies involving chapped skin or too much garlic, I grab one of them pretty much every time I drive. I may not *need* a mint or a swipe of tingling balm, but I always feel better after I treat myself.

Make a Plan

Use It When: You're feeling unmoored.

Whether I was following a training plan or not, running laid the foundation of my day. No matter what else was going on, I knew I'd find the time and motivation to get outside for a few miles. Somehow, I almost always made it happen.

Now I don't have that certainty anymore, so it's much more important to be proactive with my workout schedule. I sit down on Sunday nights with my work and personal calendars and make my workout plan for the week. My mind needs my body to move every day, and if I don't have a written plan, I can easily talk myself out of it.

Most weeks, my schedule is very routine—teach spinning on Mondays and Fridays, do strength training and ride my bike inside on Tuesdays and Thursdays, swim on Wednesdays—but the habit of writing it all out reinforces my promise to myself to make it happen. On Sundays, I also sign up for Pilates classes for the week and put them on my schedule; that way, I've committed to them financially, and I won't get shut out because I waited until the last minute.

Sometimes I hanker for a grander plan: an event to train for. Because long hikes or bike events aren't as common as running races, I need to be more intentional about planning for them. (Especially because I like to do them with friends, so extra coordination is involved.) I wanted to do a 2-mile swim in Lake Superior called Point to La Pointe, held annually in August, but I missed the registration date this year, and the event sold out in one day. Note to self: Sit down at the beginning of the year to map out potential events I'd like to do and mark the registration dates in bold on my calendar.

Love on Your Whole Body

Use It When: Unadulterated loathing kicks in.

Troubling but true: Part of running's appeal is the way it offset my dubious nutrition habits. For the three decades I ran, sugar was the fourth—and most plentiful—macronutrient on which I subsisted; a typical lunch of mine at age thirty-five was four chocolate chip cookies and a Diet Coke. When I mindlessly ate a sleeve of Girl Scout Thin Mints while watching *Survivor* at night, I didn't worry about the cumulative calories. I knew the hilly 6 miles I had cued up for the morning would burn them off and rev my metabolism so I could eat the other sleeve for lunch the next day.

When I wasn't calibrating a miles-to-cookies ratio, I was hyperfocused on any area of injury. I didn't think of my body as a whole but rather as a collection of a few strong muscles surrounded by fragile ligaments, tendons, and bones. I despised and fixated on whichever part was aching or broken. Sometimes, I'd get so frustrated that I'd smash my fist against my strained hamstring or fantasize about getting my troublesome right foot surgically removed so I could "start over" with a prosthetic.

Although running brought many good things into my life, it skewed my relationship with my body. Entire books have been written on healing the relationship with your body, so I'm not pretending I have complete answers, but here are a few ways I have tried to embrace my whole body with a healthy perspective.

Pamper Yourself

For most of my adult life, my self-care centered on trying to fix what was broken. Massages to release my lower back; acupuncture sessions devoted to helping my tight hips loosen up; ice baths to speed recovery; foam rolling to break up tight spots.

Although I still tend to my activity-related aches and pains, I also have expanded my definition of self-care: anything that helps me relax. A couple times a year, I get a regular Swedish massage from a massage chain, not my therapist who has unknotted every inch of my body. I don't give many details about what is hurting. Instead, I simply ask for a full-body massage and allow the therapist to decide if or when she needs to spend extra time on a tight spot. Having delicate fingers tend to your whole body is a very different experience than having an elbow lodged in your glute; both have their benefits, but the former leaves my body feeling light and connected, not sore.

Other spa-centric options include a facial, a body wrap or scrub, a pedicure or manicure.

A low-budget version of this practice: a long bath with Epsom salts, bubbles, a drink you enjoy, and a good book. When you get out, spend time putting lotion all over your body: in between your toes, behind your knees, on your neck. When I touch my skin over my entire body, I am reminded how much more there is to me than just legs and lungs.

Wear Clothes That Fit and Flatter

For most of my running years, I wore the same size. My miles maintained my weight and I only went shopping when I felt woefully out-of-date. Otherwise, I could wear anything in my closet.

The end of my running coincided with the beginning of perimenopause: a one-two punch that slowed my metabolism. I wore my tried-and-true (formerly) flattering jeans on a flight, and the waistband dug into my belly so deeply, I covertly unbuttoned them without even leaving my seat. (I'm pretty sure my seatmate noticed, but I was so uncomfortable, I didn't care.)

Once I got home, those jeans went into a Goodwill pile along with many other staples I'd worn for decades. I did a huge closet cleanout.

Trying on (read: not being able to close the zipper on) some of my favorites, especially low-waisted pants and pencil skirts, made me almost laugh. How did I ever fit into these?

My wardrobe excavated, I had to buy new clothes. And even though my ego wanted to buy the same sizes I've always worn, I needed larger sizes to feel comfortable in this iteration of my body. When my jeans were suctioned to my thighs, I felt trapped in a sausage casing about to burst. When I walked across the pool deck and my Speedo went up my crack, I felt exposed in a way that had nothing to do with the swimsuit.

I did my best to turn off my self-judgment and ordered a bigger size in styles I love. I also bought things I would've never considered in my running years: flowy, elastic-waist pants and billowy sundresses. When the packages arrived, I slipped on my new, bigger jeans, thinking I would hate them and begin another cycle of self-judgment. Much to my surprise, the opposite was true. I looked better in my new jeans than the ones whose seams sprang when I attempted a squat.

I'll be honest: When shopping now, I still reach for—or click on—the size I've been most of my life. I chalk it up to muscle memory and recalibrate. And I remind myself each time I choose what actually fits, I'm not just dressing my body. I'm also actively loving it.

Say Thanks

When giving advice to runners at race expos, I would often tell people to thank their legs and their lungs as they crossed the finish line. I often did that, but that was the extent of my gratitude. Finish a race, my body gets praise. Any other time, though, I was the opposite of thankful; I was not especially kind to myself through my decades of running.

The process of losing running helped me gain perspective. Now when I notice I am having a critical thought about a certain body part, I do my best to stop myself. I offer thanks: *Thank you, legs: You have carried me so far. Thank you, glutes: Your power got me up so many hills.* Recognition feels much better than criticism.

Old habits die hard, so I know this will continue to take conscious redirecting. But expressing gratitude for my body, piece by piece, is something I plan to practice for the rest of my life. It's a simple way to nurture self-compassion as I age.

Write It Out

Use It When: You need a private and reliable outlet for your emotions.

I am a middle child in a family from the Midwest; I don't do emotions well. Running allowed me to process difficult-for-me feelings, so losing my miles was huge, mentally. I started regularly journaling in 2022, two years after I stopped running, when I took an online course focused on *The Artist's Way: A Spiritual Path to Higher Creativity* by Julia Cameron. A staple of the book is morning pages, or writing three unfiltered pages about anything on your mind. The course was six weeks long, and I rarely missed a day of morning pages. Writing with no expectations of beautiful sentence structure or proper punctuation cleared my mind, helped me process my worries, and generally made me feel so much lighter.

I've continued the practice for nearly three years. When I occasionally slack off, the absence feels like missing a run once did. I'm so much more balanced and positive when I do them. Sometimes I set a timer for twenty minutes, as counselor Nicole J. Sachs recommends in *Mind Your Body: A Revolutionary Program to Release Chronic Pain and Anxiety*, and sometimes I give myself a three-page requirement.

When I'm feeling particularly anxious or angry or sad, my only goal is to move the emotions I am feeling from my body to the page and give myself some perspective on my thoughts. I alternate between two prompts. The first is "I feel [emotion] because [reason]." I start at least a few sentences with that structure, then other thoughts start to form, although sometimes I fill a whole page with simple *I feel* statements. The other prompt I use is one from Sachs: At the top of the page, I write the question "What is real and true right now?" and let my pen flow like I'm running on a slight downhill.

Plug into Another Power Source

Use It When: You're feeling disconnected.

On rare occasions, I would have a run during which I felt so connected to the earth, I was convinced my strides were helping it turn on its axis. A little dramatic, yes, but running grounded me and connected me to something bigger than myself. I soaked up the weather, the energy, the forces of the universe as I moved slowly through space. I watched the navy-blue sky, dotted with stars and a pocked moon, brighten to welcome a new day. I spotted coyotes, foxes, prairie dogs, snakes, rabbits, squirrels, and birds going about their lives. I felt the wind blast my face, the cold freeze my fingers, the sun burn my shoulders. I greeted strangers I'd never see again, I waved at drivers who stopped to give me the right of way, I chatted with my neighbors during my cooldown.

Even though I ride my bike and hike outside, it's much harder for me to access that intimate connection on a universal scale, and it's a vital one for me. There are a few ways I can get close to that feeling without running. Meditation is one avenue; it's best when I have been meditating regularly and have a routine built up around it. I sit at roughly the same time daily, I use a meditation track that resonates with me, I focus on my breath, and when that feels too hard, I do a body scan to stay present in my body.

The second way is simple: an exercise called grounding, which is, at its essence, walking barefoot outside, sitting in the grass, or otherwise finding some skin-to-skin contact with the earth. Research shows that getting in direct contact with the earth—and using the earth's mild negative charge to balance out the positive charge we internally build up—has myriad benefits, including the ability to improve sleep, normalize the day–night cortisol rhythm, and reduce stress. (Benefits that sound very similar to those offered by running, yes?)

The third is related to grounding: gardening. Trust me when I say I don't have a green thumb, but I have planted enough durable perennials that continue to bloom and grow despite minimal TLC. Walking around barefoot while noticing which buds have popped or which plants attract the bees buzzing around them reminds me I'm still a witness to the greater forces of the world.

Remember the Definition of Suffering

Use It When: You need a (compassionate) reality check.

"When we resist change, it's called suffering," writes the wise soul and Buddhist nun Pema Chödrön in *Living Beautifully with Uncertainty and Change*. My copy has a spine so worn, when I open it, it lays flat to expose multiple highlights on every page. "We can spend our whole life suffering because we can't relax with how things really are," she explains, "or we can relax and embrace the open-mindedness of the human situation."

The human situation, of course, involves beginnings and endings, birth and death, pleasure and pain, hope and disappointment. More often than not, we are not in control of when these things happen. When I get caught in the woe-is-me doldrums, I remind myself that I am the cause of this suffering. My body has changed, and it can no longer abide the demands of running. I can relax and embrace that, or I can suffer because I won't accept it. Easier typed than done, of course, so if you want to throw this book across the room and curse me, I get it. But I'll gently remind you that you've suffered enough during this process; take a deep breath and allow yourself to think about how it might feel to ease into the river of acceptance.

Go Somatic

Use It When: You need some easily accessible emotional release.

Before I knew the definition of *somatic healing*, I already used the practice copiously in my life—and I'm confident you do too. Somatic healing is a therapeutic method that connects the mind and body to process stress and emotions.

"Somatic work always involves moving some aspect of the body," says Amy Pickett-Williams, a Denver therapist who specializes in grief.

"Emotions are often stored in the body, so when you move, you release tension and promote healing."

There are three main ways to access somatic healing, and they often overlap. For instance, a yoga session includes all three elements.

Bilateral Stimulation

Bilateral stimulation is a steady physical rhythm that integrates the left and the right sides of your brain and body. Therapists employ techniques like eye movement desensitization and reprocessing (EMDR), but there are plenty of DIY ways, including, yes, running.

The alternating cadence of your legs and arms while running helps calm your mind; research has shown that a steady, rhythmic pattern with movement, touch, or sound can reduce anxiety and help you process emotions.

TRY IT

With running off the table, walking is a no-brainer. Even better? Walking without digital distraction so you can tune into your emotions. If you want more of a sweat, high-aerobic options include swimming, cycling, climbing stairs, shadow boxing, cross-country skiing, snowshoeing, and dancing. Yoga, kayaking, marching in place, and tai chi are more low-key physical options.

You can also feel bilateral benefits by typing on a keyboard, kneading and rolling out dough, drumming, knitting, or crocheting. The simplest one Pickett-Williams recommends: slathering on hand lotion. (No wonder I reach for it all the time in the car!)

Contraction and Expansion

The second aspect of somatic healing concentrates on alternating between contraction (tightening in response to stress, like clenching your jaw) and expansion (opening to release stress, like taking a deep breath). Moving between these two states, says Pickett-Williams, helps regulate your nervous system and naturally widen the emotional space in which you feel balanced.

TRY IT

Clench and Release

Sit or lie down and make your body as tight and small as possible: Pucker your face, clench your fists, squeeze your elbows into your sides, contract your calves and quads. Hold tight for five seconds, then release. Repeat two or three times, noticing the relief you feel when you unclench.

Hug Yourself

Give yourself a big hug, then open your arms wide and allow your chest to expand. Repeat a few times, being aware of how both ends of the range feel. I especially love the hugging part; it reminds me that little things and my own personal touch can instantly shift my mood.

Stimulate the Vagus Nerve

Running between your brain and heart, lungs, and belly, the vagus nerve is the air traffic controller of your emotions and mood. It helps the body shift from a stressed fight-or-flight state to a calm rest-and-digest state. Although the nerve originates in the brain, 80 percent of its signals flow from the body to the brain, so stimulating the nerve with movement sends relaxing signals to your brain.

TRY IT

Focus on the Exhale

Pause and take some deep belly breaths, consciously making the exhale longer than the inhale. An extra-long exhale, which isn't possible if you were, say, running from a tiger, signals to your nervous system that you are safe.

Sing, Chant, or Hum

The vagus nerve runs near the vocal cords, so vibrations from humming trigger relaxation.

Use Cold Water

Splash cold water on your face or stand in a cold shower; doing so activates what's called the dive reflex, which helps slow your heart rate and calms your nervous system. I'm a huge fan of cold plunges. I challenge myself to stay in a little longer than I think I can: a little dose of accomplishment on top of some healing!

Handle Your Ego

The ego is a sly little fox. She hangs out in corners, behind trees, in the way back of an SUV, waiting for a moment when you feel wounded and small.

The fox pounces when you're scrolling Instagram and see a friend celebrating her marathon PR. She whispers, "Your PR was fifteen minutes faster, wasn't it?"

The fox pounces when you walk into a Starbucks on a Saturday morning and see a group of rosy-cheeked women sitting around a table piled with ear warmers and running gloves. "Glare at them," she commands.

She pounces when you're out on a walk and a flock of runners swallows you. "Yell at them so they don't judge you," she demands. "Tell them, 'I used to run. I was a runner.'"

You hear the fox, but how can you protect yourself from her digging her teeth in?

First, stop and name the emotion that summoned the fox from her lair. *I am jealous of my friend running a marathon. It hurts to see others enjoying what I used to do. I am angry that I can no longer run. This is really hard.* The chemical reaction resulting from an emotion, like adrenaline or cortisol, has a short shelf life: ninety seconds, according to neuroscientist Jill Bolte Taylor. But very few of us allow emotions to come and go in less than two minutes; instead, we welcome the fox and tell ourselves the same stories over and over about how this isn't fair or we don't deserve this.

Instead of tuning in to that story again, identify where you feel the emotion in your body (a tight chest, lump in your throat, tingling fingers— anything goes), take a few deep breaths, then position your body and mind to let the feeling move through you.

A great place to start: Turn one or both palms upward. This simple motion signifies openness. When your palms are open, you can't grasp or cling to anything. A nice complement to an open palm is to tell yourself to hold it lightly, either in your head or out loud. You're not pretending the fox isn't lurking and your mind isn't racing with thoughts of comparison or anger. You are, however, going to intentionally accept the situation, not dig into it too deeply, and realize it will pass.

The strategy I use most often to deter the fox is a spin on metta med-itation, a style that uses benevolent statements, such as "May I be safe, peaceful, and free of suffering." With similar sentiments, it expands those feelings to close friends and family, enemies, and eventually the whole world.

When I stopped running and the fox seemed to be following me everywhere, I decided to send every runner I saw good tidings; just because I was suffering didn't mean I wanted others to. "May you run well and be well," I said internally as I drove carpool and zeroed in on a pack of morn-ing runners. "May you run well and be well," I said out loud as I pedaled my bike in the opposite direction of a runner I whizzed by.

You can do the same. When you're hiking on a trail and a fit runner passes you, think: "May you run well and be well." When you're at the gym cranking the incline on your treadmill walk, and the runner next to you has 7:30 splits queued up: "May you run well and be well."

For the first hundred or so times, it will feel forced and fake, awkward and insincere. Keep showing up and practicing. Over time, my angry glare became a quiet gaze, positive and compassionate for both the giver and the receiver.

That doesn't mean, though, that I have vanquished the fox perma-nently. Almost five years after my final run, my daughter and I were walking our dogs on the Highline Canal, the trail I traversed for years as a runner. We were quiet, so we heard two women chatting as they approached us from behind. They were talking about returning Christmas gifts, laughing about why they even try to give their teenagers anything but cash and gift cards.

I often have that same conversation with fellow mothers of teenagers, and I wanted to insert myself into theirs. The fox, recognizing where my thoughts were going, appeared in a nearby field. I didn't just want to toss a few lines into their conversation though; I wanted to run next to them, be a part of them, soak up their energy on the day after Christmas, a day that always feels deflated. The fox crept closer, realizing she had a sure thing. In fact, I thought, I want to run again with my close friends, the posse that still meets a couple times a week. *Why can't I just do that?* I asked myself. The fox was running right alongside the pair of women, laughing and striding in sync, as they passed me and my daughter.

"May you run well and be well," I whispered as the duo carried on, already twenty steps ahead of us.

The fox disappeared into the trees.

AID STATION

Dimity Needs Friends

I'm dropping Ben, my second and youngest kid, off at college for his freshman year. Although I use the word *drop* frequently to describe this trip across the country, it's the wrong verb; it implies ease, like I am leaving a forgotten water bottle on a friend's porch. It doesn't encompass the exhaustion from multiple hour-long trips to Target, the sore knees and raw thumbs from assembling particleboard furniture on a dorm room floor, the tension between us as I ask him too frequently who he is texting and what is next on his schedule and generally hold on too tight.

His adult life is about to launch, and my adult life, at age fifty-two, is deflating. My social calendar, packed for two decades with choir concerts, back-to-school nights, and the like, now has two entries per month, if that. Similarly, my friendships are dwindling. I work from home, I work out by myself, and with both kids in college, I don't have those random encounters with mom friends at football games or prom-planning parties.

While Ben is off with new friends finding art for his dorm room, I register for Venus de Miles, a women's bike event about an hour north of Denver. As my kids were growing up, I used long workouts to process transitions; the rhythm of a long run or ride helped me come to terms with their flourishing independence and my role in it. The day Amelia, my daughter, started kindergarten, I ran 10 miles; the day Ben started preschool, I climbed up Deer Creek, a near 4,000-foot grind, on my bike.

Becoming a full-fledged empty nester is perhaps the last big transition of parenthood, so Venus de Miles, a sixty-four-mile ride, fit the bill. I did the event fifteen years ago and remember its inclusive, energetic vibe fondly: women of all ages and sizes sharing a day on bikes. I have been riding my bike this summer, but not with regularity or any kind of focus on training. Before Ben and I left, I did one fifty-mile ride with my husband to see how it would feel; I had been holding Venus de Miles as a possibility, but wasn't sure I would do it. As I click *register*, I feel a jolt of fresh energy and give myself a stealth assignment for the event: Find some new friends to ride bikes with.

Two weeks later, and I'm pulling into a gravel parking park next to an SUV with bumper stickers from the Leadville 100 and Dirty Kanza 200 (now called Unbound Gravel), two ultra-challenging off-road bike races. The cyclist standing nearby has a sleek bike frame, a sleek kit, a sleek body. I have a slight freakout, wondering whether the Venus event has morphed from a sisterhood celebration of riding to a peloton of speedy cyclists.

Walking over to the bathroom, I hear somebody call my name. *Yes*, I think, *a friend already!* It's Liz, a former rugby player who is now a competitive rower; she and my husband are in the same rowing club. She'll be wearing a red-and-white jersey with the Canadian flag, she tells me, and she's riding with a few friends. "Look for us," she says, and I promise to.

I line up in a sea of bright cycling jerseys, back pockets stuffed with gels, tubes, an extra layer. Some women are pumping air last minute into their tires, others are chatting with friends. My head is down; I haven't ridden in a pack of bikes for a few years, and I hope I don't make any dumb mistakes.

The first miles, punctuated by whoops and claps by a few spectators, are effortless, setting up my expectation that things will feel this way for the full sixty-four miles. I have conveniently forgotten that every athletic endeavor entails a portion of suffering, and the smarter you are at the front end, the fewer consequences you'll face on the back end. The road is smooth under my skinny tires, the Colorado sun is behind a cloud, and although I don't realize it yet, there's a solid tailwind against my back, making me feel like I properly trained for this.

I have not. About seven months ago, I officially entered menopause, and I acutely feel the absence of life-giving hormones, from my foggy brain to my extra creaky bunion. Despite following plenty of advice—eating loads of protein and fiber, supplementing with stress-reducing ashwagandha, doubling up on strength training—I am twenty pounds heavier than I used to be. My cheeks and knuckles are puffy, my clean pajamas stink with sweat after one night, the seams of my Lycra leggings now leave indents on my calves. I did one more 50-miler upon returning home from college drop-off, so I know I can finish this, but my body feels unreliable and foreign. I don't trust its capabilities anymore.

I ride by Rhea, one of Liz's posse, and she calls out, "Aren't you Liz's friend?" "Yes!" I answer a little too enthusiastically. We chat a bit. Turns out, Rhea, also a Canadian, met Liz last year on this exact ride, so new friendships started on wheels are possible. Liz catches us from behind and proceeds to introduce me to Megan, another friend, and Dawn, yet another.

As we continue along, Megan tells me she's a gravel biker. I've thought about getting into gravel biking: It's not as technical as mountain biking, and feels much safer than sharing the roads with drivers holding their phone in one hand and the steering wheel in the other. Megan's kids are college-aged too. As we're talking about how different grocery shopping is now (*How many bananas do I buy?*), I'm picturing us doing rides together; we'll be the same pace and we'll have bonding, intimate conversations. Then she tells me she just—as in six days ago—completed the SBT GVL gravel race, a 100-miler in Steamboat Springs, Colorado, that includes 8,000 feet of climbing. "Oh, that's so cool!" I say, hopefully hiding my shock that she's so fit she can take on another big event today.

We see the first aid station, and I am anxious to get off my bike, stand up straight to unkink my back, and grab a snack. But the Canadian train decides not to stop. Swept up in their momentum, I ignore my needs and try to stay in their draft. Within a mile or so, though, I check myself. I know this pace is not realistic. I quietly tell Liz not to worry if I drop back.

They pedal off ahead of me, and I wonder whether I've given up my one shot at finding bike buddies. Most of the riders did stop at the aid station, so the road is empty. The sky is still dotted with clouds, and I tell myself to just settle in, enjoy the day. Then a woman with a gray ponytail, skinny legs, and a busy jersey who has been riding about fifty feet in front of me drops back and introduces herself. "We're about the same pace," she says, before introducing herself. Her name is Robin, and she moved to Colorado recently to help with her grandkids. Grandkids? I wince internally and judge myself immediately: I am now the pace of a grandmother.

Robin turns out to be lovely and a great conversationalist. A former runner and triathlete, she used to live on a lake in upstate New York and water ski at 6 a.m. before heading to work. Over the course of 15 miles, she tells me more about herself, and I pull out my two greatest conversation hits: the story of my name and height, both mine and my family's.*

I am uneasy, though. I'm not used to riding and talking, and I don't have an accurate reading on my internal gas gauge. And to be honest, I'm not even sure how many miles I've gone. I'm wearing my GPS, but the numbers on the display have become, over the past few years, too small for me to read on the fly. I have not been eating and drinking like I know I should, so right before the second aid station, I try to make up for lost time. I stuff a full packet (two servings) of grape GU Chews in my mouth and swig some warm water to wash them down.

At the next aid station, I creak my leg over my bike seat like a cowgirl who has been riding from sunup to sundown. A wave of nausea hits me as I stand up. I'm about to taste those chews again. The clouds have

---

* Short story: Dimity is a family name.
Longer story: My grandmother had a friend named Dimity Dorcas Davis, and she mentioned that to my dad around the time of my birth. My mom named my older sister Megan, so it was my dad's turn to name me. He wanted to name me Dorcas. My mom said, "No way." I was 11 pounds, 6 ounces and had no hair when I was born; I didn't need a name like Dorcas.
My dad asked whether *Dimity* was okay, and my mom agreed. So my birth name was Dimity Davis McDowell. Davis was chosen as my middle name because it was the same as my dad's.
Longer story continued: I married a man named Grant Davis. So my name became Dimity Davis McDowell Davis, but sometimes I say I could've been Dimity Davis Davis, or D Cubed.
As for my height: I'm just shy of six foot four. I get my height from my dad, who was six six. My sisters, Megan and Sarah, are "short" by comparison: five foot eight and five foot nine. My husband is six foot two, our daughter is six foot five, and our son is six foot nine. Robin, it turns out, has a bunch of tall relatives as well.

moved on, the sun feels too bright. I cross the street to get away from the cyclists and head for a tree. In the shade, I take a few deep breaths, reassure myself I'm okay, and spit out my grapey regurgitation. As I refill my water bottles, Robin introduces me to a group of women from the bike club she joined when she moved to Colorado. It sounds inclusive and robust, but I dismiss it because the club is based in Boulder, an hour north of where I live.

I ride alone to center myself and get my stomach back to nonvomit mode. Pedaling along, I realize I *could* actually join a bike club an hour away. My weekends used to be about stocking the fridge, watching various sporting events, running errands to make sure everybody was ready for the upcoming week. Not anymore; now I can devote the majority of a weekend day to a long ride with other women. I smile at the thought. A few more miles, and a bunch of us get stopped at an intersection by a two-mile line of Harley-Davidsons. I make a joke about how we must look as ridiculous to them as they look to us, and it gets a few laughs. I feel connected. At the last aid station, with about 17 miles to go, I sit in a chair and chug two mini Cokes, my Hail Mary to get me home.

Thank goodness I had the second one. The barely noticeable tailwind has turned into a fierce headwind and the road back to the start is a steady uphill. "I've dropped out of ultramarathons," I would overhear one woman say after the ride. "And this was harder." My inner thighs are cramping—a first for me on a bike ride—and my right foot is on fire, lit up by a pinched nerve in my lower back. Every time I push my right pedal down, it sparks. I'm sick of thinking of how much I physically hurt, so I encourage everybody I pass by saying, "This is just brutal, isn't it?" I cross the finish line by myself, unclip out of my pedals and stand there for a few minutes to orient myself and find my car.

The SUV with the badass bumper stickers is already gone. I collapse into my driver's seat, close my eyes, and heave a deep sigh. *Holy F that was hard, Dimity.* I'm tempted to start the car and skip the postride festival, which is all the way across the street, but then I remember my stealth assignment. Even though I'm confident new bike friendships won't have the depth that my running friendships did—the fact that we mostly ride single file ensures sporadic, not sustained, conversation—I still want to be part of a group, to have somebody expecting me to show up. Plus, there's always stops for coffee and parking lot chatter.

I wobble over to the festival, thankful to grab the last cold protein drink from a vendor as I walk in. The Canadian train is, impossibly, standing around a high-top table. I'm sure they're tired, but they certainly don't look it. I say hello and drag an empty chair over to sit near them. I'm too tired to engage, so I stare at their knees, listen to their chatter, and drink my supercharged chocolate milk.

Liz and her posse are very kind—Liz texted my husband later to make sure I was okay—but I feel sheepish asking any of them to ride with me soon, given how different our days turned out. I spot Robin and her teammates sitting at a picnic table and, without giving it a second thought, walk over to her and ask her to text me so we can ride together again.

As I'm driving home, Ben calls. It's the first time he's initiated contact since I dropped him off. I wipe away my tears as he talks about his professors and first week of classes. He sounds so much older than he did two weeks ago.

I pull into my driveway and pull out my phone. I read a text from Robin. "So much fun to ride with you today! [bike emoji] [bike emoji] How do you spell your first name?"

CHAPTER 8

Managing the Messy Stuff

Social Media, Friendships, and (Maybe) Menopause

Barb Eisner, who stands an even five feet tall, became a runner when she was cut during her high school basketball tryouts. Although conversations with her cross-country teammates during practices were never much deeper than "Do you have a lot of homework?" she realized how much she enjoyed running with others. "I connect best with people when I can go for a run with them," says Barb, now fifty-eight. "Nobody has a filter on, including me: I can just be myself."

For nearly three decades, Barb found community and plenty of conversation with the running group at Multnomah Athletic Club in Portland, Oregon. The self-named Early Birds meet four days per week, usually at 5:30 a.m., and Barb, a second-grade teacher, rarely missed a day. "Wednesdays' longish runs were the best," she says. "I got to run eight miles with a group of the greatest people. Heading into work, I always had a huge smile on my face."

The ages of the Early Birds span from thirty to seventy, and their connections don't end when the runs do: They chip in when a member could use a boost, whether it's painting their house, delivering a warm meal when they're sick, or sending them a good-luck care package before a big race. "It's the best kind of village," says Barb. The group's motto? What is shared on the run stays on the run.

While training for the 2016 New York City Marathon, her fourth marathon, Barb's teammates noticed her pace and potential; then fifty years old, she could qualify for Boston. And they weren't about to let her off the hook, even though Barb has always valued connection over competition. Around mile 6 of the race, one of her teammates gave her a gentle push: "You can't run with us anymore," she said. "You're capable of more." Barb took off. She crossed the finish line in 3:55, earning her Boston Qualifier.

Barb went on to run five more marathons over the next six years, chasing experiences more than PRs. Her ninth and final 26.2 was the 2022 Chicago Marathon. She stopped 100 meters from the finish line and handed a phone to a spectator to take a picture. "Time is ticking," the photographer said after handing it back. "Don't you want to cross the finish line?" Barb wasn't in a rush. "I just want to soak this up for a little longer," she thought.

Less than six months later, on March 14, 2023—yes, she remembers the exact date—Barb came down with a case of sciatica, shooting nerve pain running down the back of her legs so severe, the walk to the bathroom had her in tears. The Early Birds stayed in touch, inviting her to a beer or coffee or offering a ride to the doctor. After a few months, Barb was recovered enough to head back to her beloved Wednesday morning crew, simply to say hi. She knew she wouldn't be running a single step, but the idea of not going was out of the question. She needed her people.

The moment hit hard. After hugging everyone, she watched them run off. With her sciatica flaring up and tears running down her face, she called another Early Bird to talk it through. "She said she'd just listen to me for as long as I needed her to," Barb recalls.

Like anything, going to walk while the Early Birds ran became (a little) easier with time. Sometimes Barb walks by herself, sometimes she's got company the whole time, and sometimes somebody will run part of the route, then walk with her. "It's bittersweet. I want to be running," she admits. "But then I remember what is most important to me is being part of the group."

Deciding how to interact with your running friends is just one of the thorny issues you may face when you step away from the sport. Social media and attending races can also stir up an emotional tornado; you're watching others do what you once loved. And if you happen to be in peri-menopause as you transition out of running, you probably feel like you're going through this whole transition as you try to find a route through thick fog. As your hormones shift, everything else—your body, your emotions, your moods—does too, so it's hard to define something as simple as which direction is forward.

Here's some help navigating it all.

Staying in the Running Family

Friendships form at warp speed while running. Amy Ebeid, a psychologist in Fairfax, Virginia, remembers showing up for a group run at five thirty in the morning. One woman proclaimed she was having a bad day already, and Amy said, "Me too! My two-year-old is an asshole." The other runner laughed "Mine too!" Their friendship was cemented by running together on that mutually terrible morning.

Sharing roads, trails, discipline, and finish lines, we runners connect easily and deeply, forging a bond through a few runs that can rival the one siblings take years to create. When your body no longer allows you to run, your social network suffers as well. You feel pushed to the edge of a supportive, inclusive community when you emotionally need it most.

Losing running doesn't necessarily mean divorcing your running friends, but it does require grace and time to figure out a new configuration for those relationships. "Even though it may be difficult, try not to isolate yourself from your teammates," says Hayley Perlus, a sport and performance psychology expert based in Vail, Colorado. "Feeling supported is so important when you're grieving, and these people have been your cheerleaders and confidants."

You can be like Barb: Decide that the attachment to your group is so important, you're willing to have your running wound throb a little when you see them. One athlete, who asked to remain anonymous, also attends her group's weekly long run to walk. A few in the group have also shifted to walking, so she's not alone on the trail, but the situation can still sting. At the end of the workout, they all go to brunch. "You know how it is: After a ten-mile run, you can talk about that run for hours," she says. "I'm not riding that high. I can't lie: It feels awful." Another athlete walked once while her group ran but hasn't returned to do it again. "It's just too emotionally hard for me," she says.

If joining a postrun breakfast or coffee is appealing but you'd rather not walk while they run, consider doing your own workout first; ideally, do something that makes you feel both sweaty and strong. Then when you give them a hug hello, you'll be riding your own endorphin high, setting yourself up for a more positive mindset as you catch up.

You can also switch things up entirely. If you're part of a group, you can ask one or two friends to meet for a walk or a hike. After all, it's not just the miles that bring you together; it's also the shared time with few distractions. Or you can rally the troops and have a totally different adventure. Sarah Lightner's running group used to train for the Twin Cities Marathon together, and now they hike or ride bikes to a brewery together. "It's not the intensity or frequency of what we used to do," she says. "But it's a fun way to stay in touch."

Taking a gathering off the road might not be as smooth as you hoped. As Ingrid L. was phasing out of running thanks to two bone-on-bone arthritic knees, she went to dinner with her running group. Although she loved seeing them, she felt like an outsider. "They're all breaking out their planners to schedule runs and races," she says. "It was really hard."

Before meeting up with running friends in any capacity, sports psychologist Erin Alaya recommends taking a moment to reflect on what expectations are realistic given your emotional state. "The bigger the gap between expectations and reality, the more psychological distress you're likely to feel," she says.

If you attend a group run expecting a quick hello and goodbye, and acknowledge that walking while others run might feel flat or frustrating, you're more likely to leave with your emotions intact. But if you are anticipating a fantastic solo workout *and* the kind of deep, honest conversations you used to have mid-run, you're setting yourself up for disappointment.

And let's be honest, sometimes your former running friends ghost you.

After Ruthie McCartney told her running partner of two years that she was having a serious pain in her knee, Ruthie never heard from her again. "She dropped me like a hot potato," she says. "It hurts a lot. I thought we had a deep bond." If something similar has happened to you, I'm sorry; being ghosted by a friend when you're already down is really painful. Although empathy might not be your first reaction, you may feel less hurt when you consider they may not know what to say or do. Conversations about loss can be awkward and vulnerable, so they may be avoiding those feelings, even if it means avoiding you too.

It's also worth remembering that although losing running isn't contagious, your situation may have triggered something in them. They might not be ready to consider the fact that their running days might also come to an end.

Finally, remember friendships born on the road are also born of convenience. No matter how close you felt, the bond may have been shaped as much by shared schedules as by shared values. When you're no longer showing up for runs, it can become a case of *out of sight, out of mind*. These kinds of situation-based friendships form and fade with job changes, different stages of parenting, moving, and all chapters of life. "Sometimes we make friendships of convenience much bigger than they really are," says sports psychologist Dawson. "Even though it can be hard to see when you're grieving, pruning is a part of all aspects of life. It helps us grow."

Then again, friendships born on the road might last forever if you can find someone who is slowing down at the same rate you are. Julie Baker met her best running friend, Janet Jones, at a stoplight in Washington, DC, in the late eighties. "I noticed that we were both wearing Asics Kayanos, and I mentioned I loved the shoe," remembers Julie, now sixty-nine. They ran down the Washington Mall together that day and since then have covered thousands of miles side by side, including the Boston and Twin Cities Marathons. These days, the pair walk 4 or 5 miles most mornings a week. "We reminisce about our runs, share everything about our lives, and laugh," says Julie, who lives in Columbia, Maryland. "Our friendship is just as deep and meaningful as when we were running together."

Listening to Former Running Friends

"I felt abandoned by my running friends," says Valorie Plesha, who was part of a vibrant training group for nearly three years. "Only a few reached out to find out why I stopped coming to practice. The rest carried on as if I'd never been there in the first place."

Even if your relationship doesn't feel like it's got the substance to persist without regular runs together, I encourage you not to pretend like the person who is no longer running with you is fine. She's probably not. Connect with her at least once to let her know you're thinking about her.

Here are a few recommendations for dealing with the delicate situation of a running friend dropping from the group:

- Send a simple text or call to say hi, tell them you're thinking about them, and ask them how they're doing. By reaching out and acknowledging the situation, you help them begin to realize they are valued for more than just their running identity.
- If it feels right, ask whether they'd like to grab a coffee or a glass of wine, go for a walk, or take a strength class together. "I wish some of my running friends would have invited me to do something active other than running," says Sarah

Lightner. "I stopped doing anything, which was not good on multiple levels."

- Don't take a no personally. "Just being invited feels so huge," says Ellen Ewing. "I may not have been ready to accept an invite to try something new, but it would have meant so much for somebody to ask."
- If you get together in person, let them take the lead on the conversation about their running. (You likely passed many miles talking about everything *but* running, so don't fret about what you'll talk about.)
- If you do start talking running, don't give advice unless they ask for it. "Listen and just be there for me," says Cathy Annetta, "rather than trying to suggest solutions or say there is something more I can do." Gretchen Gibson seconds this thought. "I wish I had been told it's okay to be sad," she says, "and not just told repeatedly to find something else to pour my passion into."
- Set up another nonrunning date if it feels natural to both of you or let the relationship naturally dissolve. Either works. "I had some running friends who reached out for walks, but those relationships have faded over time," says Megan Hinckley. "I compare it to losing close touch with work colleagues. I'm happy to run into them and catch up, but they're not the most active relationships in my life right now."
- And if you're the type of friend who likes to host guests, Chris Cesena has a lighter suggestion: Throw her a goodbye-to-running party. "End her era in style."

Scrolling Through the Splits

If your social feeds are anything like mine, they're filled with fueling tips for first-time marathoners, promos for flashy shoes, and miles of postrun selfies with overlaid splits. In other words, it's too much at all once. As such, the idea of scrubbing your feed of any endurance-related content when you've got fresh scars is understandable. Do what feels best to you. Amy Ebeid, a psychologist in Fairfax, Virginia, unfollowed every running-related Instagram page when she got the diagnosis of severe insertional Achilles tendinopathy. "I just had to clean the slate," she says. "It felt like I was trying to avoid an ex-boyfriend I still kind of liked. Running still meant something to me."

Cathy Engstrom, who hung up her shoes after running for thirty years on a knee that had been severely dislocated in middle school, thought she might unfollow some people because she knew it would be hard to see their posts. But she opted not to change anything. "I still wanted to be part of the running community," she explains, noting that her son is a runner and she loves to keep up with the professional scene. "Clearing my media of running felt a bit like burning it all down."

If you're unsure of where you stand, Dawson recommends taking a moment after you're done scrolling and asking yourself, *Do I feel happier or sadder compared to before I picked up my phone?* Yes, that's kind of a basic question—and most of us instinctively know the answer—but deliberately checking in with your mood can help you make more mindful decisions in the future.

Dawson is also a big fan of distancing yourself from social media for a stretch to recenter and take care of yourself, then rejoining when you're feeling more stable. Consider deleting Instagram, Facebook, and other social media apps on your phone for a bit instead of culling your account of all running content, which you might want in the future.

Regardless of what you choose, any social media can easily conjure up beasts of comparison, resentfulness, and self-loathing; when you're feeling raw, running-centric posts can be worse than the sting of sunscreen-laced sweat in your eyes. If you stay on social media, intentionally set boundaries for yourself. Gretchen Gibson, a former half-marathoner whose knee and hip replacements have sidelined her running, continues to follow the feeds of professional runners, but prefers not to follow her local events. "It's easier for me to appreciate elite athletes thriving in the sport," the

Dover, Ohio, resident says. Similarly, she gives herself grace on social media interaction. "There are some days I just can't participate in the conversations, and other days I want to reconnect with the community," she says. "It's a lot like my recovery journey: peaks and valleys."

In 2020, when I knew my running days were over, for at least four months whenever I opened Facebook I was inevitably met with a photo of a runner and immediately closed the window before my eyes welled up. These days, the pain doesn't go as deep, but I prefer to check in on social media when I'm warming up or cooling down on an indoor bike ride; the motion of my legs doesn't allow me to get too hung up on the details. I have learned the hard way to abstain from scrolling around momentous race days like the Boston and New York City Marathons (and the days the qualifiers and lottery winners are announced). Seeing post after post of elated finishers makes me want to just crawl in bed for the day. And just keeping it real: I still have days when I fall down running-related rabbit holes, poking around and waxing nostalgic about my glory days. Sometimes it's harmless fun (*I loved that race outfit!*), but other times I catch myself becoming resentful and ask, *Dimity, is this serving you right now?* If the answer is no, I close it up and move on.

Social media can bite even if you're looking for help. Cathy Annetta, age forty-eight, was part of an injured runners group on Facebook. She mentioned in a post that she didn't think she could run anymore because of degenerative arthritis in her big toe. The comments left by fellow runners made her feel dejected, not encouraged. "The vibe was that I gave up on running," she says. "I was so shocked that people were actually arguing with me. I came for support, not judgment." Lacking the nuance of tone and often a personal connection, online comments can fall flat, says Alaya, even though the writer may be well intentioned. Don't respond, or set a boundary by typing, "I appreciate you offering me advice. I also ask that you trust I've thought through this situation thoroughly."

The flashbacks feature on social media and your photos app can also make you feel like your own worst enemy. One year ago today, you posted a picture of your race outfit, bib already pinned, and your excitement for tomorrow's 10K, and your friends pumped you up with thumbs-up emojis and go-get-'em comments. Today, you're struggling to motivate a two-mile walk. Those flashback pictures are tough because they summon a comparison so easily, says Dawson. When you start to feel emotionally pulled by a past image, she recommends three strategies:

1. **Think of the memory as a treasure, not an anchor.** "Anchors keep us stuck, not moving forward," she explains. "Treasures remind us of our past successes, which can inspire us to try other things."

2. **Ask reflective questions.** Figure out why you're feeling so nostalgic for it. Dawson, a Canadian who lives in Waterloo, Ontario, loves the mountains and ran the 10K at 10,000 Feet in Steamboat Springs, Colorado. A picture from the race recently came into her feed. She felt wistful looking at it, so she asked herself: What is calling to me? Did I like the training? Being in Colorado? The person I was running with? How young, healthy, and happy I was then?

    Although you can't travel back in time, you could reconnect with the friend and book a trip to Colorado for a challenging hike—or similarly scratch that itch.

3. **Remember all the details, not just the finish-line photo.** I'm as guilty as anyone of sharing only the victorious, smiling snapshots online. Bad training days or teary selfies? Not so much. It's okay to revel in the memory, but don't forget the full story: What else was happening in your life then? What compromises were you making around family, work, or other priorities to get that race done? Were you truly healthy? Life is always more complicated than a single curated picture can show.

Standing on the Sidelines

Postrace coffee with friends and scrolling through results is one thing, but going to a race to spectate or volunteer? You might be thinking, "That's a level of exposure therapy I don't need," and that's a valid answer. Former collegiate soccer player and counselor Niamh Rawlins is no longer able to play soccer because of multiple knee surgeries. Her wife plays in an adult league, and Rawlins realizes it's best for her not to spectate. "All I think about is that I want to be out there with her," she says. "It just plain sucks."

If you're on the fence, go watch a race before you volunteer, advises Rawlins. "That way, you're in control of how long you stay," she says. Having the ability to exit quickly allows you to honor yourself and your emotions: You don't just have to tough it out for hours. If it's too hard today, trust that it may not feel that way down the road. "Once you rip off the bandage, it gets easier," says Cathy Engstrom, who especially loves cheering for the back-of-the-packers. "I will always be wistful as a spectator, but I love acknowledging the accomplishments of others. It's not their fault my time is over."

Some, like Britt Parker, jump right in. In 2022, Britt was signed up to run the Sawatch 50/50, a 50K weekend double-header near Buena Vista, Colorado, when a high hamstring strain didn't allow her to start. She knew the race needed volunteers, so she oversaw one of the aid stations for eight hours and handed out everything from bacon strips to cinnamon-roll cake, which Britt had made for a fellow volunteer celebrating a birthday. "Before I went, I felt frustrated and sad thinking about being at an event I had been so excited to run," she says. "But being there to support the runners was a different kind of runner's high."

For others, like Stacy Bruce, feeling ready to attend a race took time. Degeneration in her lower back and a meniscus-free left knee ended her twenty-seven years of running. Even as a triathlon coach, she waited a few years before returning to the race scene. "I had to do quite a bit of mental preparation before I could attend," she says. "I knew the emotions would come—and they did."

The advice about managing expectations applies here too. "If you go to a race thinking, 'This could be a wild ride' or 'I might have an amazing time,' it's going to be much easier than expecting it won't bother you at all," says sports psychologist Erin Alaya.

Stacy started as a volunteer, a move Alaya recommends. Having a purpose—*How efficient can I be with my water handoff?*—keeps you in the moment, not yearning for your own race bib. Plus, you know exactly what to do. You know whether a runner needs a fast handoff or a quick hug. You know saying "You're almost there" is unkind. You know that pouring a cup of water over your head feels like heaven on a humid day. You know taking in a gel can be the difference between legs that feel like string and legs that feel like steel. You know all these things because you'll always have a spark for running and, quite likely, a passion to help others light up theirs. "I love seeing the achievements," says Stacy. "It feeds my soul because I know the gift of running."

Barb knows exactly what Stacy is talking about. She chased her friend Mike around the Vernonia Marathon in Banks, Oregon, as he celebrated his fiftieth birthday with 26.2 miles. She saw him three times and cheered for him and pretty much every other runner out there. "I could go to a cross-country meet where I don't know anybody," she says, "but I'll still be high-fiving all the kids. They're doing what I love to do, and I want to be a part of it."

Dealing with "How's Your Running?" Questions

Most of us don't lose running quickly via an accident, illness, or injury. Instead, it's a long, tangled process that doesn't allow you to answer in a simple way. So, when somebody asks me why I don't run anymore, I have a stock answer: "My body doesn't respond to it positively anymore."

I recommend you find your own easy-to-access answer that feels good to you. That way, you're not retelling your raw story to a potentially uninterested person, which can make things feel even more vulnerable. ("Can't you just go to the gym instead?") If the conversation and company feel right, you can, of course, go into more details.

Here are some ways people respond when asked about their running:

I typically skirt the question by asking the person about their own adventures; it takes the spotlight off me.

—*Gretchen Gibson*

I say I'm still out there putting in some miles but my knees aren't what they used to be. At first it was difficult to talk about, but now it helps me feel strong.

—*Joanne Godfrey*

I explain I was injured, but I'm slowly coming back. I've also told my running friends I'm jealous of their long runs. I think it's okay to use that word; I'm just being honest.

—*Amy Ebeid*

I say I was a runner in my former life but can't do it anymore because of orthopedic issues. But I also say, if you want to talk about running, race prep, training programs, shoes, fueling, or anything else, I'm here for you. I will never get sick of talking about running.

—*Mariah Gianakouros*

I usually say, "Not sure." Although I know people mean well, it's hard for me to handle the questions or the pity.

—*Arielle Rosson*

I say that my body decided it was finished.

—*Kristin Zosa Puleo*

I tell them I'm not running anymore. If they press for information, I add that it was a difficult decision that I made for my future self so I can remain healthy into my later years.

—*Cathy Annetta*

I retired from running, but I'm super excited about _____ coming up (fill-in-the-blank next adventure).

—*Amy Csizmar Dalal*

I say I've had to slow down and I'm not racing anymore. Sometimes I feel the need to add that I'm doing run/walks, but as I'm adjusting to my new identity of being "into fitness" instead of being "a runner," I say that less and less.

—*Jana Resch*

Navigating the Menopausal Miles

While I was writing this book, chronic pain, the thing I was sure I'd left behind when I stopped running, came back to bite me, hard. Sciatica in both legs, paired with spinal stenosis, meant that even walking a mile in my neighborhood was excruciating. I could barely stand for more than a few minutes without needing to sit.

One of the places I rehabbed was a chiropractic gym filled with people like me who were trying to get—or stay—out of back pain. Most of them did self-led workouts, following the whiteboard warm-up and workout, which took about an hour. I'd do the warm-up, then follow my personal exercises prescribed by the trainer: two sets of body-weight squats, maybe a side plank, some calf stretches. Twenty-five minutes, tops.

This chronic pain overlapped perfectly with my first true year postmenopause. I hadn't had a period in twelve months, so I was officially out of that undefined, unrelenting fog of perimenopause, when hormones jump around faster than an oversugared four-year-old on a trampoline. The transition from one phase to the next wasn't crisp though. The night sweats were gone, but the overwhelm and anxiety remained, as did plenty of other menopausal tokens. I could no longer zip up skirts whose waistbands used to hang on my hips. I couldn't remember the name of my beloved ninth-grade science teacher—or what year I graduated from high school. My creaky knees introduced me to the term *menopausal arthralgia*, or menopause-induced arthritis, and the random aches that came out of nowhere I learned also had a scientific term: musculoskeletal syndrome of menopause.

The thing that felt the most urgent, though, was my muscle tone. I felt like I was losing it by the second. Forget flattering clothes—I had a hard time finding a clean outfit that actually fit. I actively avoided the mirror. Even when I looked up from washing my face, I barely recognized myself.

Menopause wasn't just deflating my muscles like a day-old helium balloon. Social media was coming at me with best practices for athletic women in midlife who were bemoaning their dwindling muscle. Yes, the science is real: Lift heavy to maintain bone density and muscle mass as you age. But my feed was full of sculpted women doing front squats with barbells, deadlifting more than I weigh, documenting their perfect overhead presses with the camera focused on their ripped deltoids. And I was doing two sets of six body-weight squats three days per week. My body was failing me again.

Another woman came to the gym about the same time I did. We were friendly but didn't exchange more than a few sentences. She did the whiteboard workout better than anybody else: smooth goblet squats with perfect form, single-leg calf raises without a balance assist, farmers carry with kettlebells heavier than any guy there. I was envious.

A few days before Christmas, I was on the floor doing my third round of bird-dog, and she stood near me for her next exercise. "Today is my only baking day," she announced. "The days of a whole season of cookies are over. I can't have that much sugar in the house."

I laughed. "I feel you. I literally look at a Kiss cookie and I'm up a pound." We chatted. She was only a year older than me, then fifty-two. She told me about buying the same dress in two sizes for her daughter's wedding in a few months. Although the smaller one fit right now, she was also keeping the larger one just in case. She didn't want to stress about what future surprises menopause might have in store for her.

From the outside, it felt like we were on opposite ends of the spectrum. I was floundering; she was in control. But the truth is, we were more alike than different. Menopause, like puberty, is a physiological reality, and the only way out is through. You can lift heavy, eat clean, aim for eight hours of sleep (good luck with that!), and track your macros, but menopause is still a natural, nonnegotiable process.

That said, it's a process that trips up many women. "I've seen a lot of women get stuck," says Maria Luque, founder of Fitness in Menopause. "They hold onto an identity that isn't possible anymore." Here are some suggestions to help you through yet another transition.

Update Your Perspective

You're an athlete who took care of—and took pride in—your body. You can still do that, but only if you acknowledge one key truth: Your body is no longer working from the same operating system it used for most of your adult life. "The single most difficult part of menopause is the way body composition changes," says Selene Yeager, an exercise journalist who hosts the *Hit Play Not Pause* podcast. "It happens to most active women." Indeed, research shows that 60–70 percent of women gain weight during menopause, and fat-mass measures, which include body fat percentage, waist circumference, and waist–hip ratio, similarly increase.

As your hormones shift, your mindset around all exercise—not just running—needs to shift as well. "The old equation of work equals results isn't as reliable," says Yeager. "It's upsetting." That's not to say you can't still be a kickass menopausal athlete. You just can't get there using the same training methods, intensity, or expectations you had at age thirty-five.

Reconsider What Control Means

If running was your go-to method for managing your body, mood, or daily routine, giving it up can feel like surrendering control on every front. Then menopause arrives and adds another layer, forcing you to take your metaphorical hands even further off the wheel. Take time to reflect on how your need for control shows up now, especially when your body isn't responding the way it used to.

"I always say, control is an illusion," says Luque. She explains that the desire to control is often tied to how we see ourselves physically: how you look, what you weigh, how you perform, which can be manipulated via diet and exercise. When that reality changes during menopause, it can feel like everything is slipping away, especially if you're also navigating the loss of running.

Luque doesn't sugarcoat it: "We have to face our demons. People who didn't think they had a body image issue are suddenly confronting one." Yeager also hits a hard truth: "You can increase the amount of fiber and protein in your diet, get control of your sleep, and strength train, and you may still be a size bigger than you were before," she says. That reality, she admits, is psychologically tough. When she starts to feel overwhelmed, she asks herself, "Do I want to spend the rest of my life—thirty years or more—worried about the size of my thighs or living through my body image? How much of my remaining energy am I willing to give to this constant battle?"

The transition from managing your body like a project to honoring it as a companion might be a new life goal; it feels like one for me. Thinking of your body as a partner who wants to move with purpose, stay healthy, and feel energized is a great place to start.

Pay Attention to the Facts

If running has been your primary form of exercise, it's time to zoom out and think long term. "While running's high impact does strengthen your bones, it doesn't protect you from age-related muscle loss," says Luque. After age thirty, we lose muscle at a rate of 3–8 percent per decade. By our fifties, that loss accelerates to 1–2 percent per year. That's significant, whether you're trying to power up a hill on your bike or carry three bags of groceries to the car.

You don't have to put a barbell on your back or even join a gym to get stronger, but you do need to prioritize strength. "The ideal routine for most women is a full-body workout, thirty to forty-five minutes, two to three times a week," she says. "But ideal and realistic are often two different things, so start where your schedule and motivation actually meet."

If the gym isn't your thing, make strength work part of your regular movement. Do lunges on a trail hike or step-ups on a park bench during a walk. The goal with strength is consistency, not perfection. A short, accessible strength session a few times per week is more sustainable than one fifty-minute workout you dread.

Hold Hormone Replacement Therapy Loosely

Hormone replacement therapy (HRT) isn't for everyone, but the risks associated with it are not as dire as they were once portrayed. "People tend to feel very strongly about HRT, like it's either a hard yes or an absolute no," says Yeager. "But it's really just one tool, not an all-or-nothing proposition."

If HRT helps reduce your night sweats, which improves your sleep, which reduces your stress, which lifts the brain fog? That's a win. Like any other treatment, HRT is something to explore with your healthcare provider.* And if it doesn't work for you, you can stop. "It's not a forever decision," Yeager adds.

Move However Feels Best

Maybe your squats aren't as low as they used to be or your shoulder isn't thrilled about push-ups. Keep on showing up, and lean into anything that feels fun, interesting, or challenging. It could be learning to kayak or curl, taking long walks or a course in tai chi. "The more you move, the better you feel," says Luque. "That equation has never changed."

---

* Bonus if your healthcare provider is certified as a Menopause Society Certified Practitioner. Check menopause.org to find one in your area.

AID STATION

Dimity Goes on a Grand Adventure

"Is this stretch as bad as the last one?" I asked a bearded guy hiking in Chaco sandals. He was headed down into the Grand Canyon and seemed as comfortable on the trails as a mountain goat. I, with my hiking buddies Jo and Jess, were climbing up and out. No, he said. "There's shade the whole way." I felt such relief, I almost reached out to hug him. We crossed paths near the Supai Tunnel, which lies 1.7 miles below the North Rim, our destination for the day. The three of us still had about 1,400 more feet of calf-burning climbing to do to finish our rim-to-rim hike, but at least we were promised cool shade as we inched toward our car. It was early June, when the canyon floor temperatures average 100 degrees, and over the past twenty-one miles, the relentless sun made sure we felt its every ray.

The challenge of a rim-to-rim-to-rim forty-two-mile trail run had intrigued me during my running days, but one (failed) attempt at training for a 50K (thirty-one miles) killed that thought. A few months after my orthopedist said I should consider not running anymore, I had downsized the goal to one crossing and downshifted the pace to a hike. I asked Jo and Jess, two running friends, whether they were up for it. They were. I created our training plan, Jo, a snap organizer, tended to the travel and canyon details, and Jess brought nonstop good vibes.

The hike brought two terms to the forefront that I'd come to use frequently when talking about myself as I phased out of running: *athlete* and *adventure*. *Athlete*, which replaced *runner*, was a more forgiving, all-encompassing word that didn't make me feel like an imposter, and *adventure* nodded to the fact that I preferred novel experiences over fierce competition. Still, the formidable goal—twenty-three miles with a total elevation change of 10,400 feet—kept me rooted in my daily routine of endorphins and endurance.

Most weekdays, I hit the step mill at the gym, dripping sweat onto my iPhone as I watched *Last Chance U*, a compelling documentary series about football at the junior college level. On the weekends, I filled my hydration bladder with electrolytes and my backpack with Clif Bars and gels, grabbed my hiking poles, and drove to a new-to-me trail for multihour hikes. I got a little lonely on the trail—I was jealous that Jo and Jess, who both live in St. Paul, trained together—but when my mood sank, I would remember my posthike reward: stopping at Mod Pizza for a veggie-heavy pizza, a wheat beer, and their signature dessert, a Hostess Cupcakes knock-off. Tired legs and a full belly: signs of a day well spent.

We took our first steps down South Kaibab Trail just after 5 a.m. on that June day. We would descend for 7 miles and 4,700 feet before crossing the Colorado River and starting a 14-mile, 5,700-foot climb back up via the North Kaibab Trail. Our hiking poles clacked against the stone trail as we watched the sun come up on the canyon walls, turning them from a dusty brown to brick red. We were alone for about an hour before a runner came flying down the trail and passed us. We exchanged hellos, and she mentioned that she was excited for eight hours of quiet today. My mind immediately reverted to runner mode and jumped into the comparison game: *Eight hours? She's going to cross this whole thing in eight hours? Why aren't we going faster? We need to go faster! Could I have crossed in eight hours when I was a runner?* My critical stream stopped when she, a few switchbacks down, yelled up to us that she could never find two friends who would do a canyon crossing with her. I'd rather have friends with me, I thought, but I have to be honest, too: I'd rather all three of us were running.

After three hours of descending, we came to the Colorado River at 2,400 feet, which was the lowest elevation we'd see all day. My shaky quads and sore knees were grateful to be done with the downhills. We arrived at the suspension bridge across the river just in time to see a mule train heading up. Seeing people, sweating in long sleeves and sun hats, sitting on the backs of mules plodding up the trail put the speedy runner in perspective again. Even if I wasn't running, I was going to cross the canyon solely under my own power: Success depended on my legs, my lungs, my head, my will.

The so-called flats, a stretch of about 6 miles with relatively little elevation change, were lovely, full of short bridges and a stop for lemonade and potato chips at the canteen in Phantom Ranch, a camping village at the bottom of the canyon. The river flowed emerald, and the cottonwood trees on its banks fluttered their bright green leaves. The burnt-red canyon walls, streaked with grays and tans, reached up to a cloudless blue sky. So many colors, so much to take in. We took in as much as we could as we skated along, laughing that we were finally doing this thing that we'd been talking about for nearly a year.

Then we hit The Box, so named because the canyon walls narrow and trap in the heat, and the cooling river is no longer nearby. Having trained through most of the winter—and never having experienced temperatures like this—we treated these as cross-your-fingers, watch-your-pace, and sip-your-water miles.

To take my mind off the heat, I chatted with two guys we hopscotched with along the trail, a practice I used all the time in races. One was a veteran rim-to-rim hiker; his friend was on his first attempt. They were going to hit the North Rim, spend the night, then turn around and go the other way the next day. "I'm not so sure about tomorrow anymore," the newbie friend admitted as we climbed. "I feel you," I replied. I asked the veteran hiker which direction he thought was more challenging: north to south, or south to north. "Definitely south to north," he said, "because you're climbing through The Box." Score one for feeling badass.

Around mile 11, we came to an optional trailhead. Ribbon Falls wasn't on Jo's itinerary, but a couple of hikers we talked to said it was nonnegotiable. They weren't wrong. A short detour off the trail brought us to a powerful waterfall cascading onto a brilliant green, moss-covered rock mound. We lounged in the shade before soaking ourselves; when we climbed under the falls, I pretended the moss was a bathtub and took a short soak. "Remember this feeling," I said, as we headed back to the trail. "We're going to need it sooner than later."

Although we had been slowly ascending out of the canyon since Phantom Ranch, the grade got much steeper, reminding us that we had plenty of climbing ahead. My legs felt as solid as the cottonwoods we'd seen miles ago, but the cumulative fatigue of the day, in combination with blaring sun, drained me of any sense of gratitude for being here. Our chatter was also flagging. For a while, yelling out "DRINK!" reminders was all any of us could muster.

Then, beautifully, the sun positioned itself so that many of the walls of the canyon gave us shade, immediately U-turning our energy levels. "Alright…okay…alright, okay," I yelled, my voice echoing. "What song is that?" I asked. Jo and Jess laughed. "Um, what?" they asked. I repeated the lines, trying to get the rhythm and tune as close as possible to the introduction of Macklemore and Ryan Lewis's "Can't Hold Us." I felt simultaneously tiny and huge. Optimistic, I mentioned that maybe it would be this way—shady and relatively flat—all the way up to the rim. I should've kept my thoughts to myself. The sun was back on center stage for another ninety minutes before we ran into the Chaco-wearing hiker who assured us we'd be shaded for the rest of our hike.

He wasn't wrong, but even the cool temps were not enough to prevent me from breaking down. With about a mile left—a mile that would take about thirty minutes to finish—I suddenly felt crazy pukey. I didn't have enough food in my stomach, plus I'd gulped a bunch of water at the Supai Tunnel, so my stomach felt sloshy. "I have to sit down," I said. "I have to eat." I got teary quickly; I really didn't want to throw up. Everything on me was dirty and dusty, and the last thing I wanted to deal with was smelly barf and its accompanying drool. That said, I had no interest in eating the sports gels or macaroons we had left in our packs, so I picked the most appealing of the least appealing: a quarter of a clean bagel with peanut butter. Jo and Jess split the other bagel part, which was covered in Oreo crumbs.

I rose and grabbed my poles. Silent and steady, we covered switch-back after switchback. Fir and pine trees loomed above us as the temperature dropped. My mood and stomach improved; we even picked up the pace slightly so we could finish our crossing in twelve hours flat. My quads were cooked, my teeth felt scuzzy, and I wasn't sure whether my belly could stomach the beer and burger we'd been talking about all day long.

"Never again" is the refrain I heard from many first-time marathon-ers after they crossed the finish line. Even though our grand day was much harder and longer than any 26.2 I'd done, as we stood hugging on the North Rim, I knew I was hungry. Maybe not for a burger, but for the next adventure we'd do together.

CHAPTER 9

Unpacking Your Running Years

What Do You Need?

When I moved to New York City for my first job in publishing, every aspect of city life overwhelmed me, a Minnesotan who grew up on a gravel road. The sidewalks teemed with speedy self-important walkers. The subway platforms reeked of stale urine. My shoebox bedroom stretched barely wider than my full-size mattress. And endless noise. Oh, the noise: Honking taxis, echoing jackhammers, blaring sirens wore my nervous system raw.

If I didn't have my (near) daily runs, I don't think I could've lasted a month in the Big Apple. From the front door of my first apartment, I could turn right and hit Riverside Park, which featured the soothing, if terribly polluted, Hudson River. Turning left, I could head to Central Park, a hilly, tree-lined oasis with a variety of loops. Either direction offered what I needed most: quiet and space. I ran as the sun rose, when most of the pedestrians were runners or dog walkers and most of the traffic was off-duty taxis and delivery trucks that zipped down congestion-free streets.

I returned to my fourth-floor walk-up feeling as ready as I could be for another day of urban life on steroids.

Running the 1997 New York City Marathon cemented my long-term relationship with the sport, but when I think about which parts of running meant the most to me, the marathon isn't at the top. Space and quiet are, as a jumble of scenes click through my head like an old-school slideshow. Looking down at my electric-blue Sauconys, which popped against the dark gray pavement. Running on a trail with my dog Mason, my legs brushing against long, dewy grass, which soaked my shorts. Listening to "Big Parade" by the Lumineers while watching the sun rise on my way home from my favorite 6-mile route. My legs feeling as powerful as two pistons of a V-8 engine. My postrun relief, knowing that my day and thoughts would flow like a lazy river. The habit of setting my alarm, and the rhythm that followed: wake early, feel accomplished, get to bed early so I could do it again. The anticipation of running with friends.

As my running miles dwindled, I continually asked myself, *How are you going to fill the gap, Dimity? What do you need?* I needed to feel strong and capable and—just keeping it real—to be able to look in the mirror and admire my legs. I needed activities that triggered endorphins, serotonin, and other feel-good neurochemicals to reliably boost my mood. I needed a dependable workout habit. I needed to stay connected with active people. I needed to spend time on trails, in nature, feeling adventurous.

What do you need to fill the gap that running leaves? You'll see what Heather, Julie, and others found they needed and how they filled the gaps. Read through this list of ingredients that make up running and then head to page 165. Circle the items that resonate with you, then we'll work on assembling the ingredients in Chapter 10.

Physical Health

Heather Escaravage
What Running Gave Me: An antidote to the person I used to be: I was the kid in high school who did non-sports-related

things on the sports field, like smoking and not going to class. I smoked until my mid-twenties, and I told myself that, if I finished my quit-smoking program, I would reward myself with a learn-to-run program. For fourteen years, running improved my health immensely and counteracted the effects of my sedentary job in corporate communications. It also let me model the importance of exercise to my two daughters, ages ten and thirteen, who are already more active than I ever was as a kid.

How I Replaced It: Weekday mornings, I drop my older daughter at swim practice at 5 a.m., and I head to the gym and do a forty-minute strength routine and a twenty-five-minute walk with incline on the treadmill. Lifting weights, especially when I go to the space in the gym with barbells and more serious lifters, is really empowering. It reminds me of trail running: a little intimidating at first, but ultimately rewarding, a place where I push beyond my comfort zone.

Once a year, my older daughter and I do a 5- to 10-kilometer overnight hike into the coastal mountains of British Columbia. We carry our gear (about twenty pounds each) and navigate rugged trails together. Those hikes make me feel like a badass mother, showing my daughters that we are capable of whatever we put our minds to.

Mental Health

Julie Baker

What Running Gave Me: I was all about the endorphins. Running for forty-eight years balanced me mentally and anchored my physical and emotional health. It also gave me an identity; I ran twenty marathons, and that gave me a lot of pride.

How I Replaced It: I turned to walking to fill miles and hours. I walk with a friend, also a former runner, most days a week; we go 6 or 7 miles together. (I am retired and am protective of my morning time; I don't make any plans until noon.) Movement and exercise have been a core part of my daily routine for so long, I knew I had to maintain that practice so I wouldn't lapse into some kind of downward spiral. There are very few days I let the weather force me inside, and on the wettest and coldest of days, I am really proud of myself for braving the outside elements!

Community and Friendship

Pam Harris

What Running Gave Me: A group of women who supported each other in their running goals, both in person and virtually. I was a member of Moms Run This Town in Atlanta for five years. I documented my first marathon for the Another Mother Runner community, and when I ran Boston virtually during COVID, I flew to New Hampshire where two good running friends supported me throughout the day as I ran 26.2 miles.

How I Replaced It: I didn't realize how much I missed working toward a goal—preferably a big, hairy, scary goal—with a group of supportive women until my adult hip-hop class started learning our recital number. The class had already begun filling my need for community, then recital prep started. Our text chain blew up. We met for extra practices to refine our choreography, sweat, laugh, and swear. Recital day, the music started and I gave myself over to the collective joy, camaraderie, and energy of our crew and danced my ever-loving heart out. Was I perfect? Nope. Did I let that trip me up? Also, no. Was it possibly the most fun I've ever had? Absolutely.

Alisa Bonsignore

What Running Gave Me: A few years after I started running, I joined Team in Training to train for the Nike Women's San

Francisco Marathon and to fundraise in memory of a friend's husband. I stuck with it for five years, through highs and lows, injuries and health, because I loved the community there. My role was sweep, so I helped newer runners who tended to be slower, offering support when they feared that they weren't going to make the time cutoff. I like to think that we had more fun in the back of the pack.

How I Replaced It: I've been volunteering a lot within my community. I'm an adult literacy tutor; I help at the local food bank distribution event; I support a local environmental conservation facility to prepare for school events. This gets me out of the house a few days a week, helps me to meet new people, and makes me feel like I'm truly doing something useful to help others.

A Sense of Peace

Michelle Bingham
What Running Gave Me: Time to feel balanced and quiet while in the woods.

How I Replaced It: With gardening. I find so much gratification in seeing something come alive, and I find so much peace in a tired, exhausted body, especially when I can sit back and look at what I did. True joy. I love gardening so much, I began keeping a greenhouse this winter. I planted my first vegetable garden a few weeks ago and I can't wait to watch and tend to it. I also love to propagate indoor plants all year long and give them away to friends as gifts.

Maureen Powers
What Running Gave Me: Solitude, peace, and meditative movement. I always ran alone and almost always without music, and it was the best way I found to clear my head and reset my mood.

How I Replaced It: Swimming first thing in the morning, especially if it can be outside. I try to go at 5 a.m. one day a week, when the pool is quietest and I'm most likely to get a lane to myself. It is a necessary reset and replicates the beautiful, peaceful solo time that running gave me.

Meditative Time

Amy Ebeid

What Running Gave Me: As a therapist, the meditative space running provided helped me reset my entire system and let the day go.

How I Replaced It: I started swimming three or four days a week wearing underwater headphones. I listened to classical music when I ran, and now I listen to yoga music when I swim. The zen-like music allows me to zone out, forget where I am, not listen to myself breathing. It's the most glorious thing ever: just me in the water, feeling my body move.

Arielle Rosson

What Running Gave Me: Running gave me a place to process daily life: job, kids, other responsibilities, as well as heavier things. It kept me (semi) sane so I can show up as my better self in all areas.

How I Replaced It: I took a couple yoga classes during my regular running days, and I didn't particularly enjoy them because it was so different from running. After stopping running, I started practicing yoga again, embracing the mindset that this is more for my mental health than to work up a sweat. I now practice about four times a week. I now enjoy the challenge of sitting in stillness and focusing on my breath while still being able to use my physical body. Things always feel a little bit better emotionally after a yoga session.

Jenny Davies

What Running Gave Me: A break from the daily stressors of life. A friend and I would run at 4:30 a.m. and solve all the world's problems. It made me feel really good.

How I Replaced It: Knitting. I didn't think it would challenge me, but it does. More importantly, it helps distract me from everything that stresses me out on a daily basis. I'm still on my first scarf…or is it a blanket? I don't know, but whatever it is, knitting and purling takes my mind off everything.

Time Outside

Paige Sato

What Running Gave Me: The chance to prove that I could survive in any weather. I loved running in snow, in 10-degree temps, in rain, on sunny days, and even in the wind.

How I Replaced It: Dragon boating on the Schuylkill River in Philadelphia. The season starts in April, when the weather is different every.single.day. I wear my warmest winter running jacket, lined leggings, and wool hat at the beginning of the month, but at the end, we're in tank tops. We go out when it's windy (in the spring there is wind both ways!), wavy, hot, cold; the only time we don't practice is if there are thunderstorms. I get wet, but not soaked, except in competition: Sometimes there's intentional splashing during races. While paddling, we see river otters, turtles, Canadian geese, and ducks. It's pretty remarkable for a city river and exposes me to a different side of nature I didn't get while running.

Jenny Davies
What Running Gave Me: Plenty of time in the fresh air, which is essential for my mental health and well-being. I work as a research scientist inside and have plenty of chores and indoor activities; getting outside daily was an absolute must to keep me sane.

How I Replaced It: Bike riding. I had forgotten how much joy I get from riding. I love feeling the wind in my face, finding a new bike path to explore, and pedaling and watching the world go by. It really makes me feel alive. I find it's almost as good a workout as running, and I go a lot farther on my bike than I ever did on any run.

Maureen Powers
What Running Gave Me: I ran outside year-round, in Chicago, as long as it was above 9 degrees. I loved getting fresh air, seeing the world, and feeling invigorated by all the elements: wind, rain, snow, and sun.

How I Replaced It: I have become an ardent walker and take a walk almost every night after dinner and usually one or two more during the day. (This is separate from my exercise routine.) Walks are generally roughly a mile or less, so I don't need to change my clothes, and it doesn't take a lot of time. I love seeing how my neighborhood changes with the seasons, smelling my neighbor's barbecue in the summer, admiring Halloween decorations in the fall, and silently thanking everyone who shovels their sidewalks after it snows.

Structure and Routine

Mariah Gianakouros
What Running Gave Me: I loved everything about training plans: the fact that somebody else designed them so I didn't have to make any day-to-day decisions; the fact that I could see my

progress adding up as I checked off boxes; and the fact that I felt so accomplished when I finished a training cycle.

How I Replaced It: I plan my own strength-training workouts and cycles. I use a mix of Peloton workouts and free workouts on YouTube by Lift with Cee, a trainer in her mid-fifties. I plan four- to six-week cycles and write everything out in my training journal. That way I don't have to make daily decisions for a long stretch; I just follow the plan. That said, I allow for modifications for injury or when I may need to change my workout days.

Adventure

Megan Hinckley

What Running Gave Me: The chance to explore. Whether it was a new trail or a new city, I loved not knowing what I would find around the next corner; experiencing a landscape from the ground; and even the possibility of getting lost.

How I Replaced It: Backcountry skinning (climbing up a hill on touring skis). I tried it for the first time this past winter and felt the same sense of excitement at experiencing the unknown: turning a corner, seeing a new vista, wondering how I would fare on the way down. I've discovered trying new things is just as important for my mental health as it is my physical health. I'm confident that there will be many more backcountry adventures in my future.

Competition

Amy Csizmar Dalal

What Running Gave Me: I like to do things that scare me. I found it thrilling to train for an event, show up, and adjust on the fly depending on how the race was going. Plus, there's something exciting about doing hard things surrounded by other people doing hard things!

How I Replaced It: Aquabike races—an open-water swim followed by a bike—scratches that itch, for sure. Training for two events at the same time is a fun challenge, both logistically and physically. On race day, I'm at the mercy of the elements in both the swim and the bike. I make what feels like millions of decisions: when to push and when to conserve energy, when to fuel, what line to take on a turn, how aggressive to be when claiming my space in the water. I love testing my fitness, seeing my splits, and figuring out ways to improve my performance for the next race.

Ruthie McCartney
What Running Gave Me: A chance to continually challenge myself. Over fifteen years, I ran about thirty half-marathons, five marathons, a few ultras, and I have a few trophies and plaques from 5Ks and 10Ks to show I was fast at one time.

How I Replaced It: Coaching our middle school track team in its first year. Before I committed to it, I spent a lot of time contemplating whether I should coach: Would I want to coach kids at a sport I can no longer really do? Could my mental health handle it?

The answers were yes and yes. Coaching the team of thirty-two students was everything! At the first meet, when one of our girls took first in the 1600, I cried. At district conference, when our 4x200 girls relay came from behind to win, I cried again. My love of competition and my enthusiasm for the sport were reignited, and it was exactly what I—and these kids—needed.

Personal Challenge

Julie Baker

What Running Gave Me: The chance to prove to myself I can set and conquer goals and push my personal boundaries. I missed qualifying for Boston in my first marathon by three minutes but went on to qualify three more times—and run twenty marathons total.

How I Replaced It: At age sixty-nine, I signed up for the Mammoth March—a twenty-mile hike in a state park—in the Delaware Valley and trained with the Another Mother Runner group. For a long time, I just stopped having goals, and I embraced this goal of hiking 20 miles with an energy and dedication that honestly, really surprised me. Not one to follow a training plan, I followed the program almost 100 percent. The day was hard and such a reward when I finished! I liked it so much, I completed another Mammoth March in Virginia and am signed up for a third in Maryland this spring.

Jennifer Moynihan

What Running Gave Me: A chance to set ambitious goals, push myself, and run fast. I loved running as fast as I could, so any PR was a good race for me. My last PR was in 2017 in the half-marathon.

How I Replaced It: The 2025 Great Chesapeake Bay Swim: a 4.4-mile swim across the bay. I got in by lottery and had not been swimming at all, so I'm swimming three days per week to get ready. (My husband got in too; we've been training together at little date days at the pool!) This is the first big challenge I've had in eight years; I'm scared and excited at the same time. It's not a given that I can finish it!

Leah Wiesner

What Running Gave Me: A chance to continually challenge myself, whether it was a running streak or finishing a fifty-mile race.

How I Replaced It: Through the Peloton app. After getting tickets to the Oasis reunion tour, I am now on a quest to take every class on the Peloton app with an Oasis song in the playlist. I've even begun rowing to check off classes!

Metrics and a Way to Measure Yourself

Mariah Gianakouros

What Running Gave Me: A chance to continually go farther than I had before. Driving with my kids, we'd cover ten miles down the parkway, and I'd tell my kids I could run that far! When I conquered 26.2 miles, my kids all knew that was the distance we went when we drove down to the shore. It made me so proud!

How I Replaced It: Strength training has filled this void, in a sense. As I hit a new PR in strength training, I can't wait to tell my kids. Two of my kids are very into weightlifting, and it's nice to be able to share my accomplishments with them (even if it's significantly less than what my twenty-somethings are lifting). We have a hobby in common now and we can talk about form, gear, PRs and recovery. It's great to be able to share this with them and celebrate our accomplishments together.

Megan Hinckley

What Running Gave Me: A quantitative way to determine "success" in any given workout and the sense of accomplishment and pride that come with hitting a new PR.

How I Replaced It: Strength training three to five times per week. I use strength circuits from Caroline Girvan's YouTube channel, and it's been fun to incrementally add weight as I repeat some of my favorite programs. When I started following her, I was consistently using about half the weight she used, and now I am just about matching her weights. I'm progressing slowly, but it's very rewarding to look back over time and see how I am getting stronger.

Stress Relief

Jana Resch

What Running Gave Me: The rhythm of running automatically helped me process my thoughts and clear my head.

How I Replaced It: When I could only spend minutes, instead of hours, running, I felt my stress levels go way up. I started alternating walks and hiking with weight training and intentionally emptying my mental trash bin while I'm working out. Some days I make a mental to-do list, sorting through what's important and what doesn't really matter. Other days, I pick at strands of thoughts until things loosen up and make sense; it's like untangling a knotted-up necklace. By the end of the workout, I've usually discovered some worries or tasks that I can let go of. Because my workouts are shorter, I still find myself sometimes needing more time to quiet my mind, so several days a week I use an app (Headspace) to meditate; it helps me collect and process my racing thoughts.

Gretchen Gibson

What Running Gave Me: Running gave me an outlet to escape the daily stressors as well as escape larger issues for a short period of time. It was "me" time, when I could do whatever I wanted or a place to try to solve whatever may be complicating my world.

How I Replaced It: Walking my dogs, which I do almost daily. It gives me an opportunity to get out on my own and hash through things or zone out. The dogs are an addition to our family since COVID, and their unconditional love is the support I needed when words couldn't communicate my sadness of running slipping away from me. They are satisfied with a walk and their contentment is contagious.

Accomplishment and Pride

Arielle Rosson

What Running Gave Me: As a type A person, I thrive on accomplishing difficult things, particularly in terms of tough physical workouts. It's an important part of my self-identity and self-esteem.

How I Replaced It: I bought my Peloton bike a couple years after I stopped running, and it filled the gaps I had almost forgotten I was missing. In very challenging classes when I doubt if I'll make it to the end, I'm reminded of those tough runs and races. In the long endurance rides, I can let my mind wander as it used to on long endurance runs. At the end of all classes, I'm filled with a similar happy exhaustion and sense of accomplishment as at the end of a run. While it's not the same as a run, no matter what else happens on my Peloton days—usually about four days a week—I know I have a reason to feel proud.

Maureen Powers

What Running Gave Me: Running gave me tangible "proof" that I'm bettering myself and accomplishing something every day. (I'm a bit of a control freak and a striver.)

How I Replaced It: I'm in two group texts of people who do the *New York Times* puzzles daily. I wake up, have a cup of coffee, and immediately get to the puzzles. I love the achievable challenge of completing the puzzles, the chance to celebrate my fellow puzzlers, and starting my day having already accomplished something.

What Do *You* Need?

Circle all the items in the following list that were important features of your running years. If you end up circling more than three, go through a pruning process, taking time to reflect to get to your main three.

"Runners can be very siloed, thinking running is the only thing that can provide these things," says sports psychologist Kim Dawson. "It may not be one activity that fills all your needs, but they can be filled with time and effort."

Physical health
Mental health
Community/Friendship
Meditative time
A sense of peace
Time outside
Structure/Routine
Adventure
Competition
Personal challenge
Metrics/Way to measure myself
Stress relief
Accomplishment/Pride
_____ (fill in the blank)

AID STATION

Michelle Walks an Ultra

Michelle Bingham admits her body doesn't climb hills very well. Nevertheless, the self-described endurance junkie loves trails, going long, and a juicy challenge. She thrived during her first 100-miler, the pancake-flat 2021 Canal 100 in the DC area, so, after having a bourbon with friends, she put her name in the lottery for the 2022 Colorado Leadville Trail 100, a legendary beast that features over 15,000 feet of climbing. She got in. To prepare for the Rocky Mountains, she joined a friend for the Smokies Challenge Adventure Run: a 70-mile plus, 14,000-foot plus romp along the Appalachian Trail in Smoky Mountains National Park in Tennessee in March 2022. She fell around mile 20, slamming one knee into a rock, one knee into a root. "It was ugly, ugly," she says. "I finished, but I paid dearly."

No stranger to injury, Michelle has undergone surgery for four labrum tears in her hips and both knees. Trying to save her Leadville entry, she "threw all the money at it," seeing multiple doctors and physical therapists, getting MRIs and plasma-rich protein injections. The ultimate diagnosis was patellofemoral syndrome in both knees. "My knees don't track properly," she explains. "And the experts were like, 'There's not much we can do after thirty years of running.'" She didn't make it to Leadville, and spent two years away from the sport. She gardened, tried gravel biking, and hoped her knees would feel better with time. Despite her break, Michelle, now sixty years old, has been unable to progress her run/walk ratio beyond thirty seconds running/four minutes walking for a few miles before her knees start screaming at her. "What's the point?" she asks.

A running coach with a quiver of local athletes, Michelle has headed up an aid station for the Mamba 100 in Germantown, Tennessee, for two years. Appreciating her dedication, the race director offered her a free entry to his twenty-four-hour race, which features a four-mile loop on Memphis's Wolf River Trails, her favorite place to run.* "I felt a little tingle of excitement, but I put off the decision." Four weeks before race day, the director circled back, and Michelle figured, *What the heck?* She spent a couple of weeks walking the loop as fast as she could, strategizing how far she could go. Could she make 50K, her favorite distance? Possibly. Fifty miles? "Probably not," she says, "but it's fun just thinking like that again." With very little training but lots of enthusiasm, she was in.

Race prep is Michelle's jam. "I love the process of getting my gear together, thinking about what I'll need for different temperatures, running my pace numbers on a spreadsheet," she says. She recruited her long-time running friend Elizabeth and at noon, the two set off with the intention to go as long as they felt like it. Despite some wet trails that soaked their feet in chilly December temps, the two found a rhythm, talking about everything from their grandchildren to old boyfriends. Nearing the end of a loop, they'd discuss what gear changes they would need for the next round, then beeline for their car and cooler, which was filled with Michelle's favorite ultra fuel: Chick-fil-A sandwiches (quartered or halved), salted potatoes, and Pringles.†

Two loops down, three loops down. "I couldn't stop smiling," she says. "It was so fun to just hear my breath, listen to the birds, see the deer, smell the forest." One part of the loop was an out-and-back, which allowed for plenty of high-fives and chatter with other participants, many of whom she knew personally. Five loops down, the winter sun set, six loops down. "The magic of the trails at night," she says, "my favorite time." She was so entranced with the experience she resisted comparing herself to the other runners or even her former athletic self. "It didn't matter how fast I was going," she says. "I was just in the moment, moving forward, and taking care of myself during breaks."

---

* Instead of going for a specific distance, like 50K or 50 miles, in a twenty-four-hour race, you complete as many loops of a specific distance as possible.
† "I would never eat this crap otherwise."

The pair walked for thirteen hours, completing seven full laps. With commutes to the car for savory snacks, fresh socks, and hand warmers, as well as some detours on the trail to avoid water, their watches registered thirty-one miles. "I'm calling it a 50K," she says. The twenty-four-hour pressure-free format was exactly what she needed. "It didn't leave me feeling like I couldn't finish or that I would fail," she says.

Despite the unconventional format and her slower pace, the race was reminiscent of Michelle's previous long-distance events in two ways. First, she came down with a solid case of the postrace blues. "I've lost my steam," she admitted about two weeks after the race. "I haven't walked at all." Second, the inspiration to challenge herself has been reignited. As she relived her perfect day on the trails, she wondered what she'd do next: "Maybe a 25K with a generous time cutoff or even another twenty-four-hour event."

CHAPTER 10

Thriving in Your Next Chapter

The 27th Mile

At one point, you were a beginning runner. You may not have known on which side of the road to run. Going a full mile seemed almost impossible. You probably wore shoes that, when you think back on them, make you wince. Lined shorts were baffling: Do you wear underwear with them or go commando? You had no idea how to pace yourself. Words like *chafing, compression socks, GU,* and *PRs* were not in your vocabulary.

Mile by mile, month by year, you figured things out. You read about running, you talked about running, you bought things for running, you made friendships through running until running became so ingrained in you, you don't have to think twice when someone says, "I blew past the 10K mark feeling like I could negative split the whole thing, but I bonked at mile 11. I ate my last gel too early, my quads felt like bricks, and the finish line couldn't come fast enough."

"Beginnings are strange things," writes William Bridges in *Transitions: Making Sense of Life's Changes*. "People want them to be quick and to come automatically, but they don't." Embarking on your next chapter will also take the same kind of time and intention it took for you to integrate into the running world. These ten guidelines will help you slide as smoothly as possible into your 27th mile.

1. Don't Wait

Although it's important to take as much time as you need to grieve the loss of running, it's also crucial to keep your body moving most days of the week. Whether you walk, take a yoga class, or learn to dragon boat, physical movement, which releases a cocktail of endorphins, serotonin, and dopamine, is the equivalent of putting Neosporin on your running scab. Plus, being in motion, especially if you're learning a new skill or interacting with others, requires presence. It's hard to fixate on your final half-marathon when you're learning to swing a golf club or taking a cross-country skiing lesson.

Healing from an injury may physically limit which activities you can do, but try to let that—and not other factors—be the only thing that holds you back. Cathy Annetta, who works in hospital human resources, is interested in joining a local rowing club, but she's self-conscious about the weight she's gained since she stopped running. "I just need to get over it and not wait until I'm feeling good about myself," the forty-eight-year-old says. "I'm not going to feel any better doing what I'm doing, and time is passing away."

I get it: When your self-confidence is in the dump and your fitness isn't at its peak, showing up to a new athletic situation is harder than finding a Lycra-based outfit that feels flattering. One way to overcome the hurdle is to remove self-judgment from the situation—again, ridiculously hard—and look at it objectively. Cathy started running at age thirty because she wanted an activity to get her out of the house and help her meet new people. She thought she'd hate running but was quickly enamored; her first 5K turned into a 10K, and she committed to running a marathon before she turned forty. She actually finished three 26.2s: New York City, Berlin, and Chicago.

Now working from home, Cathy is in a similar spot as she was eighteen years ago: She's on the hunt for outside interaction and a community, two things she misses about running. Objectively, rowing gets her into the fresh air of Mississauga, Ontario, and gives her a boatload of like-minded teammates. Subjectively, she's a three-time marathoner and dedicated athlete, which, as a former rower, I can assure you any beginning masters rowing squad would welcome. (Also, rowing is a full-body workout on par with running's physical demands. Cathy is also missing how running made her body look; rowing will get her back there pretty dang quickly and give her solid shoulders to boot.)

2. Remember What You've Built

Even if you're feeling like Cathy and not in top form, realize that running has laid a solid foundation for your next chapter, both physically and mentally. "I am so confident when I am in the boxing ring," says sports psychologist Kim Dawson, who embraced the new sport after eight marathons and decades of running. "I know nobody will be fitter than I am." In addition to a formidable cardiovascular base, running has developed your grit, mental toughness, and drive. You know how to set a goal and chip away at it mile by mile. And, thanks to your injuries, you have a PhD in resilience.

Although every activity has its own learning curve, don't forget: You're not starting from scratch. You're starting from strength. You're already an athlete.

3. Allow Yourself to Change

During my twenties, my athletic identity shifted from being a rower to being a marathoner. My thirties were all about athletic ambition: I clocked a few PRs in the half-marathon, finished the marathon that began Another Mother Runner, and went big at one full Ironman.

I didn't make a conscious shift, but my forties weren't as race heavy. I spent most of that decade doing lots of nonrunning things—swimming, cycling, hiking, strength—in order to hold onto a little bit of running, which I stopped when I was forty-eight.

Now in my fifties, my goal is to retain the exercise scaffolding that keeps me mentally balanced and physically healthy, but in this decade, I don't want to try so hard. In my thirties, weeks with more than ten hours of training were the rule, not the exception. In my forties, my focus was on clinging to running. I don't have that kind of physical or mental energy anymore. In my fifties, I want to feel more fluid and flexible with my workouts. I want to train for challenging adventures and keep my body strong and my stream of endorphins steady, but I'm ready to ease up on the overall intensity.

"What I know is that I want to be active for my whole life," says Sarah Lightner, forty-eight. "My tendency is to plan all the things, but now I just have to step back and let this be its own path." Sarah is taking a cue from her seventy-five-year-old father, Gary Kipling, who was her first running buddy. Gary, a college football player for the University of South Dakota, ran for thirty years until his orthopedist recommended he stop because of his knees, compromised from his football years. Gary took to the pool and swam for workouts for about five years until he injured his shoulder's rotator cuff. These days, he exercises on the elliptical machine in his garage four or five times per week for thirty minutes. He opens the garage door, looks out on a lake, and spends his time thinking about past golf games and family trips. Sounds like a pretty lovely routine to me.

Suzanne Klonis, fifty-two, is also looking for longevity. "I don't need to be doing long-distance races when I'm eighty," she says. "My forties were all about marathons." Now her goal is exploring new ways to move her body, including rock climbing, swimming, and hiking, and staying active for decades to come.

4. Stay Off the Trail

There is a trail in Fraser, Colorado, that haunts me. With a gushing river, short and steep hills, plenty of shade, and very few humans, it was my pinnacle trail. "I want my very last run to be on this trail," I thought regularly, as I cruised over its roots and kicked dusty pinecones.

When I'm cycling on a narrow shoulder and cars are whizzing by, I think of that trail. When I'm flailing on Bulgarian split squats and feeling judged by fellow gym-goers, I think of that trail. When the pool water is bathwater warm and I have to share a lane, I think of that trail. By "I think of that trail," I mean I become resentful. I hate that I will never have those 5 miles of flow again.

We've all got our own version of my trail. I advise you to hold it, and your beloved running, loosely as you poke around to find your new athletic identity. Meaning: Try not to play the comparison game. Nearly every other activity, minus walking, requires something more—a pile of gear, a commute, a membership, a reservation—than running. It's easy, especially when you're in the beginning stages, to immediately default to a comparison with running.

When that happens—and if you're like me, it'll happen regularly—acknowledge the thought and hold it loosely. When I am on my game, I'll tell myself compassionately, "Yep, this isn't your trail. And, Dimity, sweetie, you're not running anymore."

5. Expect Awkwardness and Laughter

Even though you could never describe the sport of running as easy, it is one of the simplest motions, which you repeat again and again. What's more, it requires very little coordination or gear; you move solely in one direction and hold nothing, save an occasional water bottle, in your hands.

Whether you're looping your feet into straps on a Pilates reformer or dinking in the kitchen in pickleball, any activity is more complicated than running. As such, counselor Niamh Rawlins recommends not going into a new activity leading with the achievement-oriented, accomplished runner part of yourself. Instead, she says, embrace a beginner's mindset, something most of us as adults don't have to do regularly in our everyday lives. Remember how awkward and clueless you felt at your first 5K? Yep, that's the feeling we're looking to find again.

Similarly, don't let one bad outing determine whether the activity is right for you. Give yourself a few chances to feel more comfortable and then decide. Ann Callarman stopped running after moving to Pea Ridge, Arkansas, a short drive outside of Bentonville, a mountain biking mecca. Her husband has ridden mountain bikes for thirty years, and she wanted to join the local fat-tire culture. She crashed on her second ride out ("embarrassing and painful, especially when your nine-year-old son leaves you in his dust") and had a few other spills, including one that kept her sidelined for a few weeks because of a bruised collarbone. "I made it a point to get back in the saddle as soon as I could," she says, adding that she picked a very easy path for riding after the crashes. "I didn't want fear to hold me back."

As you pack your gear, remember your sense of humor. Laugh at the enormous backpack you take to the pool or even the fact that you have to get in a car to get to a workout. "Humor helps to mitigate tough situations," sports psychologist Kim Dawson says. "Just say, 'I hate this shit,' but this is my new reality."

6. Find Your People

You wouldn't register for a 50K trail run if the longest event you've done is a 10K and you've never run on trails. You know that as a runner, but you might not have that seasoned knowledge about cycling or swimming or any new activity piques your interest. There's a big difference in vibes between a Soul Cycle class and a YMCA spinning class.

Finding your next community is a bit like dating: You need to get out of your comfort zone. Look for events held by community organizations, gyms, or local stores, or search social media for clubs or groups that might be a good fit. Once you've zeroed in on a few, email or call the contact person, and tell them exactly who you are—athletic background, age, physical limitations, if any—and what you're looking for. Review your what-you-need list on page 165 so you don't get caught up in a speedy pack when you were hoping for a no-drop, casual bike ride.

Ann, the mountain biker, found the Women of Oz through a local bike shop and took their fundamentals clinic, a two-hour course, which included basic skills and an easy group ride to practice them. At that clinic, the leaders told participants about their club's monthly flagship ride, an all-riders-welcome event where participants are encouraged to exchange numbers at the beginning and socialize over a potluck at the end. "I started to meet people and make friends," she says. These days, Ann heads out with cyclists with similar abilities at least twice a week. "They want to empower other women to embrace this male-dominated sport," she says, adding that she recently became a group ride leader. "I lead the green [or easy] or green-plus groups. I don't like a lot of challenge on the bike; I ride to have a good time."

7. Invest in Yourself

As you explore different activities, ask yourself, *What do I need to feel competent and confident?* It could be a ten-pack of personal training sessions so you don't have to slink around the squat rack at the gym. Or a Peloton so you can stoke your competitive side as you drip sweat on the basement floor. Or a babysitter so you can join your friends for a daylong hike. Or all the swim accessories, including a cute new suit, so you feel legit at lap swim.

To be clear, I'm not condoning retail therapy to charge your way out of feeling blue. I am saying, if you have the means, make an investment to solidify your commitment to this new pursuit—and to the mindset that you're not just killing time until you can run again. (Remember, sweetie, you're not running anymore.)

When I stopped running, I already owned a bike and swim equipment, but I bought a smart trainer for my bike and a subscription to Zwift, a gamified riding app. The two combined let me virtually race on a beginner-friendly team (two of the female members "picked me up" during a random group ride), ride with cyclists from around the world, and climb routes that mimicked stages of the Tour de France. If I hadn't invested about $900, my bike would mostly gather dust over the winter, plus my fitness—and my mood—would have bottomed out.

8. Prepare to Mix and Match

A typical runner's weekly calendar: running four to six days, with at least one rest day and a little strength, cross-training, yoga, or mobility thrown in for good measure. Each workout is linear, each run promises a satisfying finish. Your weeks of running can all look very similar—Tuesdays are hill repeats, Saturdays are long runs—as can your years: a late half-marathon in the spring leads into training for a fall marathon. It all feels very crisp and orderly. (Until you get sidelined, but I don't have to tell you that.)

In your next chapter, in your 27th mile, you can certainly train with focus in one sport or have competitive seasons, but chances are, you're going to have more diversity in your sweat sessions. "There isn't any one thing that can give me everything that running gave me," says Maureen Powers, who swims, walks, and strength trains, among other activities. "It's hard, but I have found multiple things that each satisfy some of the benefits of my running."

Arlene Barr, who regularly finished at the top of her age group at races and has two hip replacements, walks every day wearing a weighted vest to add extra challenge and help satisfy her need to push herself. She also gets her heart rate up on the elliptical, rowing machine, and exercise bike, and she supplements with resistance training and Pilates. Pamela Wakeman, a trail runner who did an Ironman and also has two bionic hips, swims three or four days per week, strength trains three times per week, and walks regularly. Pamela lives in Tucson, where scorching temps limit her outside time; she adds in mountain bike rides when the weather allows. She's also planning on doing a 5K once per year and will add in some runs when the race date nears.

Although mixing and matching might not be as reliable as your running schedule, it does have one important thing going for it: It keeps injuries and chronic pain to a minimum thanks to a more balanced blend of low-impact activities.

9. Take Care at the Gym

The gym is a great place to keep up with the Kardashians or otherwise sweat and binge some bad television. But I advise you to take care. For at least six months after my breakup with running, I avoided the cardio room at my rec center. The treadmill, where I often did speed work, and the step mill, where I climbed and climbed while injured, brought back too many unfiltered emotions. As my grief subsided and acceptance set in, I was able to use those machines again without getting worked up.

One other bit of advice on cardio workouts: Preplan them or use a workout programmed into the machine. An easy forty-minute run outside naturally provides visual stimulation, terrain changes, and effort variation. An easy forty minutes on the stationary bike can feel like forty hours. Changing effort, incline, and cadence keeps your mind engaged—and not feeling frustrated or too nostalgic.

These days, armed with a set workout, I use both the treadmill and the step mill. Yes, I glance too often at the person next to me running 6.4 mph as I'm simulating hiking at 3 mph and a 12 percent incline. If I start to play the comparison game too hard, I remind myself to be grateful both for the past, when I hopped on a treadmill and cranked the speed, and for today, when I hopped on and cranked the incline.

10. Aim for a B Minus

If we were grading activities, running, with its accessibility, ease, simplicity, continual challenge, community feel, and metabolic burn, would get an A. In your 27th mile, make it your goal to find activities that, combined, net a B–. That may sound like a low bar, especially to us overachieving runners, but it sets up the expectation it's not possible to 100 percent replace running, which, sadly, is the truth.

That said, can you find good enough alternatives that build on your athletic foundation and keep your body, mind, and spirit in a healthy, positive place? Absolutely. My laundry bag still overflows with sweat-soaked workout gear. I challenge myself regularly with extra-long hikes and bike rides that require training programs and focus. I'm surrounded by friends: some who ride, some who lift, some who walk right alongside me. It's not running, and it's not an A, but strung together, these B– activities provide a life that's still strong, joyful, and fulfilling.

Find Your 27th Mile

Now that you've got the guidelines, it's time to go spelunking (literally, if that's your jam) into the wide world of possibilities beyond running; former runners are mountain biking and aquabiking, learning tae kwon do and boxing. Here are twenty-two of them, with Dimity McDowell Running Transfer Scores (yes, ™) and first-person endorsements:

Aquabiking
The Basics: A race that is two-thirds of a triathlon: You swim, then bike, and then don't run. (Aquabike's tagline is Swim, Bike, Done!)

Running Transfer Score: Medium. Although the skills and the gear don't overlap with that of running, the training concepts, endurance mindset, and overall vibe do.

Pros: You're staying in the endurance world and repeating the same physical motion while swimming or biking, as you do when running. Both sports are low impact.

Cons: You need to know—or learn—how to swim and bike. Also, trigger warning: At a race, you'll see a lot of running. Aquabikes are typically a division of a triathlon; they are rarely held solo. You likely will have to run during the race: from the swim to the bike, and from the bike area to the finish line. You can walk these, of course; your race ends when you cross the timing mat in the bike area.

Gear: High. You'll need a bike, plus a helmet and bike shorts. You'll also need a swimsuit, goggles, and cap and access to a pool or lake. If you get into it, you'll likely want to invest in a wetsuit for the swim.

Competition Possibilities: High and growing as more triathletes get older and want to keep competing. The length of races varies, from a super sprint distance 0.5-mile swim and 12.4-mile bike to an Ironman-length 2.4-mile swim and 112-mile bike.

Community Vibe: The only time I—Dimity—felt community with my fellow aquabikers was at the end of a race, when the staging area is almost empty because most athletes are out on the run. We chatted about why we no longer run, which was cathartic. That said, joining a triathlon club to participate in swims and bike workouts will give you like-minded teammates.

First-Person Perspective: "As somebody who thrives on structure and relies on an early-morning workout to gather energy for the day, registering for an aquabike event was a good call for me when I was craving an athletic goal. A former triathlete, I already owned all the gear I needed for training and competition, so it wasn't much of a financial investment. I enjoyed training hard and becoming more fit via nonimpact sports; I loved that the dark cloud of running injuries wasn't shading my mindset. The only drawback with training is that I did most of it solo, and it can get a little lonely at times. I've done a handful of aquabikes of varying distances, and the race can be exactly what you want it to be: a chance to challenge your limits or to soak up the experience. Even though I was a little envious of people who could do the full triathlon, I still had the tired legs and satisfaction of racing when I crossed the finish line." (Dimity McDowell)

Barre Class

The Basics: Barre class is like ballet's sweatier cousin; tiny moves provide a big burn. Your legs will shake (in a good way).

Running Transfer Score: Low. It's a primarily strength-based class held inside. But you'll need to draw on your resilience. "I lift weights. I run marathons. I do boot camps and have been able to keep up," says Leah Wiesner, who goes to barre regularly. "Pure Barre kicked my butt."

Pros: Your legs are strong and will become stronger—and more injury-proof—during this low-impact total-body workout.

Cons: Logistics and finances: You need to buy, drive to, and schedule classes. Classes can cost anywhere from $20 to $35 (at time of writing).

Gear: Minimal. Your leggings will get good use, and you don't wear shoes in barre class.

Competition Possibilities: None.

Community Vibes: Many barre studios make a concerted effort to foster community. Obviously, chatter is at a minimum during classes, but some studios have happy hours, hikes, birthday celebrations, and other ways to connect. Plus, like many running clubs, there are women of all ages and sizes.

First-Person Perspective: "I love that barre class is physically hard, but the pain is only for seconds while you're holding a specific pose. I also love that the overall structure is predictable, but each class is a little different. When I stopped running, I never would have thought I would be somebody who enjoys a studio or classes, but I've taken over eight hundred classes now, and I don't see myself stopping anytime soon." (Jen Rucker)

Boxing

The Basics: You know the professional, pay-per-view kind; this is much more low-key. You can take anything from a one-time class to more structured training at a boxing gym.

Running Skills Transfer: Low. Your endurance will come in handy, but the coordination and cognition required are significantly higher than for running.

Pros: Engaging your brain and using your whole body. "If you're punching with your left arm, you're also stepping with your left foot, which is counter to what your body normally does," says Pam Harris, who boxes a couple times per week.

Cons: Keeping your eyes open as things are coming at your face. "The first time I got punched in the face, it was a shock, but I kept going. In a way, it was like the first time I ran a new distance. I didn't think I could do it, but I did," says Pam. "It was bad, but not as bad as I thought it would be."

Gear Commitment: Most gyms have gloves available to borrow, but you may want to invest in your own if you enjoy it. "Gloves get pretty gnarly," says Pam. "All that enclosed sweat with nowhere to go!"

Competition Possibilities: They exist, but you never have to step foot in a ring if that's not your thing.

Community Vibe: Most boxing gyms embrace all levels, including beginners, as well as all ages and backgrounds. (Pam loves the diversity of her fellow boxers.)

First-Person Perspective: "The first time I tried boxing, it felt so good. A total release. I was working through a lot of big feelings—I had just been diagnosed with cancer—so the opportunity to just really punch something felt really cathartic. I love that it demands full presence of your mind and body. It's kind of like chess; you have to be thinking about your next move as you're executing your current one. At the end of a class, I am super sweaty and have that just-exercised buzz. Mentally and physically, I'm both drained and energized." (Pam Harris)

Cycling

The Basics: Two wheels can take you anywhere, from a short trip to the grocery store to a 100-mile tour. *Wheels* is loosely defined here: You can ride a cruiser, a hybrid, a road bike, or even a recumbent. (Check out mountain biking later in this list if you want to go off the pavement.)

Running Skills Transfer: High. Pedaling a bike is a lot like running: You want to keep your cadence high as you ride on flats, up inclines, and down hills. If you don't know how to ride a bike, you can learn as an adult.

Pros: You're outside, feeling the sun and wind on your face—and you're going much faster than you ever did on foot. Also, it's a great way to exercise on a hot day.

Cons: Lots of gear (and the potential for a flat tire or other gear malfunction mid-workout). You're on the road with cars, which can feel dangerous. It takes some effort to get in a workout. "After riding for an hour, I look at my stats, and they're nothing like what I would get in thirty minutes of running," says Ingrid L., who rides with a women's group a couple times a week. "But I'm getting there; the faster I learn to bike, the more I feel something akin to a runner's high."

Gear Commitment: A heavy lift here. You'll need a bike, of course. If you don't currently have one in your garage, ask a friend of similar height if you can borrow hers. If that's not possible, check online for used ones. When you're first starting to ride for workouts, any kind of bike will work: A hybrid, which features flat handlebars and more upright positioning, might be the most comfortable call. Two other pieces of must-have gear: a helmet and cycling shorts that feature a padded chamois in the crotch to cushion your most delicate parts. Neither of these things is very flattering, so just remind yourself you're going for function over fashion.

Competition Possibilities: Although there are bike *races*, chances are you'll be drawn to bike *events*, which feature well-stocked aid stations, a critical mass of cyclists (read: safer than riding alone), and no chip time. Events range from 25-milers to multiday events.

Community Vibes: Riding with a friend is not like running with a friend; having a side-by-side conversation is tough because you're often riding single file. That said, riding in pairs is my—Dimity's—preference in case of a flat tire or other incident. Cycling clubs offer community; you ride together on a preplanned route, sometimes with a stop for coffee or a snack along the way. (Look for "no drop" rides if you're a beginner.)

First-Person Perspective: "I've always loved riding a bike: The sense of freedom I feel when I'm out on the road is unparalleled. (Seriously, just feeling the wind blow in my face is worth the effort of getting out.) I mostly ride a road bike, and I have a few go-to routes, mostly in parks or on bike paths around the Denver area, that allow me to focus on getting a workout without worrying about traffic. I like that I can just go for an easy ride or I can train for something like a century (100 miles) or an event with a lot of climbing. When the weather won't let me ride outside, I use my indoor trainer and queue up some bad reality TV to help me pass the time; it's not ideal, but it does the job for getting in a good workout. I do worry about having mechanical mishaps on the road, but I don't let that stop me. I always carry my cell phone, and I've taken a few bike clinics that show you how to do basic repairs, including how to change a flat." (Dimity McDowell)

Dragon Boating

The Basics: Eighteen paddlers, along with an oarsperson and drummer, sit in a long, skinny boat and paddle in unison at a quick pace. "The 'in unison' part is key!" says Paige Sato, a member of the women's Schuylkill Dragons team in Philadelphia.

Running Skills Transfer: Minimal, save for the fitness and competitive spirit you honed on the road. In dragon-boat paddling, your legs don't move; your core, hips, and lats provide the power. "There's a lot of torque involved when doing it properly," Paige says.

Gear Commitment: You should be able to try dragon boating without buying anything. When you commit, you'll need a butt pad ("There's a lot of friction"), a paddle, a PFD (life jacket), and either gloves or Gorilla Grip to "sticky up your hands."

Pros: You'll get an intense physical workout. "You don't do dragon boat to get in shape," says Paige. "You do dragon boat because you're in shape."

Cons: You need two not-super-common things: a nearby body of water and a local dragon boating club.

Competition Possibilities: High. Races are various lengths. The longest is 2,000 meters, which is like "a roller derby," says Paige. "You can hit other boats."

Community Vibe: Twenty people in one boat automatically means a built-in community. Paige's team has women from their late twenties to their eighties in all professions and stages of life.

First-Person Perspective: "When my husband and I moved to Philadelphia, Facebook fed me an advertisement for a five-week Learn to Paddle program with the Schuylkill Dragons, an all-women's team. I did it but broke my wrist in the middle of the season—I tripped while running—so it was challenging for me to solidify my stroke technique. When my wrist healed, I practiced my stroke at winter paddling sessions held at indoor pools, and my skills really improved. On the water the following spring, I felt so much more confident. From the shore it looks like a bunch of flailing about, but there are a million and one steps to each stroke, and it requires intense concentration to keep everything moving properly. I'm so into the sport, I attended a dragon-boat camp in Florida in April for five days. Dolphins swam beside us as we were paddling—so cool!" (Paige Sato)

Fitness Instructor
The Basics: Stand in front of a group of people and lead them in kickboxing, Body Pump, spinning, strength circuits, yoga, or anything else that interests you.

Running Skills Transfer: Low. That said, if you led group runs or loved helping beginning runners, your enthusiasm for fitness and helping others goes a long way.

Gear Commitment: Minimal. Gyms (read: your potential employers) have the equipment you'll need.

Pros: You'll learn much more about human physiology and fitness. Plus, you get to work out and get paid for it while helping others stay fit.

Cons: It costs money and time to get certified, and then you'll need to find a job. (But, like many professions, once you're in the door, hearing about opportunities is much easier.)

Competition Possibilities: None.

Community Vibe: High. Once you start teaching classes, the same crowd of people will attend, and you'll get to know them. I—Dimity—teach spinning twice per week, and a high point of classes for me is chatting with the participants and hearing about their lives.

First-Person Perspective: "I started taking kickboxing after my fiftieth birthday, which is also when I started running. Kickboxing really complemented my running, not just physically but mentally. I learned how to push through pain and calm my mind, which was invaluable as I took on longer and longer races like 200-milers. When I could no longer run, I became a kickboxing instructor. I knew I wanted to help women feel that kind of power. Although I walk around and help by holding pads for people, I like to participate in the class myself. I'm now sixty-four years old, and women come up to me after class and tell me, 'I see you doing it, so I know I can do it too' and 'This class makes me feel so badass.' That's the way I want them to feel." (Louanne Wiant)

Golf
The Basics: Otherwise known as a good walk spoiled—sorry, former runners, no golf carts allowed—golf challenges you to hit a tiny white ball into nine or eighteen holes in as few strokes as

possible. Along the way, you may have a few choice words with your clubs or the opportunity to quote Happy Gilmore ("It's all in the hips.")

Running Skills Transfer: Minimal. Golf is a precision sport.

Gear Commitment: You'll need a set of clubs and golf shoes, but most courses have clubs for rent for a few trial rounds.

Pros: A competitive way to get in your steps, play with people who are a variety of ages and aren't necessarily endurance athletes, and focus on a sport that feels nothing like running.

Cons: Costs can add up with course, club, and tournament fees. The full-body dynamics of the golf swing can cause injuries. "I have pulled muscles in my back and popped a rib out of place twice," says Christina Smith, who plays a couple times a week.

Competition Possibilities: High. Every time you play golf, you're competing, even if it's a round among friends. Christina plays in a women's league and a mixed league weekly during the summer.

Community Vibe: Also high. "I have a group of friends I golf with; we are outside, walking, sometimes with cocktails, enjoying each other's company while we chase a white ball around," she says.

First-Person Perspective: "I didn't pick golf up naturally like some do, so learning the sport can get very frustrating. It seems like when you fix one thing about your swing, then something else goes wrong. But my husband is a patient teacher, and I've slowly found my groove. I've been playing consistently for about five years, and I really enjoy it. Golfing nine holes, which is what I do after work and in my leagues, takes about ninety minutes to two hours. On the weekends, I golf eighteen holes; we take day trips with other couples to courses around the area. My community around golf is so positive. I love walking with a pull cart for my clubs. I've spent a lot of money to be in golf tournaments, but when the weather doesn't cooperate—whether it's rainy or cold or it's kind of a miserable day—when you're with the right people, it makes for funny stories later." (Christina Smith)

Hiking
The Basics: Walking in nature, usually on trails or paths in the mountains, forests, or countryside; a hike can be anything from a short few miles in a park to a challenging, all-day adventure across the Grand Canyon.

Running Skills Transfer: High. The pace is slower and trails are different from pavement, but the fundamentals are the same.

Pros: Being out in nature and a chance to catch up with friends. You can make it quite strenuous and get in a fierce workout. Depending on the trail, there's a sense of adventure and solitude.

Cons: Hiking requires considerably more time than running does. First, there's a commute to and from the trails. Then there's the time on the trails: Running 6 miles on flat pavement takes much less time than hiking 6 miles on rugged trails.

Gear Commitment: Minimal. You probably already own the essentials, like running shoes and a hydration pack or hand-held water bottle. If you want to tackle more technical terrain, some trail running shoes and hiking poles are helpful. Trail map apps are plentiful, so if your orienteering skills are minimal, don't fret; if you have cell service, you should be (mostly) good. (Knowing how to read—and bringing along—a real map is still a good call.)

Competition Possibilities: High. Hiking events like Mammoth March are springing up everywhere, and with research, you can find trail ultras with a generous cutoff time or a looped course, making them accessible to your current pace.

Community Vibe: Incredible and inclusive. Hiking groups are as popular as running groups; whether you're after camaraderie or a new workout buddy, you'll have no trouble finding your crew here.

First-Person Perspective: "For me, running was always about carving out time for myself and chasing a challenging goal that kept me moving forward. I've always needed time outdoors, and I'm lucky to live in Colorado Springs, a place with a wide variety of trails. As I transitioned away from running, I found myself spending more time hiking solo.

"That space allowed me to truly appreciate the benefits of hiking—to slow down, soak in the views, and fall in love with a different kind of movement. Hiking has helped me maintain a solid base of fitness, and when I'm craving a goal to chase, I can usually find an event that is hiker-friendly. I've completed several, including an overnight ultra that turned out to be one of my top-three favorite races *ever*! I still get that sense of achievement, the structure of a training plan, and the satisfaction of a start and finish line. And with so many trails around the world, the adventure possibilities feel endless." (Cathy Engstrom)

Mountain Biking
The Basics: Trail running on steroids: Instead of using your own two feet on rugged trails, you ride a bike with knobby tires and suspension.

Running Skills Transfer: Medium. Your legs and endurance will shine; the rest depends on the technical difficulty of the trails:

A flat gravel path can feel like running; a rocky, rooty downhill, not so much.

Gear Commitment: High. You'll need a bike (which you can rent at many ski resorts and bike shops) and a helmet. Bike shorts are also a good call; mountain bike shorts typically have an inner layer with a crotch-protecting chamois under a pair of hiking-like shorts.

Pros: Low-impact, fabulous way to get out on trails and explore more than you could on foot. Lots of opportunities to get better; many mountain bike parks have trails of all levels. Presence is required. "You can't think about anything else but what is in front of you," says Ann Callarman, who mountain bikes three or four times per week.

Cons: The possibility for bruises, broken bones, and other injuries is higher than most other sports. The cost of equipment, if you end up loving it, can add up quickly.

Competition Possibilities: High. You can ride solo or in teams in many races, which often feature a looped course. Ann tried a 6-mile looped race with her friends, and it wasn't her thing. Slower riders need to pull over for faster riders, which messed with her flow. "I'll volunteer at any race though," she says.

Community Vibe: Medium. If you live near a popular mountain biking spot like Ann, finding a group at your level should be fairly easy. If you're in sparser fat-tire territory, finding a riding friend may take some work.

First-Person Perspective: "My first ride with my husband, a long-time mountain biker, was on a greenway trail. It was instant love. I thought, 'I am on a trail, I am on a bike. And this is so cool.' I wanted to get better at it, so I found the Women of Oz, an all-levels mountain biking club. They were so welcoming, and I appreciate having somebody other than my spouse be my coach, you know? I ride with them or friends from there all the time. I always try to get 10 miles in when I go out, and sometimes I'll ride in the morning, head home for lunch, and then go out for a shorter ride in the afternoon. I'm stronger now than I was as a runner, because you use your whole body in mountain biking: You need core and arm strength to hold yourself up. When I'm riding, I just focus on the trail and enjoy being in the woods; that's huge for me." (Ann Callarman)

Nordic Skiing

The Basics: Hitting snowy trails on skinny skis. There are two styles of Nordic skiing: classic, which uses a motion much like walking and is typically done in groomed parallel tracks; and skate-skiing, which uses a skating motion and uses a groomed wider course.

Running Skills Transfer: Medium for the classic style: It's much like walking or hiking, although there's an additional balance element. Low for skate-skiing: You'll need a lesson or three to get the technique down. With either style, your endurance base and your capacity to repeat the same motion for miles come in handy.

Gear Commitment: Medium. You need skis, boots, and poles, and you can rent equipment at most Nordic centers to see if you like the sport before you commit to buying equipment. REI and ski shops often rent equipment as well.

Pros: A great, low-impact cardio workout in fresh air; depending on length and terrain, a Nordic ski session can be more challenging than a run. Plus, you have the chance to explore new trails and parks.

Cons: You need to live in a northern climate—and then actually get snow during the winter. There's a possibility of injury, especially on downhills, but the snow provides a (relatively) soft place to land.

Competition Possibilities: You may have heard of the legendary races like the American Birkebeiner (which features a 50K and shorter distances) in Hayward, Wisconsin, but there are also plenty of smaller local events that welcome beginners.

Community Vibe: The best way to find a skiing friend or group is by taking a class, says Anne Heinrichs, a Nordic instructor in the Twin Cities area. "Having a skiing buddy is so helpful," she says. "When it's cold outside, it can be hard to rally solo, but it's much easier with a friend."

First-Person Perspective: "Because Nordic skiing is easier on your body than many other sports, it's a lifelong activity. I love seeing other people in their seventies and eighties out on the trail. I love being outside; if you're dressed correctly, you won't be cold. It's a great workout, no matter what your skill level is. Classic Nordic skiing is especially forgiving; you'll work up a sweat even if your form isn't perfect. I burn a lot of calories, increase my cardiovascular fitness, and technique-wise, there's always room for improvement, which feels really good." (Anne Heinrichs)

Peloton
The Basics: An at-home fitness app with thousands of workouts led by a squad of energetic, inspiring instructors in a worldwide community. You can take classes live or on replay, using your own or Peloton-branded equipment.

Running Skills Transfer: High. The cardio workouts use running-specific language (intervals, power zone), and the endurance you've built on the road transfers to the bike or rower.

Gear Commitment: High. For cardio workouts, you either need to buy the Peloton equipment (treadmill, bike, or rower) or use the app with a treadmill, indoor bike, or rower at home or at the gym. For strength workouts, you'll need dumbbells, at a minimum.

Pros: A range of workouts from yoga to Pilates to a hilly bike ride to a mountain hike are available on one app. The workouts are all different lengths, so if you're crunched for time, you can still get in a fifteen-minute session. Suzanne Klonis, who got the Peloton app in 2020 and followed up with a bike purchase four years later, likes to stack workouts: For example, she'll bike for thirty minutes, then do ten minutes of core, followed by a twenty-minute strength session.

Cons: It's costly. New equipment starts at $1,500 for the bike (although you can likely find deals on secondhand equipment) and you'll pay a monthly fee for the app, regardless of which equipment you used.

Competition Possibilities: Not in a traditional sense, but you can compete against yourself in workouts or with others who are taking the same class via the leaderboard.

Community Vibe: High. Classes feature leaderboards, shout-outs, and virtual high-fives, and you can form communities with virtual workout buddies. What's more, you can attend live classes in New York City or London, if you're lucky enough to get a spot.

First-Person Perspective: "My orthopedist who saw me regularly for knee issues suggested I try to expand my passion outside of running. I used my mom's old stationary bike with the Peloton app for about a month. I liked it so much I invested in a Peloton bike in February 2022, which was so helpful when I got my hip replaced; it allowed me to push myself when walking far distances wasn't an option and to increase the difficulty in small doses. I bought the rower about a year later, which helped when I had my knee replaced. It helped me increase my degree of knee flexion in small doses. These days, I use Peloton four to six times a week. I like to use the bike for endurance work and the rower for interval work.

"When I'm traveling, the app is great to use in a hotel gym, and if I don't have a gym, I can do a Pilates or barre class. I am absolutely certain I wouldn't be where I am right now, both physically and mentally, without the Peloton equipment and workouts. It gives me purpose and options, which are key for me right now." (Gretchen Gibson)

Pickleball
The Basics: A Ping-Pong-meets-tennis hybrid in which you hit a plastic ball back and forth across a net with a paddle with one (singles) or three (doubles) other players.

Running Skills Transfer: Low. Not much except when dashing toward the net to (hopefully!) return an opponent's well-executed drop shot.

Gear Commitment: You can rent paddles at most indoor pickleball places or ask your PB-obsessed friends if you can borrow a paddle. You can also get starter kits at Target or Walmart.

Pros: A highly social sport, pickleball is a great way to make new friends or spend time with your family. Relatively simple to learn, especially if you have prior experience with racket/paddle sports. It's a highly addictive sport, which could be a pro or con, depending on the amount of free time you have.

Cons: Need access to courts—and other players. Rules can be a bit confusing to newbies. Can't play outside in wet weather, and indoor court rentals can be a bit pricey.

Competition Possibilities: Besides every game offering a chance to win, local tournaments are held year-round at parks and indoor facilities. Many pickleball facilities and health clubs also offer organized leagues.

Community Vibe: Incredibly social. At public parks nationwide, folks convene to play games with people they've possibly never met before. Multiple apps allow players to find local sessions, ensuring that there will be players at the courts when you show up.

First-Person Perspective: "I fell hard for the sport when I took an introductory pickleball class at a fitness resort—I was playing a basic game with three other novices by the end of the hourlong class! Back home, I played once with a paddle I borrowed from a friend, then I bought a $90 paddle, and I've been addicted ever since. I play six to ten hours per week, usually for two hours at a time. I'm a competitive person, yet what I love best about pickleball is the camaraderie—striking up random conversations with other players and laughing in between points. I've played in numerous places across the country, and there's truly a shared sense of humor and joy on every pickleball court I've ever stepped on to. I've made so many friends in the three plus years I've been playing, and my life is infinitely richer because of both the friendships and the sport." (Sarah Bowen Shea)

Pilates

The Basics: Done on a mat or a reformer, a low-impact exercise that uses controlled, slow movements coordinated with your breath to build functional strength, improve your posture, and increase overall flexibility.

Running Skills Transfer: Low. There is very little crossover, but your strong legs will come in handy.

Gear Commitment: Low. You may want a pair of grippy socks, but the Pilates studio will have either mats or reformers.

Pros: A different way to move your body if you've been an endurance athlete your whole life. I—Dimity—often feel like I stand up straighter and have more space in my body after a class.

Cons: It takes a little time to get used to the language and positions; you will likely need to take an introductory session if you're new to the reformer. Classes are pricey; they typically run $25–$40 per class (at time of writing).

Competition Possibilities: None.

Community Vibe: If you attend the same class at the same time each week, you'll end up becoming friendly with the regulars.

First-Person Perspective: "My sixteen-year-old daughter asked me last summer if we could try Pilates together, and I have kept it up. I go twice a week right now to a reformer class. I like that the springs on the reformer can be adjusted to different resistances; our instructor gives us options for all the different moves. I like challenging myself, and I like that it's a total-body workout; we work the core, of course, but also the upper body and lower body, and then stretch at the end, which I never do on my own. I think Pilates has this impression that it's all ballerina types, which is not true. There are all shapes and sizes in classes." (Chris Cesena)

Rowing

The Basics: In narrow boats with one, two, four, or eight people, rowers hold either one or two oars to propel the boat forward. If you prefer to stay on terra firma, rowing machines are common at most gyms.

Running Skills Transfer: Medium. The rowing stroke requires much more concentration than running does, but the cardiovascular fitness and leg strength built through running come in handy in the boat. With every rowing stroke, you push with your legs, then swing your torso, then pull with your arms.

Gear Commitment: Low, because you'll likely join a rowing club that owns oars and boats. You'll probably need to buy a PFD (life jacket).

Pros: A full-body, low-impact, challenging workout that you can do on the water (amazing) or in a class (not as fun, but more efficient).

Cons: Most practices are held at the crack-o-dawn (6 a.m. or earlier) to avoid motorboat traffic and accommodate working schedules. Costs can add up: club dues, plus travel to races.

Competition Possibilities: High. Competitions include sprint races (1,000–2,000 meters) and head races (about 3 miles). Master rowers often compete at the same regattas as high schools and colleges, which makes the sport feel inclusive.

Community Vibe: High. If you're training for a race, you'll practice regularly with your boatmates, and there's plenty of time for chatter when you're not in the middle of the workout.

First-Person Perspective: "When I was forty-six, I saw these boats on a lake when I was out for a morning run and had no idea what they were. When I got home, I figured out it was the Rocky Mountain Rowing Club and emailed to get involved. I was hooked from the moment I tried it. I value being challenged, and it's a very intricate sport with delicate boats that requires full attention. I loved learning everything about how to carry the boat properly to how to get your shoulders to properly engage in the stroke. When I'm rowing, there's no room for anything else in my mind; I'm more present than I am in any other part of my day.

"During the season, I try to row every day. In the winter, I train on an indoor machine. During a workout, the sun rises, and the birds fly over my head, and I think, *How lucky am I to be here?* Races are challenging in the best way. When I get close to the finish line, I'm so tired, it feels like the gates of heaven are going to open. Then I cross the line, and it's just pure exhilaration." (Danielle Waagmeester)

Rucking
The Basics: Walking or hiking while wearing a backpack loaded with extra weight (beyond your necessities).

Running Skills Transfer: High. The movement is the same; you're just slowing down and adding weight.

Gear Commitment: Low. You likely already own a backpack, and you can put in dumbbells, liquids (a box of wine weighs about 7 pounds), and other heavy household objects to weigh it down. If you want something sleeker, you can purchase a rucking-specific backpack with removable weight plates.

Pros: Load 'em up: Rucking is a more challenging cardiovascular workout than simply hiking or walking because of the added weight, which also helps maintain bone density, strength, and muscular endurance. It's also super accessible, just like running.

Cons: If you have chronic neck or back issues, check with your doctor first before rucking.

Competition Possibilities: Yep, you can ruck for time, and events are growing in popularity; they range from fun rucks to a brewery to twenty-four-hour team events.

Community Vibe: Rucking has military roots, and many rucking groups and races include former and current military members; that said, all are welcome to join. The pace of rucking makes conversations on the trail more accessible than running.

First-Person Perspective: "I started rucking when I met my now husband; he is a big backpacker, and I wanted to go on trips with him. These days, I'm a working mom of teenagers, and it's easier for me to throw on a heavy backpack and go up a mountain than it is to be consistent with runs. I'm lucky, because I live in Utah, and have trails right near my house. Depending on my route and training goal, I put between twenty to thirty pounds in my backpack. I use a combination of weights and full water bottles. (I'll drink from one bottle during the workout.) I typically ruck three or four days a week for three or four miles, which takes me at least an hour.

"Rucking has definitely made me stronger. I used to struggle with sprained ankles, and my ankles feel much sturdier. I also notice that I climb hills more efficiently; I can feel my glutes and quads getting much stronger. My endurance has also increased substantially because I spend a lot of time in Zone 2, the heart rate zone optimal for building a wide aerobic base." (Jennifer Hickenlooper)

Skinning (Alpine Touring)
The Basics: Instead of riding a chairlift up a ski hill, you climb up using special ski equipment and your own power then ski down.

Running Skills Transfer: Medium. Leg strength and cardiovascular endurance are key ingredients for skinning.

Gear Commitment: High. The required gear includes touring skis (thinner than regular downhill skis); skins (synthetic strips for the bottom of the skis so you don't slide backward); special bindings that allow your heel to be free on the way up and locked in for the ride down; touring boots (which offer ankle flexibility for climbing), and adjustable poles. You'll also need goggles, a helmet, and all the clothing you'd wear for a day on the slopes. Megan Hinckley, who skins twice per week during the winter, typically wears a T-shirt and jacket when she's going up, then changes into her regular winter layers at the top. "It's unusual, but it works well for me."

Pros: A sense of freedom: You're outside in the elements and fresh air. If you like to climb or enjoy a repetitive physical challenge, skinning could be your nirvana.

Cons: At a minimum, you need a snowy hill and the skills to ski downhill.

Competition Possibilities: Yes! Ski mountaineering (skimo) races are becoming popular; in fact, skimo makes its Olympic debut in 2026. To get a sense of the sport, look for introductory skimo clinics or uphill nights at your local hill.

Community Vibe: Like running; you can join a group for a mass climb, grab a friend and climb together, or go solo and enjoy the alone time. It's also great for all ages; Megan's twelve-year-old son has skinned with her, and her seventy-three-year-old mom tried the learn-to-skin program at their home hill of Cranmore in North Conway, New Hampshire. "She's hooked!"

First-Person Perspective: "I thought skinning might be good rehab after I had surgery for hip dysplasia, so I rented equipment first to see if I would like it. During my first climb, I was like, 'This is awful, this is really hard, I'm going to keep doing it.' Now, I skin both days on the weekend, going up a 2.5-mile trail with 1,000 feet of climbing, for about an hour. I love it: My heart rate is elevated, I'm working hard, I'm sweating, I'm outside. I just feel really alive; it's very similar to the high I used to get while running. (And it's like running in another way: If I can't skin for some reason, I feel disappointed and a little antsy.) Now my son has caught the bug, and we've gone a few times together. A few years ago, I never would've imagined doing this, and now I get to go have adventures with my kid until he surpasses me, which I'm sure will be very soon." (Megan Hinckley)

Stand-Up Paddleboarding (SUP)
The Basics: Standing or kneeling on a large, stable board, you use a long paddle to propel yourself across a lake, river, or bay.

Running Skills Transfer: Minimal. You're balancing on a board on the water and your upper body is your main source of power.

Gear Commitment: You can borrow or rent paddleboards (and a life jacket) at many resorts or lakes. If you enjoy it, you can invest in a board; many boards are inflatable, so storing them doesn't require as much space as you'd think.

Pros: You're outside on the water, and it's a great activity for hot summer days. Plus, it's a total-body workout: Your core activates with every paddle stroke; your upper body provides the power; and your lower body works to keep you stable. You can have a leisurely paddle, dipping your toes in the water, or a power paddling session.

Cons: If you don't know how to swim, you may not feel comfortable on the water.

Competition Possibilities: Races range from sprints to ultra-long-distance events.

Community Vibe: Find fellow paddlers at organized sunrise or sunset paddles or SUP yoga classes, often held through a rental shop or recreation center. You can also recruit a friend and rent boards for a fun afternoon on the water.

First-Person Perspective: "I love paddleboarding. There are several rivers and lakes near me [in Pitt Meadows, British Columbia]. I'll grab a friend and use our paddle as my social time. We get caught up, it's a good workout, and it's just beautiful. We usually go for about two hours, and I feel it in my shoulders, my core, and even my quads because they stabilize it so much.

"I also take my board on vacation. I usually go for about an hour in the morning. I take my tea with me and start the day in peace and quiet." (Heather Escaravage)

Strength Training
The Basics: Hopefully you're somewhat familiar with this one from all your years as a runner. You use your own body weight or external resistance (dumbbells, barbells, kettlebells, bands) to build muscle mass and get stronger.

Running Transfer Score: Low. Which is why most runners don't like to strength train.

Pros: High accessibility; body-weight exercises (push-ups, wall sits, step-ups, and the like) are both challenging and effective. Building and maintaining muscle mass is hugely important for quality of life for everybody, but especially for women in perimenopause and beyond. Strength classes are inclusive; everybody lifts to their own ability.

Cons: The gym can feel intimidating to newbies, and proper form is important so you don't get injured.

Gear Commitment: Medium. If you're strength training at home, you'll need some bands or dumbbells and a mat, but they're a one-time purchase. Joining a gym gives you access to much more equipment.

Competition Possibilities: Although there are bodybuilding competitions, most of us compete against ourselves to build strength and improve running. "Much like running, it never really gets easier," says Britt Parker, who goes to a strength class three days per week. "Though you will be less sore as time goes on."

Community Vibe: Medium, depending on whether you strength train solo or with a class. Britt loves the community she found at her 6 a.m. strength class. "We support each other when lifting, and between sets there are discussions of kids, parents, work, and other life joys and pains."

First-Person Perspective: "I never thought I would be a gym rat. A massage therapist I worked with suggested strength class when I was lamenting the loss of running and needing something to fill the void. I was dubious, even more so walking in the first morning to the gym and seeing eight power racks and chalk dust on the floor. Once I got going, the intimidation factor dropped to zero, and now, I am hooked! I honestly feel stronger and fitter than when I was just running, and I like that I'm doing the recommended thing for my menopausal body. While strength training does not give the same endorphin high as running, I feel so much better on those mornings that start bright and early in the gym. At home when I am in a sour mood, heading to the basement to pump some iron shifts my mindset." (Britt Parker)

Swimming
The Basics: You can swim laps in a pool or outside in a lake, pond, or river. Most people use freestyle to swim, but you can mix it up with backstroke, butterfly, side stroke, breaststroke, and even a little dog paddle if it feels good.

Running Skills Transfer: Low. Unlike the motion of running, which is fairly intuitive, swimming relies heavily on technique. Don't despair; you can learn to swim as an adult. That said, the strength you built on the road benefits you in the pool. Amy Ebeid swam a timed 100 meters per month after she stopped running, and her coach was impressed. "Those are my running legs working," she told him.

Gear Commitment: Low. You need a suit, a pair of goggles, and a swim cap: The three of those combined cost less than a pair of running shoes. If you enjoy swimming, you might buy a pair of flippers, a kickboard, a pull buoy, and paddles: All are one-time investments. If the sensory deprivation of the pool feels suffocating, not soothing, you can invest in a pair of Bluetooth waterproof headphones.

Pros: A full-body, low-impact sport that offers support to your body, which is especially divine after the impact of running. "Swimming is the only activity that didn't hurt my herniated disc," says Alison Pellicci. You may love the rhythm of simply swimming, but if you thrive on metrics like distance and time, you can continually switch up your workout to keep it fresh.

Cons: To feel like you're getting a workout, you need to know how to swim efficiently, which means taking lessons if you don't know how to swim well. Logistically, a lot of steps for a workout: drive to pool, change, potentially shower, swim, shower again, change, drive home.

Competition Possibilities: You can enter local meets or national meets—or not at all. There are also competitive swims in open water around the country and world; races can range from fairly short to 10K and beyond. (And relay swims are also a thing!)

Community Vibe: Low to medium. Most masters swim teams are inclusive, but the fact that you have your face in the water for most of the workout limits interaction. But that's not always the case: "We mock-complain to the coaches and crack bad jokes and groan over certain drills and sets," says masters swimmer Amy Csizmar Dalal. "We also share stories about our kids and our jobs, give each other advice, and pick each other up when one of us is having a bad day."

First-Person Perspective: "I signed up for an adult beginner swim class when I was fifty years old. I was so nervous. I took a few lessons when I was young and wasn't afraid of the water, but I hadn't swum in over thirty years. I didn't know the rules or etiquette of the pool, and just showing up in a bathing suit is uncomfortable.

"The classes turned out to be great; I spent about nine months in various rounds of lessons. The big things we learned were how to kick and breathe efficiently, the correct head position, and how to pull. I wasn't using my arms right at all. Now I swim twice a week; I would go more, but I'll be honest: the biggest barrier is having to wash my hair after the workout. I love that it gives me time by myself to be alone with my thoughts, and that there's infinite opportunity for improvement. I can focus on technique and get faster.

"In the three years I've been swimming, the time it takes me to swim a mile has dropped considerably. I also love the metrics of it: How many yards did I go, how does that compare to my previous session? After I swim, I feel so good, even if I do smell a little bit like chlorine for the rest of the day." (Maureen Powers)

Tae Kwon Do

The Basics: A Korean martial art that involves punching and kicking and focuses on courtesy, integrity, perseverance, self-control, and indomitable spirit.

Running Transfer Score: Low. You wear a uniform in a dojo (a martial arts practice room).

Pros: It's easy to learn the basics, but there's always a better way to perform a kick or execute a form or throw a block or hold a stance. A great workout that improves your balance, core strength, timing, and reaction.

Cons: You can't just zone out while practicing, unless you want to get punched or kicked.

Gear Commitment: To start, you'll need sparring gloves (less-padded boxing gloves), a uniform, and of course your belt.

Competition Possibilities: Available, but not mandatory. You can go your entire martial arts career going to classes and taking your belt rank tests.

Community Vibe: The vibe varies a lot from dojo to dojo. Amy Csizmar Dalal chose her studio because it's a family school; there are no separate kid or adult classes, and the emphasis is on fun and community, as well as hard work.

First-Person Perspective: "I started tae kwon do when my youngest was in kindergarten; I thought, instead of watching, I could be on the floor with him. As soon as I started punching and kicking the bag, I liked it immediately. I love the feeling of power it gives me, and that it's a very cerebral sport, especially sparring. I'm thinking, *What is my opponent going to do and how am I going to not let them hit me?* (When I'm sparring, I'm completely padded up, and the punches are light.) I'm now working toward my fourth-degree black belt. The best part? I get to break boards and play with weapons, which is usually frowned upon in running." (Amy Csizmar Dalal)

Walking
The Basics: Exactly what you did running, just at a slower pace and with less impact on your joints.

Running Transfer Score: Extra high.

Pros: You can walk with all kinds of friends, not just endurance athletes, and you can go out your front door and get a new perspective: "I am on the same route that I used to run, but I never saw the stuff I am seeing now that I am walking," says Barb Eisner, who walks a couple days per week. Plus, walking is a lifelong endeavor (truly!) that benefits your health, whether you're forty-five or eighty-five.

Cons: None, except for the potential for comparison with your running miles. "Try not to think of walking as running downsized," says Sage Rountree, who now walks on the trails she used to run. "Change up your routes so it feels fresh."

Gear Commitment: Minimal—and you already own everything you need. Wearing a weighted vest during your walk ups the intensity by challenging both your cardiovascular and musculoskeletal systems.

Competition Possibilities: There are plenty of places to pit your walking pace against the clock, including the Honolulu Marathon and Portland to Coast, the walker's version of the popular Hood to Coast Running Relay.*

Community Vibe: High if you want it to be. You can gather a group of friends and set up regular walk dates or train for an event together.

First-Person Perspective: "I started walking in high school. My best friend and I walked 4 miles a day, no matter the weather; our goal was always to try to make it in under an hour. These days, when there's more daylight, I walk between 3 and 4 miles a day, at least six days a week. In the winter, I'll either walk on the treadmill or after school. I'm a math coach who loves numbers, and I'm naturally programmed to try to get incrementally better every day. I think, *I did yesterday's walk in this much time, so let's see if I can beat that time.* I keep track of my mileage on my watch app. Some mornings, I listen to the outdoors, and other times I listen to a podcast I save just for walking (the same way I saved the *Gilmore Girls*

---

* Visit 27thmile.net for a list of walking-friendly races.

for watching when I had treadmill runs to do). I typically walk by myself now, and I think of my walks as both a good workout and important downtime for myself." (Alison Pellicci)

Yoga

The Basics: A mind-body practice that combines physical postures, breath control, and meditation to cultivate strength, flexibility, and inner awareness.

Running Transfer Score: Low.

Pros: There are so many varieties of yoga, from restorative yoga (gentle emphasis on healing) to Bikram yoga (twenty-six poses done in a 105-degree room), you can find a style that works for you. Traditional yoga is a spiritual practice with breathwork; most yoga classes include some components of this, where the teacher weaves in reflections or themes that pertain to matters off the yoga mat. Yoga helps with flexibility and mobility, both extremely important for healthy aging.

Cons: Cost of classes, although there are plenty of free sessions on YouTube, and the process of finding a studio and teacher that is right for you.

Gear Commitment: Minimal. Just a yoga mat.

Competition Possibilities: There are a few yoga competitions, even though it feels at odds with the practice.

Community Vibe: Going to the same class at the same time brings a sense of community, and you may find a favorite teacher who cultivates community as well.

First-Person Perspective: "Yoga gives you so many opportunities to explore different sides of yourself. Most endurance athletes are good at pushing and embracing discomfort, but yoga allows you to embrace the ease, not the effort. Not everything needs to feel strong all the time. Instead of pushing, you let; instead of doing, you undo. Yoga allows you to look inside with focus and so you get better at reading your internal gauges.

"At the end of every class is the Shavasana pose. *Shava* means 'corpse,' and as one of my teachers said, 'It's the only pose you really need to master.' Yoga helps you explore accepting the inevitable, which can help you process the end of your running days." (Sage Rountree)

START WITH A BASIC: MAKE WALKING A WORKOUT

When I was a runner, I thought walking had two speeds: one for when I was at the mall, one for when I was about to miss a connecting flight. Turns out, walking has plenty of gears in between, with plenty of opportunities for an effective workout.

First, a quick form review for efficient, speedy walking:

- Just like you eased into your runs, ease into a power walk. Walk for five minutes at a casual speed before you pick up the pace.
- Roll through your entire foot: After your heel touches down, roll through the ball of your foot, then push off with your toes.
- Really push the ground away with your toes, which naturally engages your glutes to propel you forward.
- Let your hips rotate naturally; they should guide your stride, not lead it. (Leave the exaggerated side-to-side swaying to the Olympic racewalkers.)
- Pump your arms with purpose: crisp, tight elbow swings. (Your arms set the rhythm for your foot cadence.)
- Take short, quick steps; aim for more steps per minute rather than more inches per stride.

- Keep your shoulders back and relaxed.
- At the end, if it feels good to stretch your quads, calves, hamstrings, and/or glutes, have at it!

Here are five ways to break a sweat while walking:

1. **Add intervals of fast walking.** Use time (for instance, 1 minute of fast, 30 seconds of slow, repeat 5–10 times) or objects (walk fast to that mailbox, slow to the next) or fartleks (random bursts of speed when you feel like it).

2. **Head for the hills.** Walk a hilly route, and emphasize speed on the climbs: How fast can you get up the hill? You can also do hill repeats; they're not just for runners.

3. **Add stairs.** Head to a high school stadium or public building with flights of stairs and climb and descend for a set period of time (5–10 minutes is a good place to start).

4. **Stop for strength.** At regular intervals, stop to do a circuit of body-weight exercises. Without your hands touching the ground, you can squat and lunge, and if you pass a bench, you can do push-ups, triceps dips, and step-ups.

5. **Wear a weighted vest.** Adding weight to your walk naturally increases the cardiovascular demands, and you'll build core strength, improve your posture, and help your bone density as well.

Ten Activities That Don't Require a Sports Bra

As you mix and match different activities to replace what running gave you, consider nonathletic hobbies to help fill the void. Here, ten athletes share what they enjoy about their newfound pastimes.

Baking Sourdough Bread

Sourdough bread was the trendy thing to make during COVID, but it didn't interest me at the time. By the end of 2021, though, I felt a desire to be more creative. I tried watercolor painting, but that didn't stick. Then my niece shared a story on Instagram about how she was making a sourdough starter, so I decided to try it myself.

Growing a starter and baking loaves of bread totally scratched the itch to be more creative. I thought my first loaf was the most beautiful thing, but it probably wasn't that good. I've simplified my method and keep it very basic. Sometimes I'll add a mix-in, but I keep it simple: If I'm making garlic rosemary, I'll just add those two ingredients.

I love the repetition and routine baking provides. I usually make ten loaves a week. My starter makes two loaves at a time, so I put one out to rise when I go to work, and another one to rise when I go to bed. I store them all in the fridge, then bake them at the end of the week.

On Saturday, I put them in the Bread Box on my front porch. Anybody can come and grab a loaf and either make a donation or give the bread to somebody in need. I also love a barter system: Bring me a bag of flour or some salt in exchange for a loaf.

Because I just make one thing, I kind of feel like a one-trick pony, but I really enjoy the process. Everybody I share my bread with seems to like it too.

—*Gina Brown*

Creating a Decade List

I have a few inspirational quotes (*Do your crazy ideas; All great things come from a dream*) framed in my bathroom. I've always applied them to my running, but now that I'm not running anymore, I realized they can apply to more than my miles.

So I decided to make a list of things I want to accomplish in the next decade, the first time I've done something like that. The items range from the professional (work abroad, work in human resources to help others grow and develop) to financial (write a will, put more money in savings) to travel (take my mom on a trip that I pay for, go to a new continent) to personal (read 500 books, go to a major sporting event like the Kentucky Derby or an NHL playoff game).

I keep the list in my workout area, so I look at it almost every day. One of my mentors suggested I concentrate on getting one item done at a time, a process that feels a little like training. The one I'm working on now is a physical one: hiking the Ice Age Trail in Wisconsin. Next weekend, I'm going out of my comfort zone by hiking 10 miles with a friend on Saturday, camping overnight—I haven't slept in a tent in twelve years—then hiking 10 more miles on Sunday.

—*Leah Wiesner*

Gardening

In 2022, the year before I got diagnosed with follicular lymphoma and diverticulitis, my husband and I bought a house in Delaware on an acre and half of land, which was essentially brown dirt. Over the past three years, we've done a major overhaul: seeding the lawn, planting trees, creating gardens, building raised beds for fruits and vegetables.

I've been interested in gardening for as long as I can remember— I took farm as a daily class at 4-H sleepaway summer camp—so I have some general knowledge, but I am also mindful of planting native plants that are good for pollinators. We've planted everything from hydrangeas and raspberry bushes to peach trees and wildflowers. In the raised beds, we have a bounty of vegetables and fruit, including peppers, cucumbers, mini watermelons, and radishes. (Potatoes are so fun to dig up in the late summer; it's like digging for treasure.) It's incredibly satisfying to pick something in the backyard, bring it directly into the kitchen, and make a salad, soup, or roasted veggies.

My husband and I spend most of Saturday, usually around seven hours, doing gardening and yardwork. I love being close to the land and seeing how things evolve through the season. I often feel sore, tired, and fulfilled at the end of the day, reminiscent of how I used to feel after a long run. If I were still doing long runs every weekend, I wouldn't have enough time for both.

—Debra Helfand

Knitting

I taught myself how to knit through watching YouTube videos during COVID. (My husband says I learned how to knit and our children learned how to curse.) After about two months of frustration, it all started to click. I made my first full (basic) sweater within four months of learning. Now I can knit anything: sweaters, hats, mittens, you name it. I've made sweaters for my two daughters and me, and we wear them together. I always have one project—and sometimes more than one—going. Right now, I'm making a beautiful wrap sweater on a tiny needle. It feels like it's taken me years to finish it, but I love following a complicated pattern.

On weekends, I'll sit on our back porch and knit while watching football. This year, I worked on what I call my Detroit Lion sweater. It's not blue and silver, but I worked on it during football games. I'm three-quarters of the way through the sweater and would love to finish it, but I think it brought the Lions luck: They had their best season since 1991. So, it's on hold until the NFL starts back up in September.

Knitting is a lot like running. Both offer hours of repetitive movement toward a final goal that gives you a satisfying sense of accomplishment.

—Lisa Payne Kirker

Music

For Christmas in 2019, my husband gave us the gift of music: He rented stringed instruments for us (violin for me, viola for him), bought beginning music books, and scheduled lessons with an instructor. He had this vision of the two of us standing and playing together, but that didn't work out. He's not playing anymore, but I consider the violin one of the best gifts I ever got!

I have a lesson a couple times a month and practice daily for forty-five to sixty minutes; the time flies because I'm concentrating so intensely. Right now, I'm working my way through a book of etudes—basically, study pieces—that are hard for me but help me with technique. I play for my own satisfaction; I'll never join a group unless it's the Really Terrible Orchestra.*

The violin lit a creative spark in me; I took piano lessons for ten years when I was young and played through college, and I recently bought a refurbished baby grand piano. I spend at least an hour practicing piano on Saturday and Sunday, trying to get back the level of play I had fifty years ago.

Running truly defined the person I am. I mastered something that did not come easily to me, and that perspective has translated into many areas of my life. The same persistence that got me to run marathons keeps me trying to improve my skills on both instruments.

—*Jeanne Hanisko, who also plans to get into welding and stained glass when she retires*

Painting

Before I had my knee replaced, I signed up for a watercolor painting retreat in Agadir, Morocco. I knew my pace of life would be different and thought I might need something new to focus on.

---

* A real thing. "You can only be a member if you can't play well; once you become too accomplished, you have to move on," she says. The orchestra is based in the UK, where Jeanne lived for three years.

The retreat was held by my friend, an accomplished artist, who I met in a barbell strength class at our gym.

I hated art class as a kid; I couldn't figure out how to get the image from my head on the paper. But I love to travel, and I've always wanted to go to Morocco, so I figured even if I don't like painting, I'll enjoy being in a different country.

Turns out, I really liked it. Everybody was very welcoming to me, a total novice, and I appreciated the pace of sitting down, studying something, and trying to get it on paper. I often thought of running as my sanctuary. I loved listening to my breath, my feet hitting the ground, the gravel under my shoes and just having time to reflect. Sketching and painting, while not a replacement for running, offer me a similar way to interact with the world.

I love that watercolors are portable; I brought them to Mexico on a trip, and I'm about to head to France, where I'll be painting on a boat as we float down the Canal du Midi. I haven't yet started painting at home, but I've taken lots of pictures during my travels that I plan to paint in the future.

—*Kara Neuse*

Pottery

I am a ferocious knitter, love to mosaic, dye my own yarn, make jewelry. You name it, I've probably done it. I loved my high school pottery class and started taking classes as an adult in 2019; as my running started taking up less time, I found more space for creative outlets. For our twenty-fifth wedding anniversary, my husband bought me a pottery wheel and kiln for home. (Both arrived in the nick of time; they got delivered the week before everything shut down for COVID in March of 2020.)

There is so much space for creativity in pottery. Besides deciding what to make, I choose what type of clay, the technique to use, as well as the surface decoration with underglazes and the final glaze. My favorite thing to make is mugs on the wheel; I love the feeling of a warm cup of coffee in my hand, so I like making a big-belly mug with a smaller neck. I pull each handle by hand, which makes each piece unique.

My beloved neighbor, who passed away unexpectedly last year, had a favorite tree in her yard with the most beautiful branches. I imprinted the branches on clay and made earrings and mugs for her husband and children. Doing that brought me so much joy!

I don't spend as much time as I'd like making pottery, but I'm trying to do better with scheduling at least a few afternoon sessions. I call it my "Mariah Time"; it always puts me in such a good mood, which benefits everybody in the house.

—*Mariah Gianakouros*

Quilting

I was a passionate quilter before I took up running at age fifty, but it took a back seat while I focused on training. I was working full-time and commuting 30 miles to join a run group four days a week.

I got back into my sewing room as I transitioned away from running. These days, I am retired and spend between twenty and forty hours a week either at my sewing machine or doing hand-work on the couch. (In other words, I have plenty of time to finish the UFOs—unfinished objects—in my sewing room.)

I've been sewing since I was seven years old and started quilting about thirty-five years ago. I went on my honeymoon to Hawaii and saw Hawaiian quilts for the first time. They're a traditional art form that typically feature a bright, symmetrical design of flowers or another natural element on a white background.

I'm a baseball fan, and I like to have the game on when I sew. I also listen to music. Much like running, quilting blocks everything else out; it is an addiction that I hope never ends.

—*Valorie Plesha*

Reading

After I was diagnosed with salivary gland cancer in 2022, I knew I needed to expand my mental health toolbox; I couldn't just rely on running to disperse all the clouds hanging around.

Before my diagnosis, I read a couple books a year; I was working full-time and raising kids, so time was at a premium. I signed up for a free trial of Kindle Unlimited after my diagnosis, and a friend recommended the Ratchel Hatch series by L. T. Ryan, which was easy and entertaining; radiation made concentrating for more than fifteen minutes a huge challenge.

Now I'm reading at least two books a month. Some of my recent favorites are *Lessons in Chemistry* by Bonnie Garmus, *The Dutch House* by Ann Patchett, and *The Midnight Library* by Matt Haig. I also love memoirs; I read *What a Fool Believes* by Michael McDonald. I'm a huge Doobie Brothers fan, so this was fangirling at its very best!

Reading keeps me connected to running; my online running posse make excellent recommendations, as does my best running friend Sara, who taught me how to check out library books on my Kindle using Libby, so I don't have to pay for them anymore!

—*Alison Taylor*

Writing

In the over thirty years that I've been running, I've also been a writer. I have an MFA in creative fiction and have taught writing classes to high schoolers. But after I had babies, I let writing go in favor of running. Finishing a whole slew of endurance events post-babies was empowering and gave me a quick hit of the good stuff during a difficult time for me.

Writing is a slow burn and requires (at least for me) much more sleep than I was getting for a decade to be able to think creatively. Now that my kids are older and my body isn't as resilient, I have circled back to working on writing projects in the hours I might have spent training for marathons. The emotional energy, time, and center of interest has switched, but being out on the trails is part of my process.

Some days, I bring a notebook and stop to do some writing while on the trail. Or sometimes I hike with my Speechify app so I can listen to my work as I'm out in nature. The red dirt and junipers and sandstone inspire me and reset me; being among them is part of my creative routine.

—*Paige Kaptuch*

AID STATION

Dimity Turns Fifty-Two

It's May, and I'm fifty-two today. I haven't run in over four years.

I wake up in a bad mood. I thought I would go swimming, but it just feels like too much. The drive to the pool, the sucking a swim cap over my head, the fact that I may need to share a lane with a breaststroker whose limbs cross the line, the stray hair clogging the shower.

Okay, no swim. Just get moving.

I need to do my exercises that loosen everything up: cat/cow, pelvic tilts, groin rocks, 90/90. Small movements that remind my joints how they're supposed to behave. But it's bleak down on the floor. The other day, I spied a dead fly in the corner, and used a nearby massive dust ball as an ersatz rag to pick it up.

Still, I get down. I queue up a thirteen-minute story from *This American Life*, about a cop who chases a squirrel around a new house. It's funny and light. That's my goal these days—and has been for pretty much my whole life: Hold it lightly. Don't force it. Unclench. Relax.

My body unlocks with each pelvic tilt, and I'm feeling better. I remind myself for the 4,867th time: Just as I wouldn't judge a run by the first mile, I shouldn't judge my day based on its first ten minutes. I want to be out in the fresh spring air; I want to move through space and feel like I'm a part of this world.

I get ready to ride. Arm warmers, gloves, extra chamois cream and A + D diaper ointment to my delicate parts to counteract the fact that my cycling capris are so old, the chamois may as well be a couple Bounty paper towels.

In my neighborhood, I follow a teenager, responsibly wearing a helmet, until she turns off into the orthodontist's parking lot. I catch a green light at the intersection where I never catch a green light. I cross a creek on a wooden bridge and remind myself I want to come back here with the dogs and let them play in the water.

My effort feels hard, but I am consciously trying to keep it light, keep it easy. Relax. Don't force it. On a short hump of a hill, I click into my easiest gear and don't judge myself for doing so. I notice the cars on the nearby freeway, clogged with red brake lights as far as I can see. I am not clogged. I am not braking.

I ride past a small mountain bike course where I used to cheer for my youngest as he navigated the trail, rolling down hills that made me wince from the sidelines. I notice prairie dogs popping up everywhere, a town of little mounds as they chitter good morning to each other. On top of one mound, there's a mom with her two babies clinging to her. Did I appreciate the clinging days enough? Hold it lightly, Dimity.

A neighbor passes me with a smile on her face. She's the type I've rarely seen scowl. How would my life be different if I were more smiley? If I didn't have to consciously tell myself to relax? I get excited that we're both here, near Cherry Creek, on bikes at 7:47 a.m. on a Wednesday morning. Maybe she's my new riding buddy?

But I remember a run I did with her years ago, and the conversation felt forced, not flowy. Also, she was faster than me, and I didn't really like that. Plus, having a conversation while you're on the bike is so hard. Without even applying, she's already lost her gig as my new riding buddy. Don't force it, Dimity.

I keep riding. I see my husband, fresh off his morning crew practice, leaving the park in his big truck. "Fancy meeting you here," I say, telling him that I've picked the longest loop, so don't expect me home too soon. I can tell he's both surprised to see me and proud of me for being out here. I feel light.

I keep riding. I see two large, well-fed coyotes far enough away that I want to stop and take a picture, but I don't want to stop my momentum. They're next to another town of prairie dogs, which is probably why their bellies look so full. "I've seen two coyotes, tons of prairie dogs, and so many birds," I tell myself as I pedal by green fields that have yet to turn brown in the intense Colorado summer sun.

I say good morning to every pedestrian I pass after warning them "On your left" as calmly as possible. I notice a woman walking who has beautiful calves. I immediately think, *Runner*, and then wonder why she's walking. I hope she's not injured.

I want to take her on a bike ride. I want to buy a mountain bike, a gravel bike, and a cruiser bike. I want to bring a group of women to ride across the state of Iowa in RAGBRAI.* I want to keep riding forever.

One guy with meaty thighs passes me on my way home. He's pushing a big gear. He doesn't say good morning or anything, actually, as he passes me on the left; instead, he just flicks up his pinky in acknowledgment. Whatever, bro.

I get home, down a glass of chocolate milk with a scoop of creatine mixed in, and go to make my morning latte. We are out of oat milk, but this doesn't set me off.

In fact, in a few minutes, I'll calm down a heated discussion between my husband and our daughter about transporting her stuff to a new apartment. "You both feel disrespected right now," I say, amazed that this insight has come to me so clearly. "This isn't about moving furniture."

My legs are pleasantly tired, my mind has bathed in the fresh air, I'm spinning in this big world, and I'm ready to hold it all lightly—at least for today.

* RAGBRAI stands for Register's Annual Great Bicycle Ride Across Iowa, which was started by two columnists for the *Des Moines Register*.

THE ATHLETES AND EXPERTS

I'm so grateful for the accomplished women who shared their stories and expertise in these pages, and I wanted to bookend their wise contributions with one of my favorite literary devices: the six-word sentence. I asked the athletes to capture their life after running in just six words and the experts to offer their best six-word advice to those navigating this transition. Their sentences made me nod, laugh, tear up, and feel a little less alone. I hope they do the same for you.

The Athletes

Cathy Annetta, 48 years old
On the road for: 17 years
Off the road for: 1 year
Stopped running because: Hallux rigidus (degenerative arthritis and stiffness in big toe)
Her six words: Never give up. Keep moving forward.

Julie Baker, 69 years old
On the road for: 48 years
Off the road for: 1 year

Stopped running because: Osteoporosis, a dropped toe, and a history of fractures

Her six words: Happy meeting myself where I am.

Arlene Barr, 55 years old

On the road for: 47 years

Off the road for: "Nearly five heartbreaking years."

Stopped running because: Dual hip replacements

Her six words: Two hip to quit. Ever hoping.

Michelle Bingham, 60 years old

On the road for: 30 years

Off the road for: 2 years

Stopped running because: Four labrum tears in her hip and patellofemoral syndrome in her knee

Her six words: Finding joy but never giving up.

Alisa Bonsignore, 50 years old

On the road for: 10 years

Off the road for: 8 years

Stopped running because: "I was always injured. When I balanced the injuries and time running required against my enjoyment, it just didn't make sense to continue."

Her six words: Avid walker, fitness explorer, runner emeritus.

Andrea Brown, 66 years old

On the road for: 10 years

Off the road for: 5 years

Stopped running because: Religion; she joined a convent that doesn't support running

Her six words: Now I run toward something else.

Gina Brown, 53 years old
On the road for: 13 years
Off the road for: 2 years
Stopped running because: Surgery for tailor's bunions on both feet
Her six words: My heart runs. My hands bake.

Stacy Bruce, 52 years old
On the road for: 27 years
Off the road for: 2 years
Stopped running because: Lower-back and hip issues
Her six words: Footsteps fade. Evolving. Fire still burns.

Ann Callarman, 46 years old
On the road for: 20 years
Off the road for: 1 month
Stopped running because: A move to Pea Ridge, Arkansas, right outside of Bentonville, a mountain bike mecca. "Running isn't as accessible, and I'm gravitating toward the local culture."
Her six words: I love to ride my bike.

Chris Cesena, 51 years old
On the road for: 37 years
Off the road for: 1 year
Stopped running because: A bone marrow lesion in her foot
Her six words: Searching for a new runner's high.

Amy Csizmar Dalal, 52 years old
On the road for: 32 years
Off the road for: 1 year

Stopped running because: Eight years of consecutive and cascading injuries

Her six words: Who knew I'd actually like biking?

Britta Czapla, 50 years old

On the road for: 29 years

Off the road for: 2 years

Stopped running because: Severe knee pain that occurred "during runs, after runs, at night when turning over in bed"

Her six words: Why just run? Do it all!

Jenny Davies, 48 years old

On the road for: 9 years

Off the road for: 2 months

Stopped running because: "I can't seem to run long distances without getting injured."

Her six words: Finding love in movement *is* enough.

Becca Dinsdale, 51 years old

On the road for: 30+ years

Off the road for: 1.5 years

Stopped running because: A bulging disc in her lower back. "I was told by a spine specialist that some days would be fine, and others would suck."

Her six words: Learning to like this new normal.

Amy Ebeid, 47 years old

On the road for: 27 years

Off the road for: 5 months—but back on it again

Stopped running because: Severe insertional Achilles tendinopathy

Her six words: I go forward because I can.

Barb Eisner, 58 years old

On the road for: 45 years

Off the road for: 4 months

Stopped running because: Lower-back issues, including stenosis, sciatica, and disc bulges

Her six words: Moving and fellowship equal bonding time.

Cathy Engstrom, 52 years old

On the road for: 30+ years

Off the road for: 1.5 years

Stopped running because: Ramifications from severely dislocated kneecap

Her six words: Still an adventure enthusiast, just slower.

Heather Escaravage, 42 years old

On the road for: 14 years

Off the road for: 2 years

Stopped running because: Patellofemoral pain syndrome in her knee

Her six words: Moving in the direction of aliveness.

Ellen Ewing, 47 years old

On the road for: 12 years

Off the road for: 3 years

Stopped running because: Plantar fasciitis in both feet ("So many cortisone shots!")

Her six words: Cats, reading, stress, curiosity, love, laughter.

Mariah Gianakouros, 50 years old

On the road for: 10+ years

Off the road for: 1 year

Stopped running because: A surgery for her foot, which stemmed from long-term steroids she took to help her sinuses, which flared up when she ran

Her six words: Mother, maker, mover, anchored in faith.

Gretchen Gibson, 46 years old

On the road for: 14 years

Off the road for: 2.5 years

Stopped running because: Hip and knee replacements within six months of each other

Her six words: Slaying dragons amid chaos and uncertainty.

Heidi Gillenwater, 58 years old

On the road for: 40 years

Off the road for: 1 year

Stopped running because: Surgery for a torn meniscus and ACL she sustained while skiing

Her six words: ACL torn; Peloton brought me back.

Joanne Godfrey, 59 years old

On the road for: 20 years

Off the road for: 3 years

Stopped running because: Arthritis in both knees

Her six words: Get your ass in gear, Joanne! ("Scott, my former husband, wrote this on a sign at a race I was in. It's still a mantra I use no matter what I walk, hobble, run, trot, or meander.")

Jeanne Hanisko, 64 years old

On the road for: 50 years

Off the road for: 1 year

Stopped running because: COVID-related effects on her body's energy systems

Her six words: Never natural; always determined; still aspiring.

Kim Harland, 57 years old

On the road for: 20 years

Off the road for: 6 years

Stopped running because: Unsuccessful surgery for a torn hip labrum and stress-fracture-prone feet

Her six words: You ran. You can do anything.

Pam Harris, 43 years old

On the road for: 15 years

Off the road for: 2 years

Stopped running because: Thyroid cancer

Her six words: Rewrote my rhythm. Reclaimed my joy.

Debra Helfand, 57 years old

On the road for: 13 years

Off the road for: 1 year

Stopped running because: Follicular lymphoma and diverticulitis

Her six words: Walking is the dessert after running.

Jennifer Hickenlooper, 39 years old

On the road for: 17 years

Off the road for: 2 years

Stopped running because: Uterine fibroids and too many life stressors

Her six words: In wildness, we find each other.

Megan Hinckley, 46 years old

On the road for: 9 years

Off the road for: 2 years

Stopped running because: Hip dysplasia and subsequent surgery

Her six words: Looking ahead with joy and gratitude.

Paige Kaptuch, 45 years old

On the road for: 33 years

Off the road for: 3 years

Stopped running because: Herniated discs and back surgery

Her six words: Creative process: write, trail, listen, think.

Lisa Payne Kirker, 48 years old

On the road for: 20+ years

Off the road for: 3 years

Stopped running because: Heart attack

Her six words: My heart asked to be still.

Suzanne Klonis, 52 years old

On the road for: 25 years

Off the road for: 6 months

Stopped running because: A meniscus tear, repaired by surgery; a
  stopgap for a total knee replacement

Her six words: Kinda miss running; love Peloton coaches.

Ingrid L., 56 years old

On the road for: 33 years

Off the road for: 4 months

Stopped running because: Severe osteoarthritis in both
  (bone-on-bone) knees

Her six words: Same me? Yes. Just different miles.

Sarah Lightner, 48 years old

On the road for: 35 years

Off the road for: 1 year

Stopped running because: A bulged disc

Her six words: Highs less high, lows less low.

Morgan M., 34 years old

On the road for: 15 years

Off the road for: 6 years ("I remember the exact month, even though it was six years ago!")

Stopped running because: A partially torn Achilles tendon and chronically torn foot ligament

Her six words: Today's tragedy may be tomorrow's advantage.

Joan Machanic, 60 years old

On the road for: 20 years

Off the road for: 1.5 years

Stopped running because: Age and the demands of training

Her six words: Retired runner still moving and grooving.

Ruthie McCartney, 55 years old

On the road for: 15 years

Off the road for: 6 months

Stopped running because: An arthritic knee

Her six words: Legs remember. Body hurts. Heart breaks.

Angie Melton, 53 years old

On the road for: 10 years

Off the road for: 10 years

Stopped running because: Osteoarthritis in both knees

Her six words: Swimming across large bodies of water!

Jennifer Moynihan, 46 years old

On the road for: 33 years

Off the road for: 6 years

Stopped running because: Plantar fasciitis, recurrent ITB syndrome, chronic glute and hip pain

Her six words: More swimming, still running a little.

Donna Nash, 54 years old

On the road for: 35 years

Off the road for: Still contemplating the end but has significantly cut back

Stopped running because: A hip that needs replacing

Her six words: Slower strides, fuller heart, joy remains.

Kara Neuse, 53 years old

On the road for: 35 years

Off the road for: 2 years

Stopped running because: Complications with a total knee replacement

Her six words: My forward pace chases blue skies.

Cathy Nickels, 51 years old

On the road for: 15 years

Off the road for: 6 years

Stopped running because: Double Achilles tears

Her six words: Will I ever be whole again?

Britt Parker, 50 years old

On the road for: 30 years

Off the road for: 3 years

Stopped running because: A high hamstring strain and lower-back issues

Her six words: Slowly accepting walks in the woods.

Jill Passarelli, 49 years old

On the road for: 12 years

Off the road for: 4 months

Stopped running because: Hip and lower-back pain

Her six words: Moving forward on my own terms.

Alison Pellicci, 48 years old
On the road for: 10 years
Off the road for: 4 months
Stopped running because: Herniated discs. Plus, she moved and lost her best running friend.
Her six words: The pace changed. Acceptance took longer.

Valorie Plesha, 61 years old
On the road for: 8 years
Off the road for: 5 years
Stopped running because: Two partial knee replacements and a lymphoma diagnosis
Her six words: Let go. Explore, discover, find joy.

Maureen Powers, 52 years old
On the road for: 31 years
Off the road for: 2 years
Stopped running because: A variety of injuries, but chronic plantar fasciitis combined with what looked like a torn meniscus in her knee was "the final nail in the coffin"
Her six words: New motion, new joy, no rollercoaster.

Kristin Zosa Puleo, 43 years old
On the road for: 28 years
Off the road for: 1 year
Stopped running because: Severe lower-back / piriformis / hip pain
Her six words: Dear black toenail: I miss you!

Jana Resch, 53 years old
On the road for: 15 years
Off the road for: 1.5 years

Stopped running because: Low energy and joint pain due to two bouts of COVID, high stress, and menopause

Her six words: Running faded; hope is still moving!

Arielle Rosson, 38 years old

On the road for: 27 years

Off the road for: 6 years

Stopped running because: Knee issues that required three surgeries

Her six words: Grateful for all I can do.

Sage Rountree, 51 years old

On the road for: 30 years

Off the road for: 2 years

Stopped running because: Arthritic, fracture-prone ankles

Her six words: You see more by going slower.

Jen Rucker, 45 years old

On the road for: 7 years

Off the road for: 8 years

Stopped running because: Back surgery for a disc pressing on a motor nerve

Her six words: Stronger each day, many different ways.

Paige Sato, 58 years old

On the road for: 15 years

Off the road for: 1 year

Stopped running because: Multiple falls that broke bones and required stitches

Her six words: Life shifted: trainers out, paddles up!

Christina Smith, 54 years old

On the road for: 42 years

Off the road for: 1 year
Stopped running because: Excruciating hip pain due to hip drop
Her six words: I wrapped my arms around myself.

Alison Taylor, 62 years old
On the road for: 15 years
Off the road for: 1 year
Stopped running because: Salivary gland cancer; she donated 8 inches of her right fibula to replace her palate
Her six words: Happy, strong grandma doing endurance differently.

Heather Treptow, 47 years old
On the road for: 33 years
Off the road for: 1 year
Stopped running because: A pinched nerve in neck, compounded by knee issues
Her six words: Without running? More books and coffee.

Danielle Waagmeester, 53 years old
On the road for: 30 years (off and on)
Off the road for: 1 year
Stopped running because: A knee that might need a total knee replacement
Her six words: Less impact, more insight, still moving.

Pamela Wakeman, 55 years old
On the road for: 12 years
Off the road for: 2 years
Stopped running because: Double hip replacements
Her six words: I am a work in progress.

Louanne Wiant, 63 years old
On the road for: 15 years

Off the road for: 6 months

Stopped running because: MAC lung disease ("Basically, a non-contagious version of tuberculosis.")

Her six words: I can still walk very fast.

Leah Wiesner, 39 years old

On the road for: 15 years

Off the road for: 6 months

Stopped running because: Severe arthritis in knees and Hashimoto's disease

Her six words: Strong, motivated, unstoppable; finding new challenges.

The Experts

Erin Alaya

Professional credentials: PhD in counseling psychology; licensed psychologist; Certified Mental Performance Consultant; member of the USOPC mental health directory; founder of Skadi Sport Psychology in Minneapolis; specializes in working with female endurance athletes

Athletic credentials: "Running is my first love." Ran in high school, became an adult marathoner and triathlete. For eight years, focused solely on bike racing, especially gravel ultra cycling, but finished her first 50K in 2025. "I'm going back for more."

Six words of advice: Remember your why, adjust your how.

Kristin Armstrong

Professional credentials: Master's in clinical mental health; founder of Kristin Armstrong Consulting in Austin; specializes in life and career transitions; currently pursuing a PhD; author of seven books, including *Mile Markers: The 26.2 Most Important Reasons Why Women Run*

Athletic credentials: A runner for twenty-six years—and counting. "I'm so grateful to still be running—and I still love it all: trail running, running treks, hiking, marathons, half-marathons!"

Six words of advice: Every finish line a starting line.

Kim Dawson

Professional credentials: PhD in psychomotor behavior; professor in the Department of Kinesiology and Physical Education at Wilfrid Laurier University; owner of Mind2Achieve in Waterloo, Ontario; specializes in helping amateur and elite athletes, artists, and health practitioners reach their performance potential

Athletic credentials: A runner for forty years. "Moving has always defined me. I have two tattoos: One is a stick 'running girl' and the other is my mantra: 'Keep a steady stride.' My goal is to keep a healthy perspective and a consistent temperature: not too high or low."

Six words of advice: Do not mentally box yourself in.

Maria Luque

Professional credentials: PhD in health sciences; Certified Health Education Specialist; ACE Certified Personal Trainer; founder of Fitness in Menopause in Austin; specializes in helping women in midlife reimagine exercise, body image, and well-being

Athletic credentials: A former sprinter. "My entire life, I've loved the fast and furious." Off the track, she's competed in everything from handball to Ping-Pong.

Six words of advice: Hung up your shoes? Grab dumbbells.

Haley Perlus
Professional credentials: PhD in sports psychology; speaker, consultant, and coach; specializes in applying sport-specific techniques to help athletes, business leaders, and high achievers optimize their mental game

Athletic credentials: An occasional runner who likes to be on trails. "I prefer hiking, biking (mountain, road, and fat tire), and stand-up paddleboarding for endurance."

Six words of advice: Running reveals values, pursue them everywhere.

Amy Pickett-Williams
Professional credentials: Master's in social work and yoga teacher (RYT 200); founder of LIGHT Movement (Love in Grief, Held Together), a nonprofit dedicated to ensuring that no one grieves alone in Denver; specializes in grief therapy integrating somatic practices

Athletic credentials: A competitive swimmer. "I ended up with a serious injury, so could not compete in college."

Six words of advice: Movement shifts when awareness guides healing.

Niamh Rawlins
Professional credentials: Master's in clinical mental health counseling; owner of Sequoia Counseling in Nashville; specializes in working with life transitions, trauma, and LGBTQIA+ individuals

Athletic credentials: A soccer player from childhood through college. "Outside of soccer, running was my emotional reset button and my favorite outdoor activity." Following multiple knee surgeries, she had to step away from soccer and running in her mid-twenties.

Six words of advice: Peace and purpose in today's body.

Shawn Snelgrove
Professional credentials: Senior leadership consultant and executive coach based in Denver

Athletic credentials: A runner for a decade: "I ran to process the stress of being a consultant." She now thrives in activities that allow her to process her emotions but don't hurt her joints: hiking, yoga, Pilates, and skiing.

Six words of advice: Relish now to greet what's next.

Selene Yeager
Professional credentials: Health and exercise science journalist; contributor to over two dozen books, including as coauthor of *ROAR* and *Next Level* with Dr. Stacy Sims; host of the *Hit Play Not Pause* podcast and author of the *Feisty 40+* newsletter; specializes in helping active, performance-minded women whose best years are not behind them

Athletic credentials: Former All-American Ironman triathlete and semiprofessional mountain biker; even though she doesn't lead with "I'm a runner," she has been running for thirty-five years and now runs three days per week, including trail running on the weekends.

Six words of advice: Cycling: joy like running, with coasting.

RECOMMENDED READING

These eleven books kept me company while I was writing, offering perspective on transitions, values, grief, and the human condition. If they look familiar, it's because I've referenced most of them in this book. Turns out my Recommended Reading list is basically my Bibliography, too.

The Artist's Way: A Spiritual Path to Higher Creativity by Julia Cameron, with Mark Bryan

Comfortable with Uncertainty: 108 Teachings on Cultivating Fearlessness and Compassion by Pema Chödrön

From Strength to Strength: Finding Success, Happiness, and Deep Purpose in the Second Half of Life by Arthur C. Brooks

Life Is in the Transitions: Mastering Change at Any Age by Bruce Feiler

Living Beautifully with Uncertainty and Change by Pema Chödrön

Mind Your Body: A Revolutionary Program to Release Chronic Pain and Anxiety by Nicole J. Sachs

My Stroke of Insight: A Brain Scientist's Personal Journal by Jill Bolte Taylor

Quit: The Power of Knowing When to Walk Away by Annie Duke

Transitions: Making Sense of Life's Changes by William Bridges, with
  Susan Bridges

The Way of Integrity: Finding the Path to Your True Self by Martha Beck

What's Your Grief? Lists to Help You Through Any Loss by Eleanor Haley
  and Litsa Williams

ACKNOWLEDGMENTS

I never stood on a podium during my running years, but I've got something far better: I've been supported by a fantastic team for all my miles, including my 27th.

For over fifteen years, the Another Mother Runner community—and my business partner, Sarah Bowen Shea—has been a steady source of encouragement, acceptance, and love. That energy didn't end when I stopped running. You supported my decision to step back, and when I put out a call to hear your stories about how your miles have changed over time, those of you facing the end of your running years didn't disappoint. You, as well as a handful of other athletes, spilled all the details, and that collective wisdom shapes this book. To be clear: Any mistakes in telling your stories are mine alone.

To the experts who shared their time and insights: Thank you for validating how rocky transitions can be and reminding us that grace and patience are key.

"Not running anymore" is a clunky pitch, especially to a running-focused publication, and I thank editors Jen Ator and Melanie Mitchell for giving me the chance to share my story in the pages of *Women's Running* magazine. Drafting a book proposal about endings is much tougher than writing one about beginnings, and my agent, Kendall Berdinsky, a newly minted marathoner, helped me shape it so that Renee Sedliar, an editor I immediately loved when she said she used to run but now does trapeze, could see and trust the vision. Tish Hamilton, who has been instrumental in developing my career writing about running, lent her sharp insights on my first draft, even after responding, "You know I'm not a book editor, right?" when I first asked for her help.

From her hospital bed, Rachel Walker, less than a week out of two emergency spinal surgeries, delivered me the kind of pep talk every writer needs. Thanks also to my Fab Four writing group—Dorian Yates, Martha Tissot van Patot, and Wendy Ward Hoffer—who cheered me on when writing about loss felt like I was perpetually stuck at mile 11 of a half-marathon. Cathy Engstrom, April Hopkins, and Sarah Wassner Flynn gamely picked up the slack around my day job while I wrote. And I'm so grateful for Joann Verweij, Jessica Johnston, and Holli Driesbach, who are always up for adventure. (Mount Whitney next?)

Mom and John: Thank you for giving me a quiet space in the mountains to write and, along with Sarah and Megan, for always encouraging me to be my true self. Finally, many thanks to Grant, Amelia, and Ben: my home team. Here's to family hikes and shared miles, whatever form they take, for decades to come.

INDEX